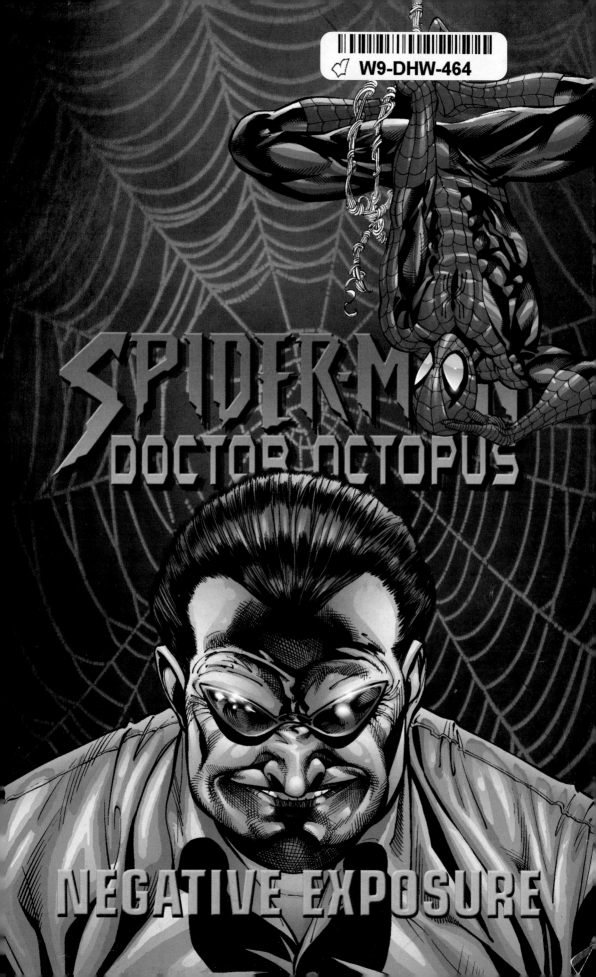

SPIDER-MAN
DOCTOR OCTOPUS

NEGATIVE EXPOSURE

SPIDER-MAN
DOCTOR OCTOPUS

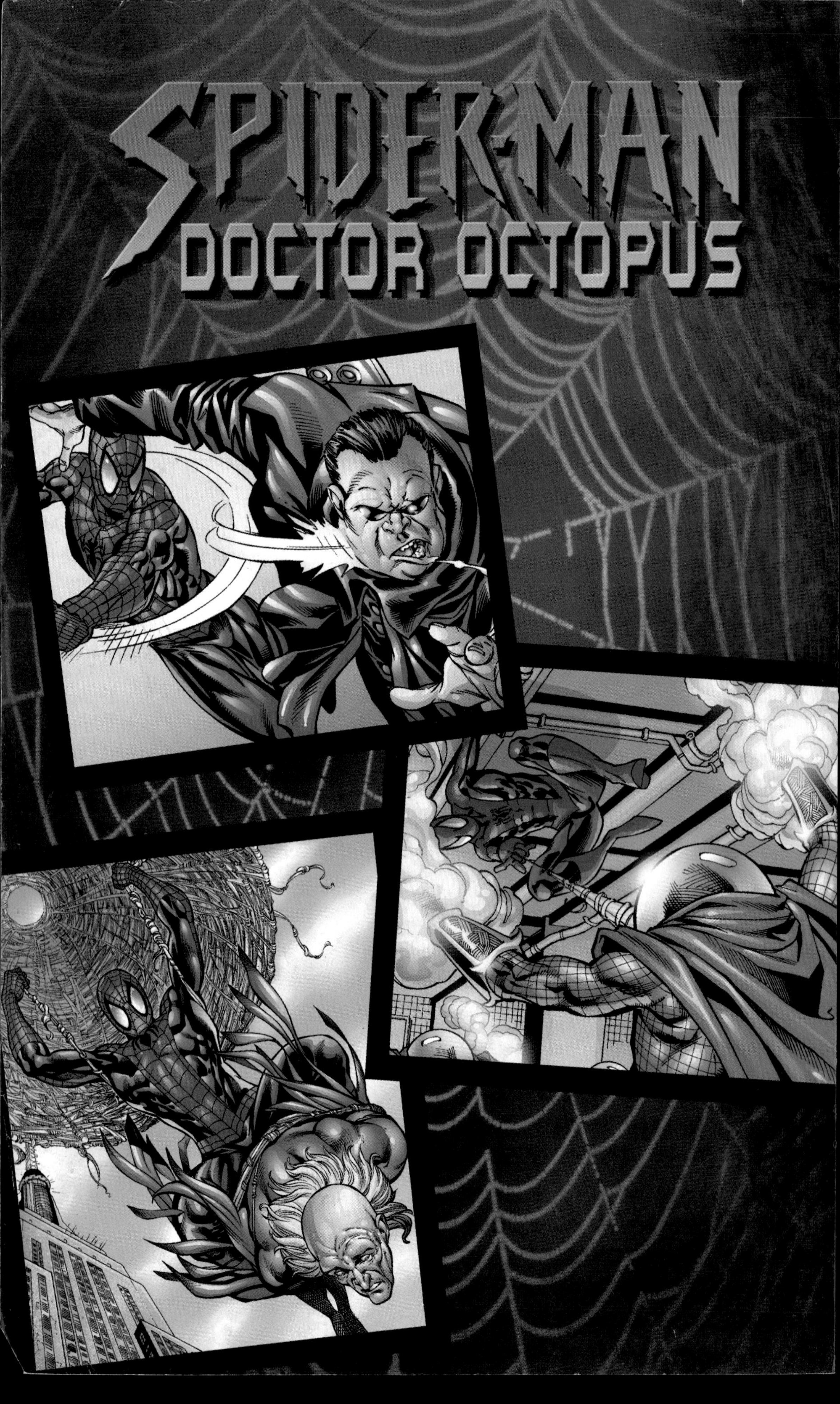

NEGATIVE EXPOSURE

writer
BRIAN K. VAUGHAN
pencils
STAZ JOHNSON
inks
DANNY MIKI

colors
AVALON STUDIOS' MATT YACKEY
letters
VIRTUAL CALLIGRAPHY'S RUS WOOTON
doctor octopus costume design
HUMBERTO RAMOS
cover art
TONY HARRIS
editor
WARREN SIMONS
supervising editor
AXEL ALONSO

collections editor
JEFF YOUNGQUIST
assistant editor
JENNIFER GRÜNWALD
book designer
MEGHAN KERNS

editor in chief
JOE QUESADA
publisher
DAN BUCKLEY

#1

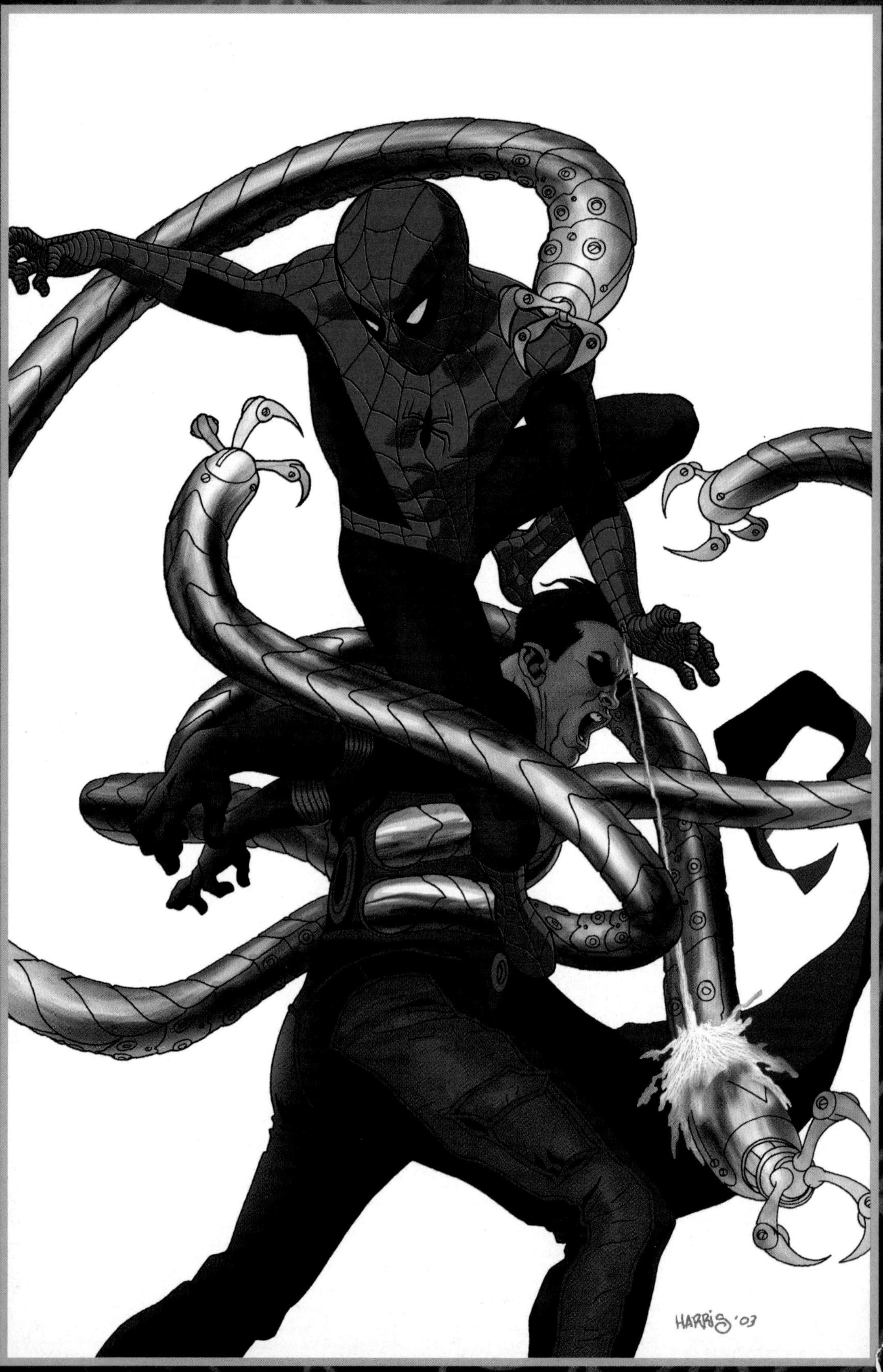
HARRIS '03

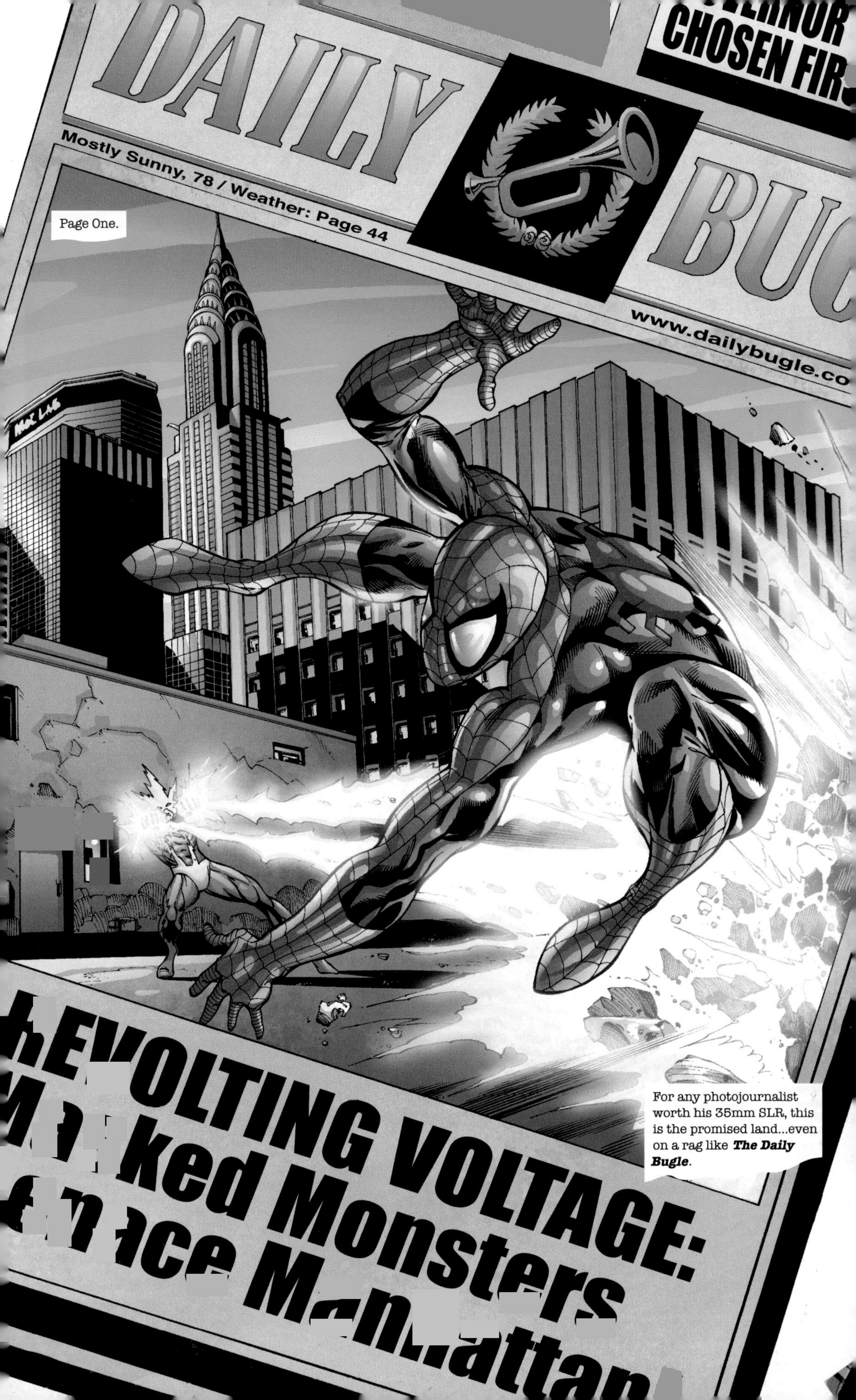
DAILY
Mostly Sunny, 78 / Weather: Page 44
CHOSEN
Page One.
VOLTAGE:
Monsters
For any photojournalist worth his 35mm SLR, this is the promised land...even on a rag like ***The Daily Bugle***.

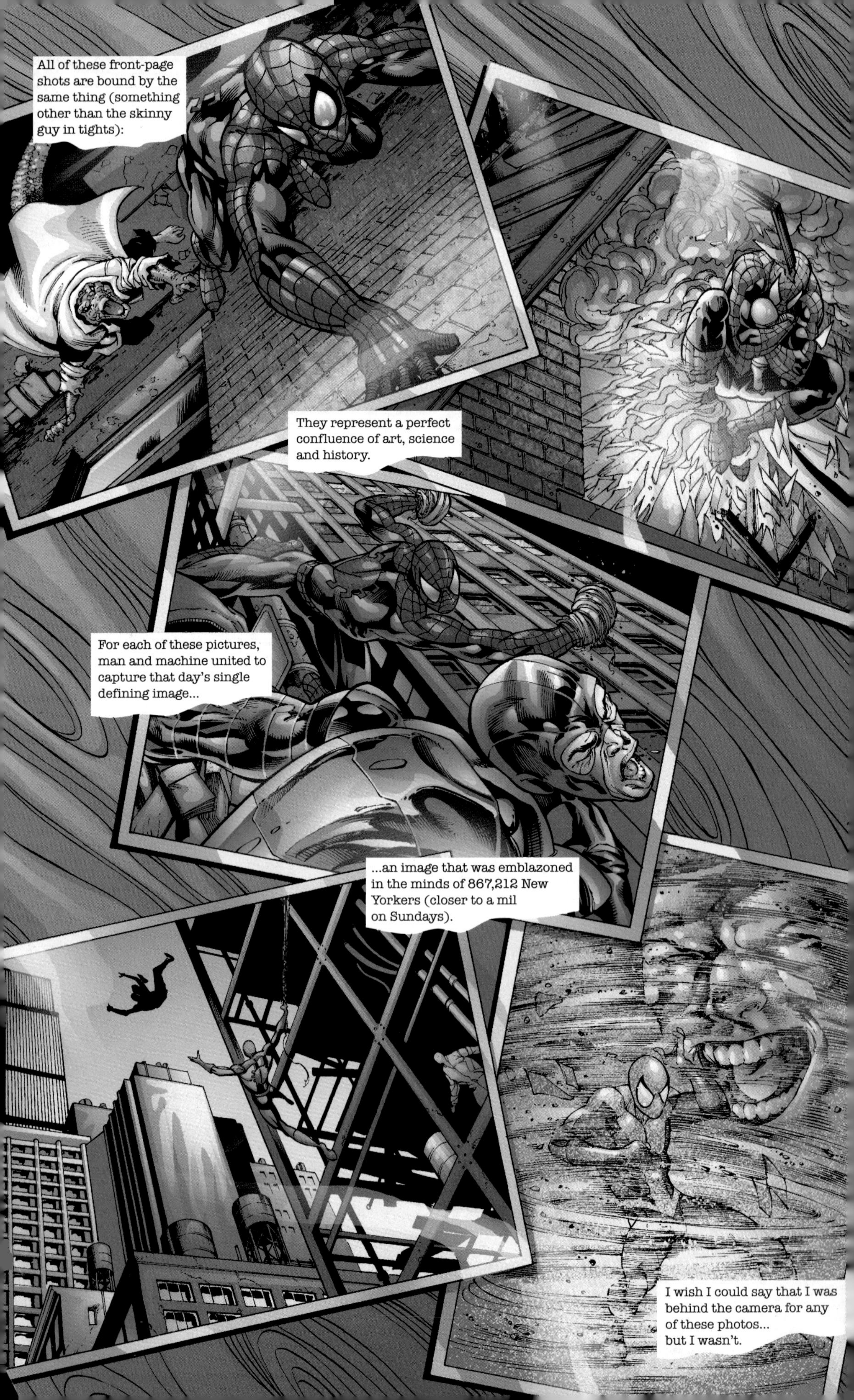
All of these front-page shots are bound by the same thing (something other than the skinny guy in tights):
They represent a perfect confluence of art, science and history.
For each of these pictures, man and machine united to capture that day's single defining image...
...an image that was emblazoned in the minds of 867,212 New Yorkers (closer to a mil on Sundays).
I wish I could say that I was behind the camera for any of these photos... but I wasn't.

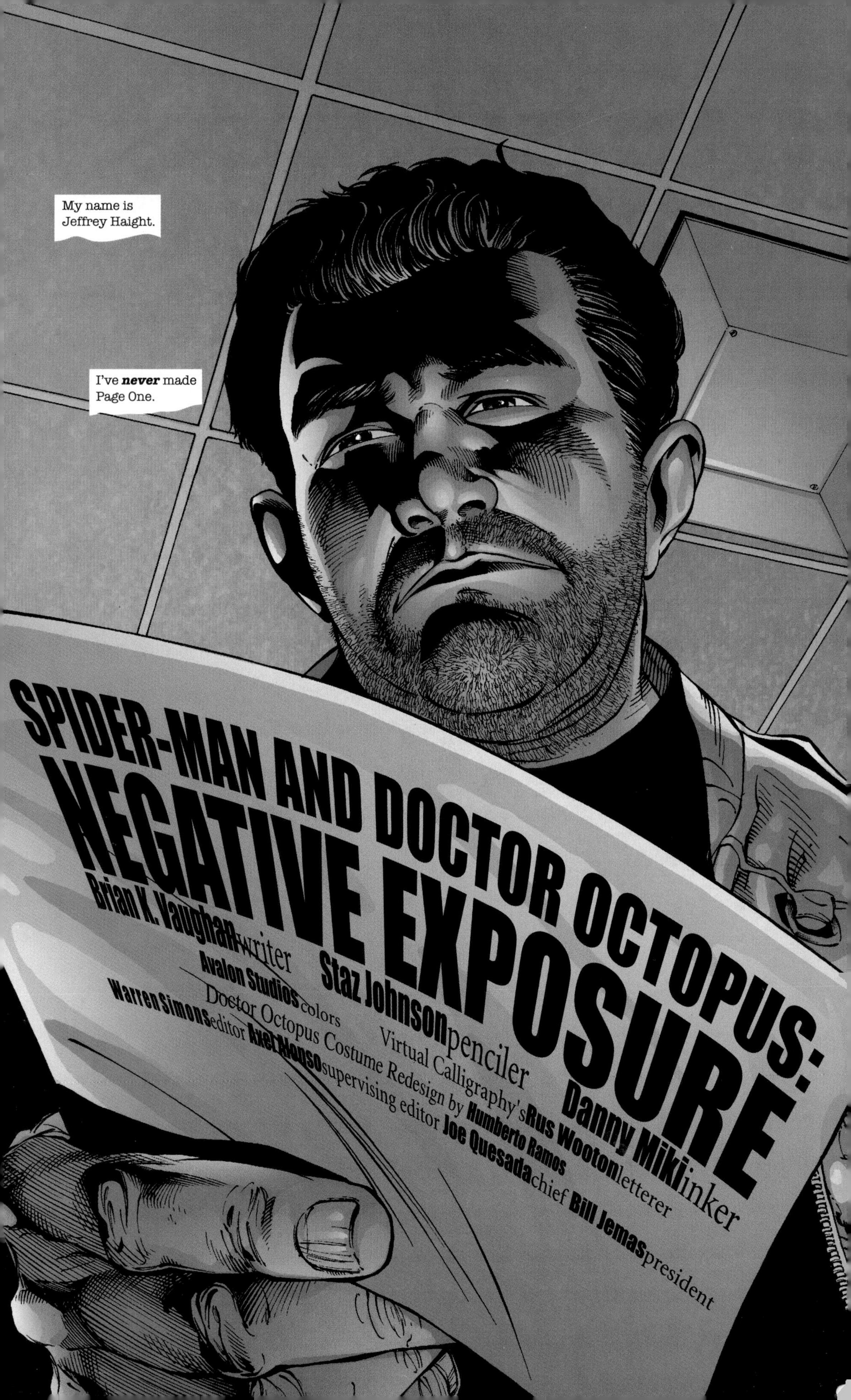

My name is Jeffrey Haight.
I've ***never*** made Page One.
SPIDER-MAN AND DOCTOR OCTOPUS:
NEGATIVE EXPOSURE
Brian K. Vaughan writer
Staz Johnson penciler
Danny Miki inker
Avalon Studios colors
Virtual Calligraphy's Rus Wooton letterer
Doctor Octopus Costume Redesign by Humberto Ramos
Warren Simons editor Axel Alonso supervising editor Joe Quesada chief Bill Jemas president

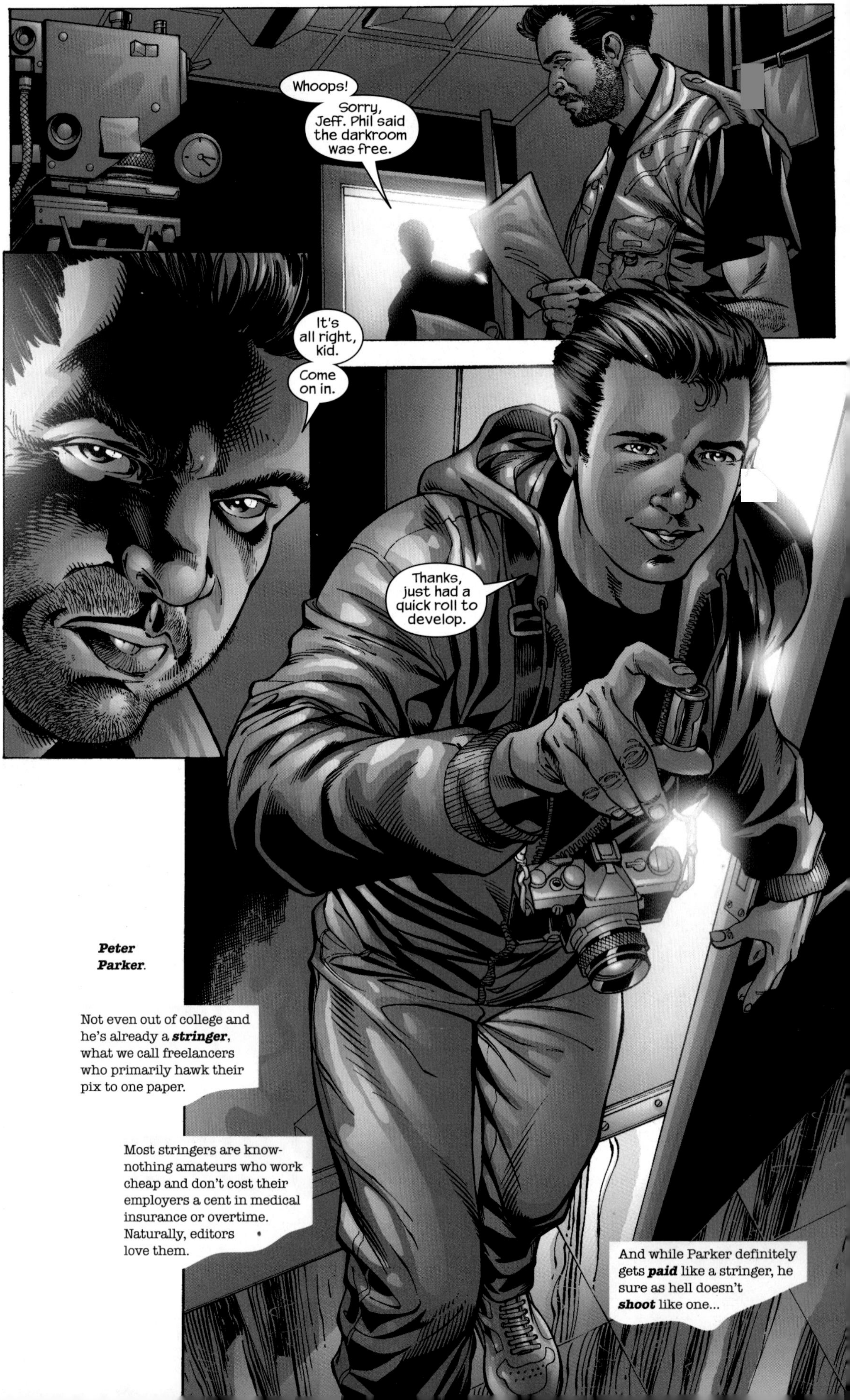
Whoops!
Sorry, Jeff. Phil said the darkroom was free.
It's all right, kid.
Come on in.
Thanks, just had a quick roll to develop.
Peter Parker.
Not even out of college and he's already a ***stringer***, what we call freelancers who primarily hawk their pix to one paper.
Most stringers are know-nothing amateurs who work cheap and don't cost their employers a cent in medical insurance or overtime. Naturally, editors love them.
And while Parker definitely gets ***paid*** like a stringer, he sure as hell doesn't ***shoot*** like one...

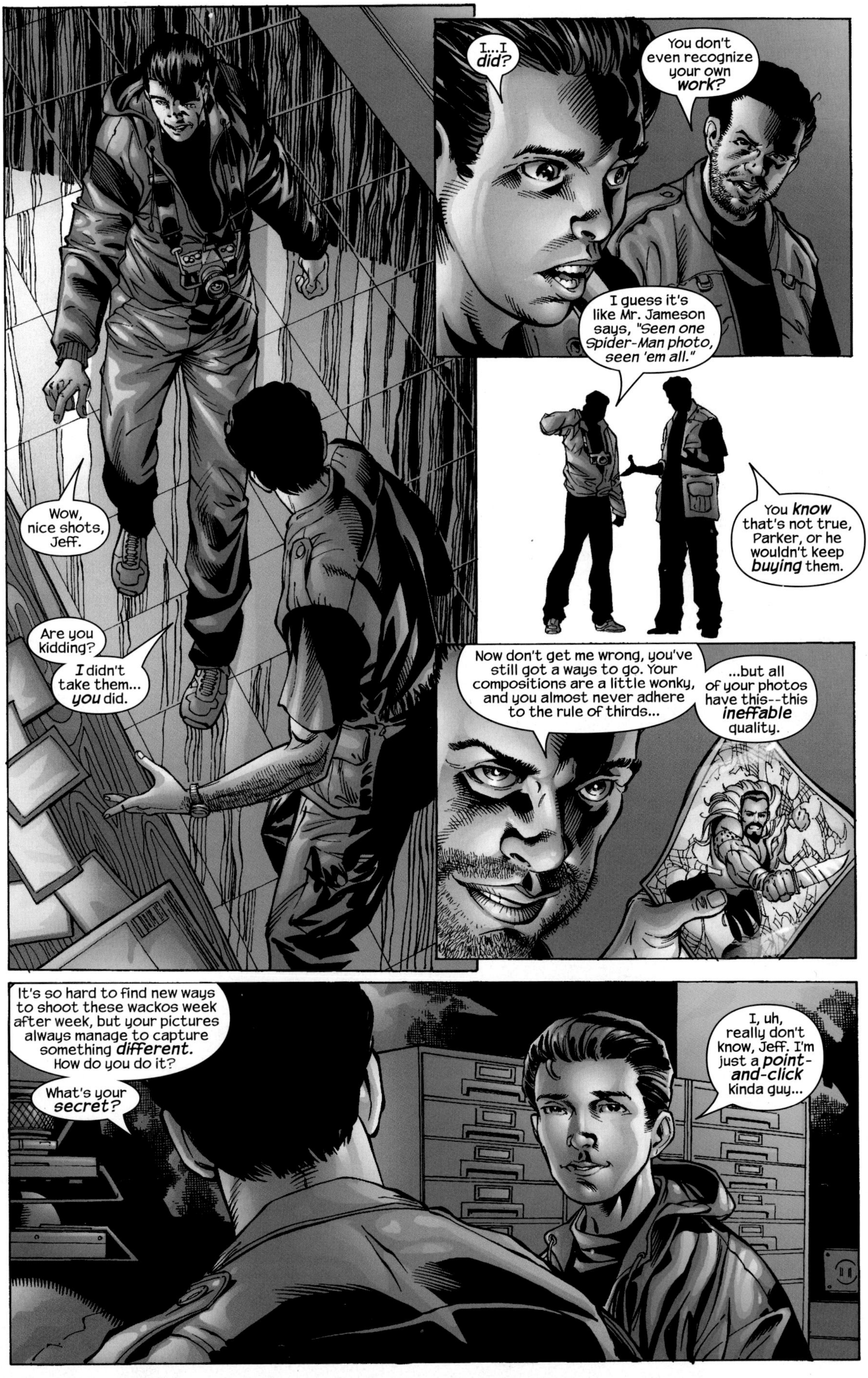
Wow, nice shots, Jeff.
Are you kidding?
I didn't take them... you did.
I...I did?
You don't even recognize your own work?
I guess it's like Mr. Jameson says, "Seen one Spider-Man photo, seen 'em all."
You know that's not true, Parker, or he wouldn't keep buying them.
Now don't get me wrong, you've still got a ways to go. Your compositions are a little wonky, and you almost never adhere to the rule of thirds...
...but all of your photos have this--this ineffable quality.
It's so hard to find new ways to shoot these wackos week after week, but your pictures always manage to capture something different. How do you do it?
What's your secret?
I, uh, really don't know, Jeff. I'm just a point-and-click kinda guy...

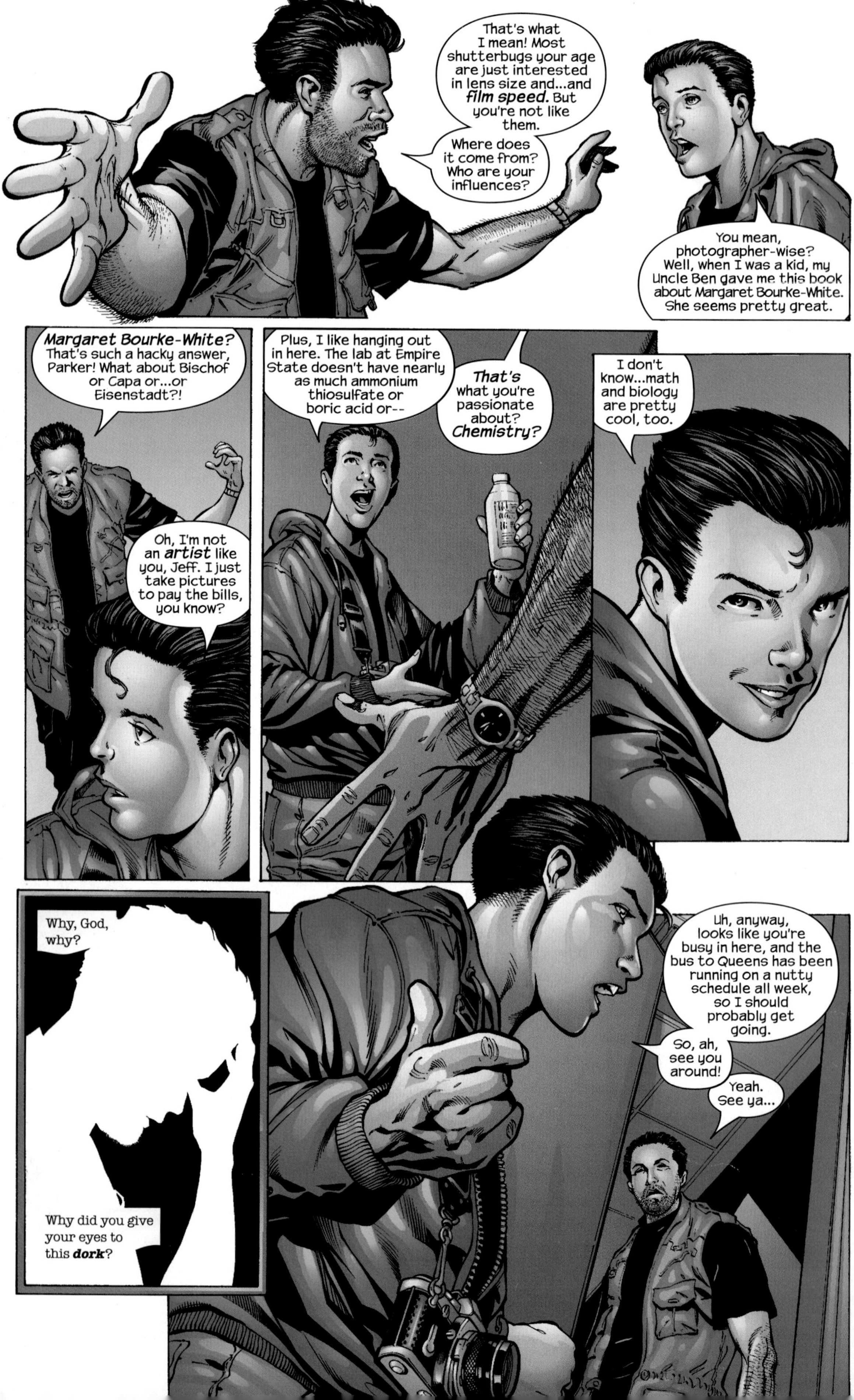
That's what I mean! Most shutterbugs your age are just interested in lens size and...and **film speed.** But you're not like them.
Where does it come from? Who are your influences?
You mean, photographer-wise? Well, when I was a kid, my Uncle Ben gave me this book about Margaret Bourke-White. She seems pretty great.
Margaret Bourke-White? That's such a hacky answer, Parker! What about Bischof or Capa or...or Eisenstadt?!
Oh, I'm not an ***artist*** like you, Jeff. I just take pictures to pay the bills, you know?
Plus, I like hanging out in here. The lab at Empire State doesn't have nearly as much ammonium thiosulfate or boric acid or--
That's what you're passionate about? ***Chemistry?***
I don't know...math and biology are pretty cool, too.
Why, God, why?
Why did you give your eyes to this ***dork***?
Uh, anyway, looks like you're busy in here, and the bus to Queens has been running on a nutty schedule all week, so I should probably get going.
So, ah, see you around!
Yeah. See ya...

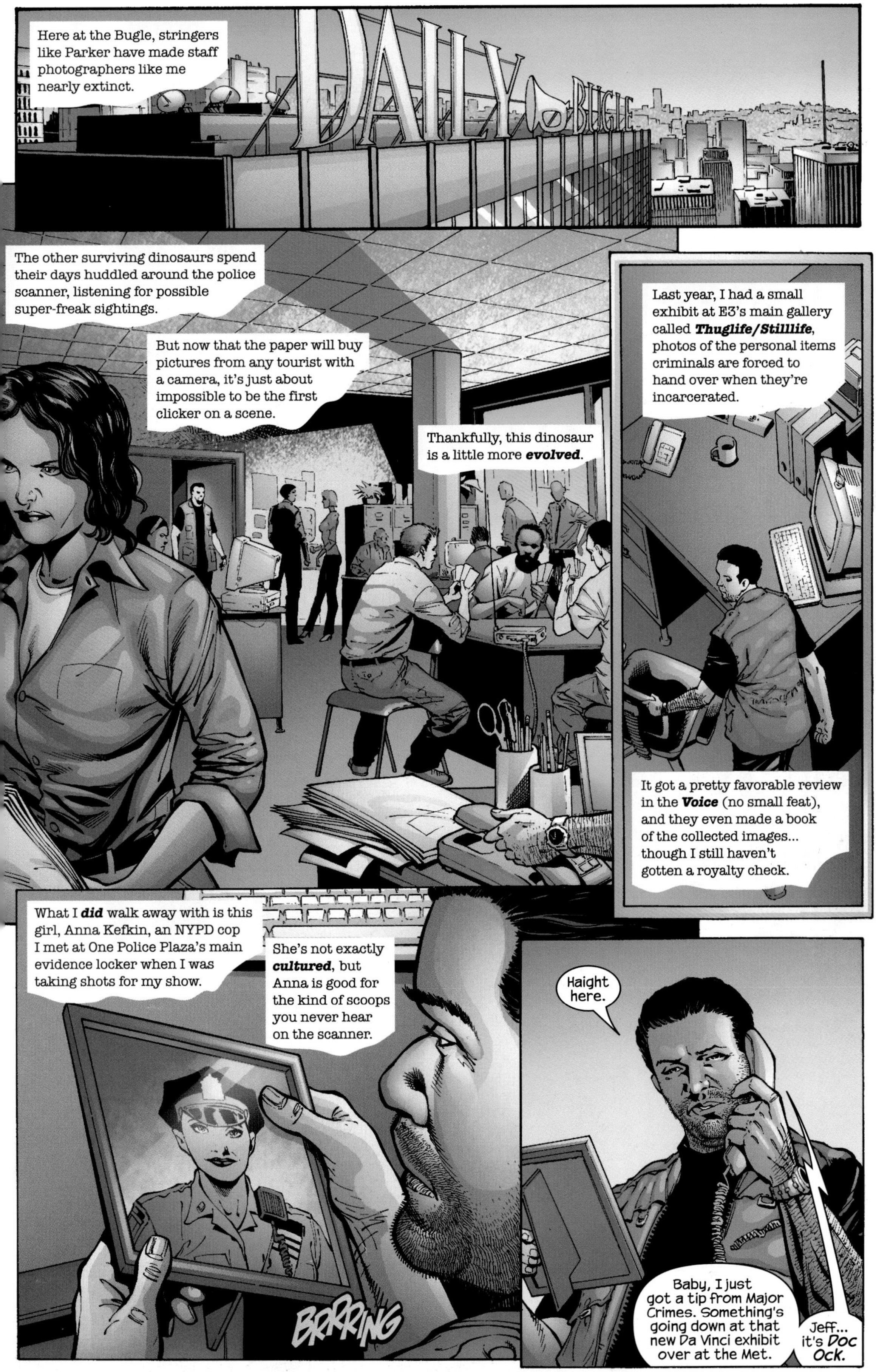
Here at the Bugle, stringers like Parker have made staff photographers like me nearly extinct.
DAILY BUGLE
The other surviving dinosaurs spend their days huddled around the police scanner, listening for possible super-freak sightings.
But now that the paper will buy pictures from any tourist with a camera, it's just about impossible to be the first clicker on a scene.
Thankfully, this dinosaur is a little more ***evolved***.
Last year, I had a small exhibit at E3's main gallery called ***Thuglife/Stilllife***, photos of the personal items criminals are forced to hand over when they're incarcerated.
It got a pretty favorable review in the ***Voice*** (no small feat), and they even made a book of the collected images... though I still haven't gotten a royalty check.
What I ***did*** walk away with is this girl, Anna Kefkin, an NYPD cop I met at One Police Plaza's main evidence locker when I was taking shots for my show.
She's not exactly ***cultured***, but Anna is good for the kind of scoops you never hear on the scanner.
BRRRING
Haight here.
Baby, I just got a tip from Major Crimes. Something's going down at that new Da Vinci exhibit over at the Met.
Jeff... it's ***Doc Ock.***

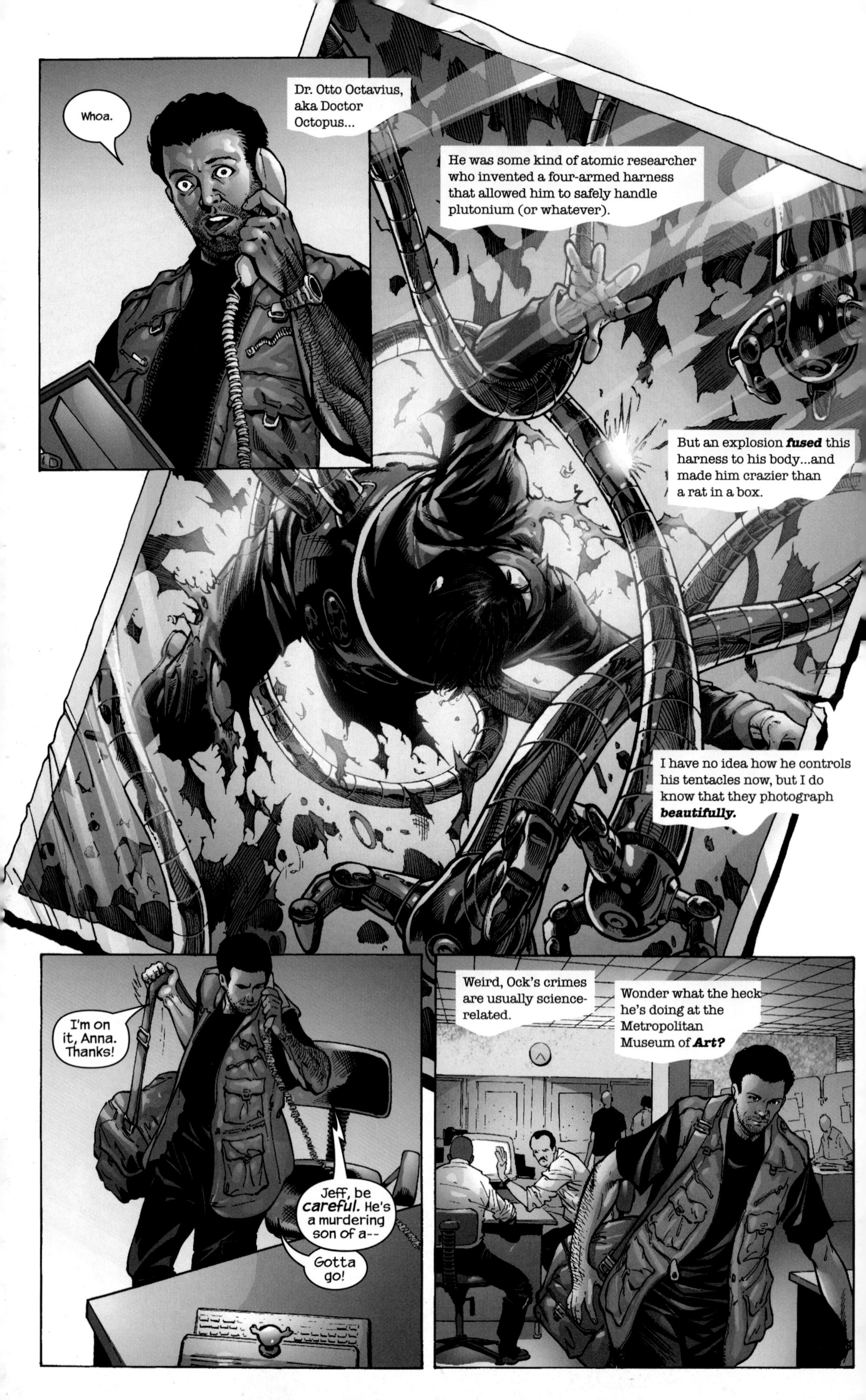
Whoa.
Dr. Otto Octavius, aka Doctor Octopus...
He was some kind of atomic researcher who invented a four-armed harness that allowed him to safely handle plutonium (or whatever).
But an explosion *fused* this harness to his body...and made him crazier than a rat in a box.
I have no idea how he controls his tentacles now, but I do know that they photograph ***beautifully.***
I'm on it, Anna. Thanks!
Jeff, be ***careful.*** He's a murdering son of a--
Gotta go!
Weird, Ock's crimes are usually science-related.
Wonder what the heck he's doing at the Metropolitan Museum of ***Art?***

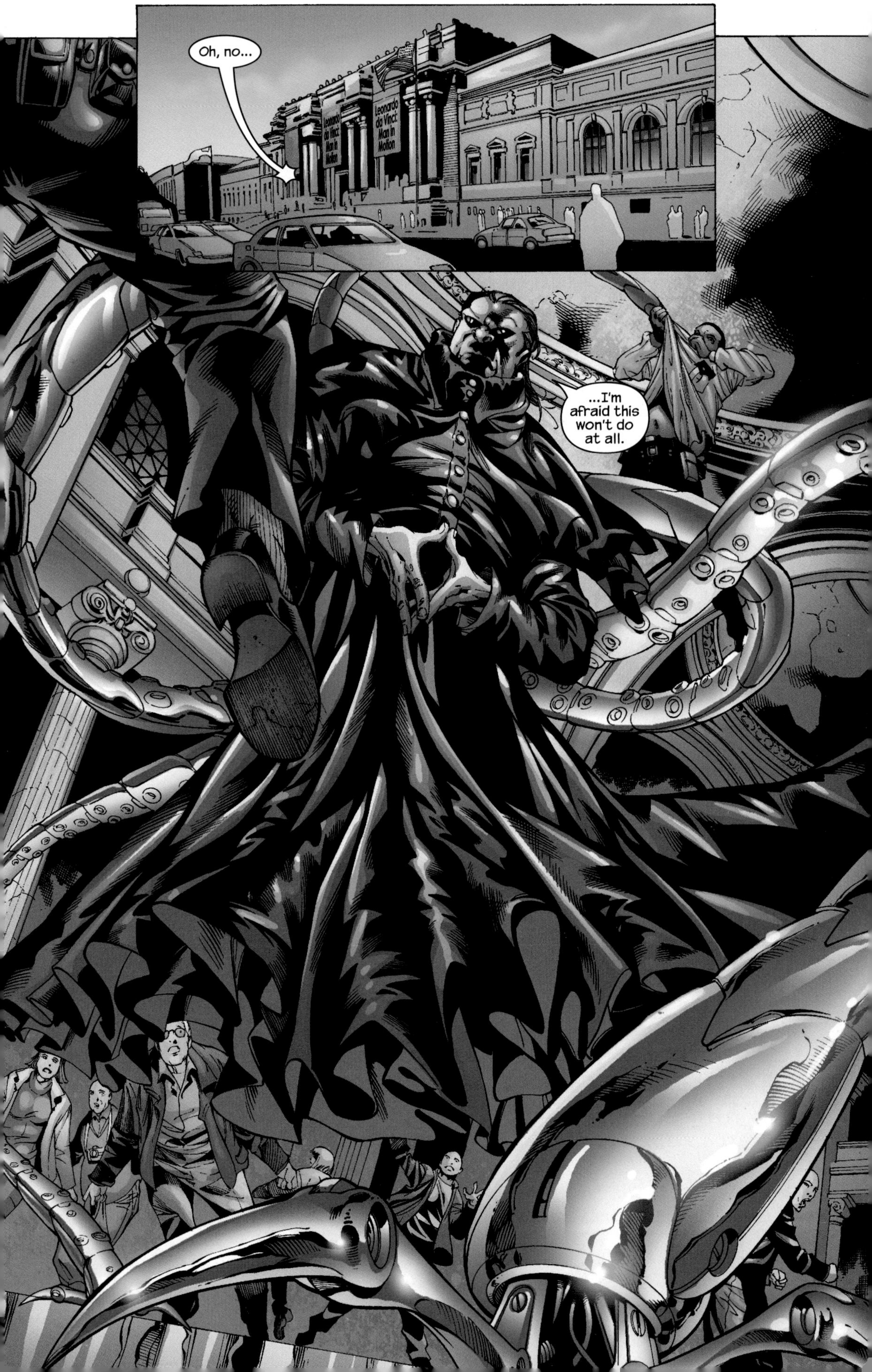
Oh, no...
Leonardo da Vinci: Man in Motion
Leonardo da Vinci: Man in Motion
...I'm afraid this won't do at all.

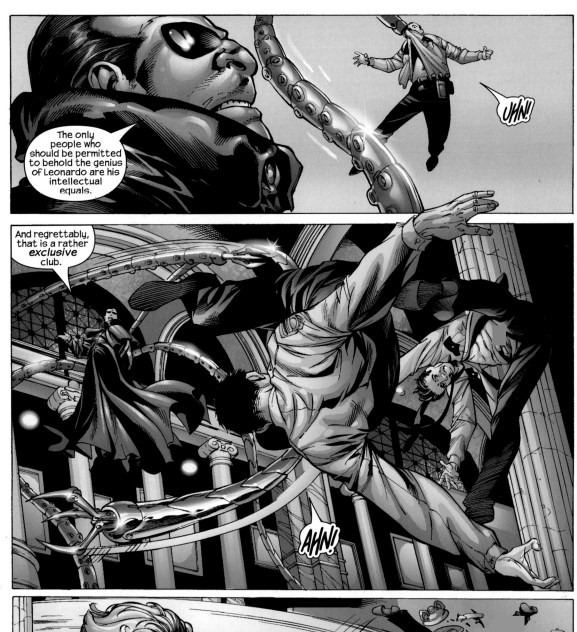

The only people who should be permitted to behold the genius of Leonardo are his intellectual equals.

UHN!

And regrettably, that is a rather *exclusive* club.

AHN!

KERRASH

Now then, *il miglior fabbro*, it's just you and I...

As I was saying, it was *this*, your seminal sketch, "*Proportional Study of Man in the Manner of Vitruvius*," which forever changed my life.

Your perfect human specimen, with his eight gloriously symmetrical appendages, inspired *my* humble contribution to the world of invention.

A work of such significance deserves to be in the possession of one who *appreciates* its true importance, don't you think?

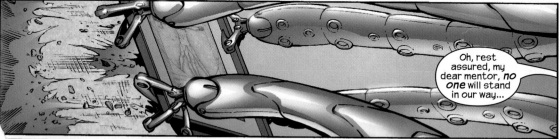

Oh, rest assured, my dear mentor, *no one* will stand in our way...

M4 BUS STOP

Leonardo da Vinci: Man in Motion

Darn it. I *knew* I should have taken the subway.

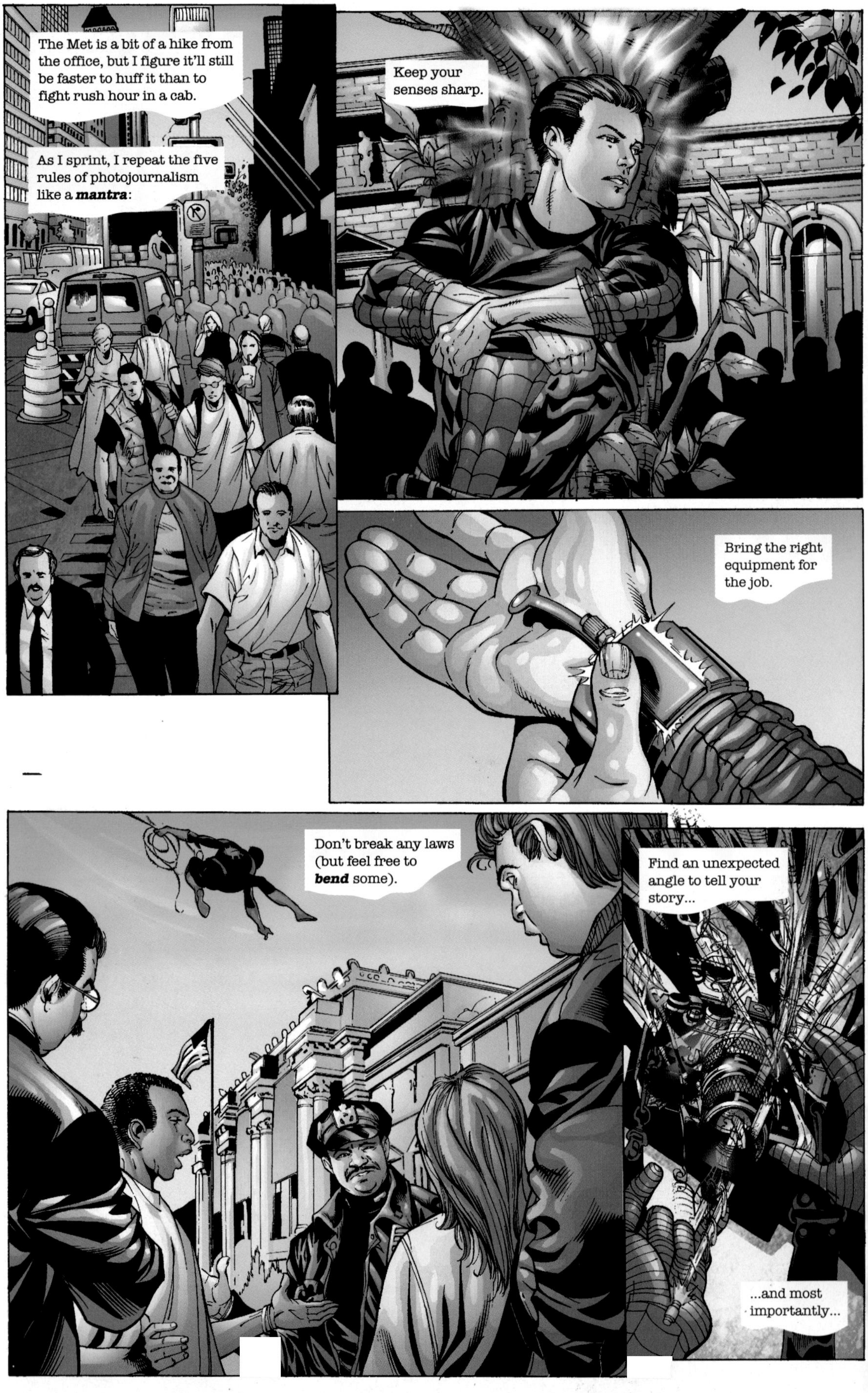

The Met is a bit of a hike from the office, but I figure it'll still be faster to huff it than to fight rush hour in a cab.
As I sprint, I repeat the five rules of photojournalism like a *mantra*:
Keep your senses sharp.
Bring the right equipment for the job.
Don't break any laws (but feel free to *bend* some).
Find an unexpected angle to tell your story...
...and most importantly...

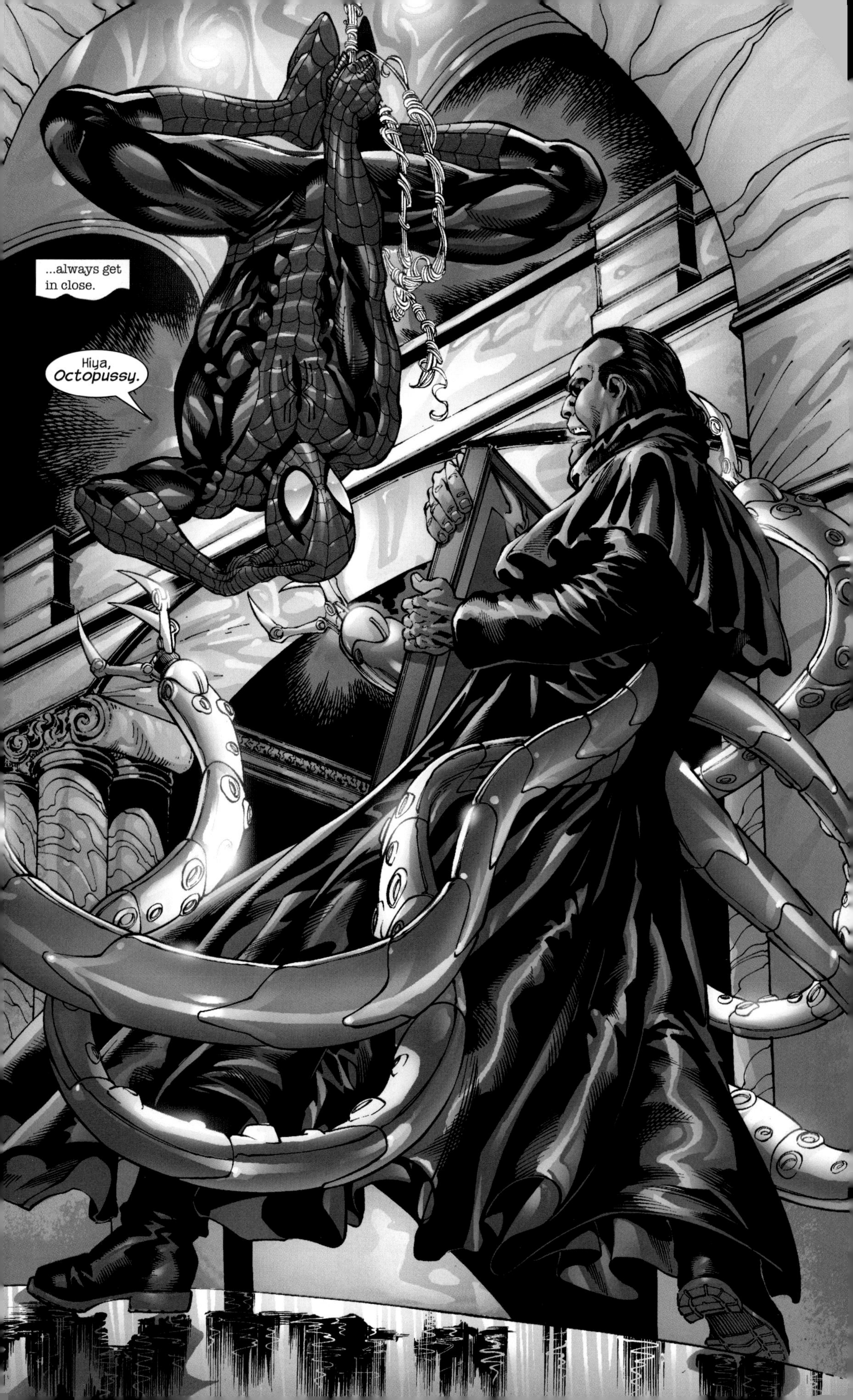
...always get in close.
Hiya, Octopussy.

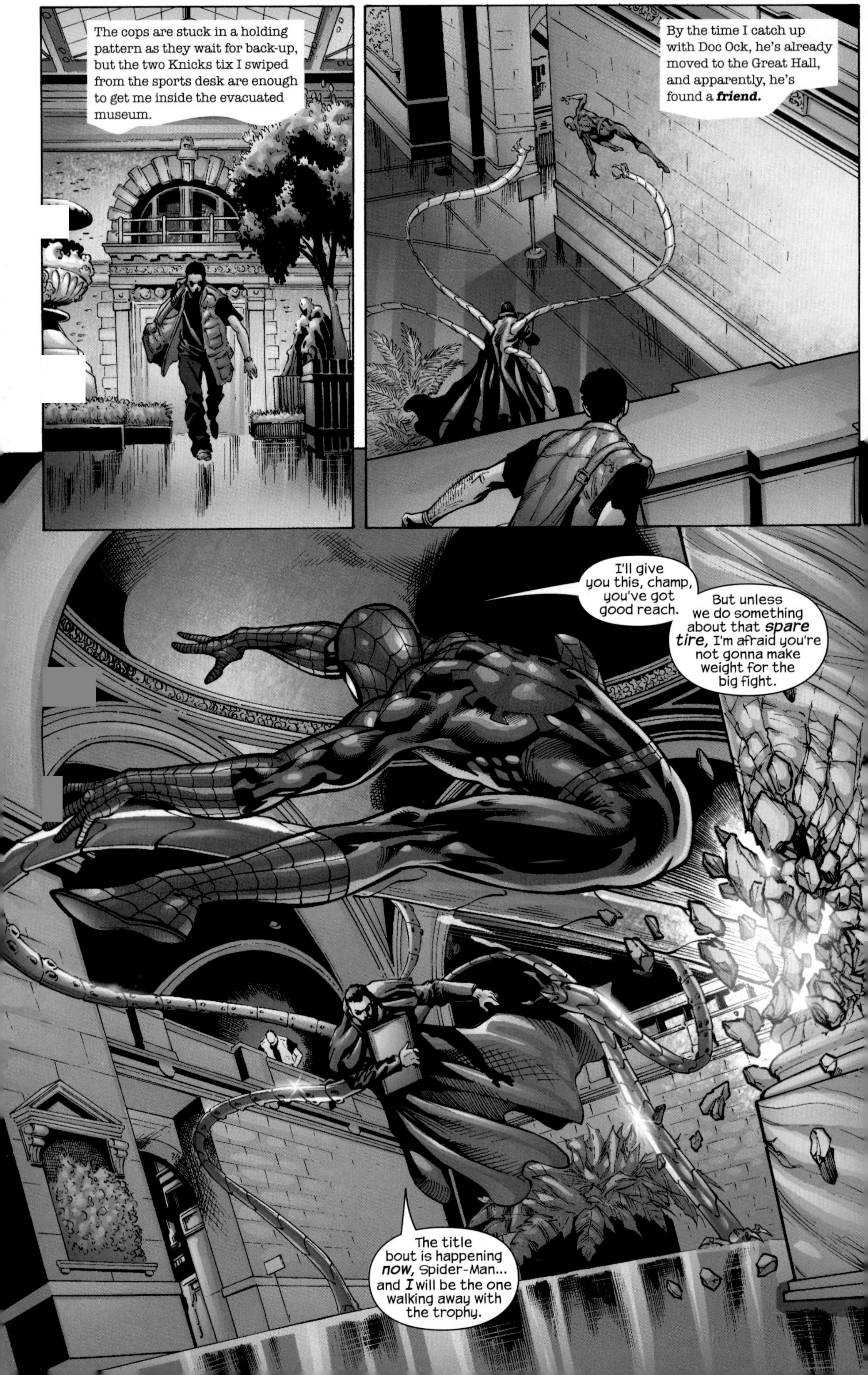

The cops are stuck in a holding pattern as they wait for back-up, but the two Knicks tix I swiped from the sports desk are enough to get me inside the evacuated museum.
By the time I catch up with Doc Ock, he's already moved to the Great Hall, and apparently, he's found a **friend.**
I'll give you this, champ, you've got good reach.
But unless we do something about that **spare tire,** I'm afraid you're not gonna make weight for the big fight.
The title bout is happening **now,** Spider-Man... and **I** will be the one walking away with the trophy.

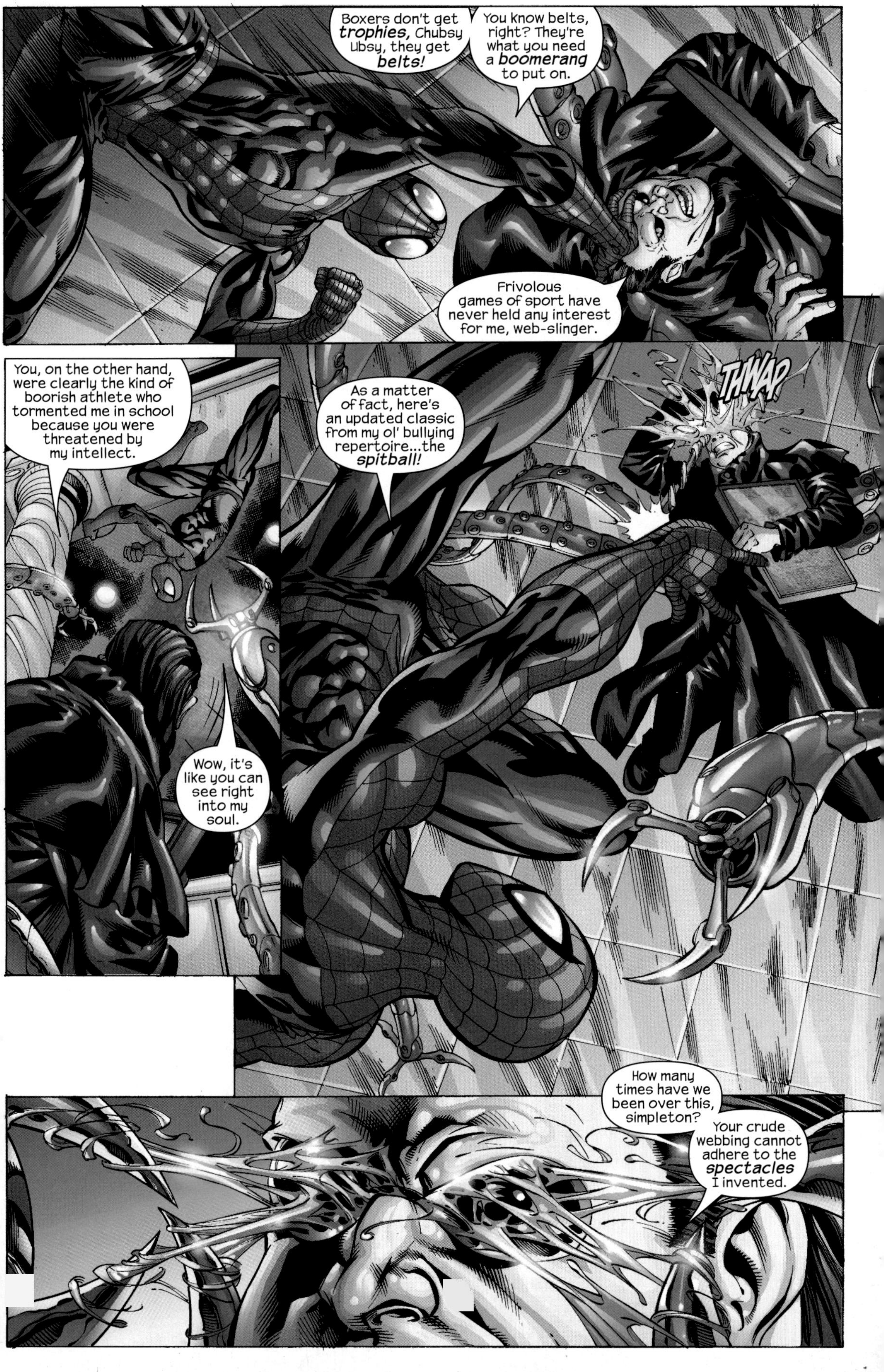

Boxers don't get trophies, Chubsy Ubsy, they get belts!
You know belts, right? They're what you need a boomerang to put on.
Frivolous games of sport have never held any interest for me, web-slinger.
You, on the other hand, were clearly the kind of boorish athlete who tormented me in school because you were threatened by my intellect.
Wow, it's like you can see right into my soul.
As a matter of fact, here's an updated classic from my ol' bullying repertoire...the spitball!
THWAP
How many times have we been over this, simpleton?
Your crude webbing cannot adhere to the spectacles I invented.

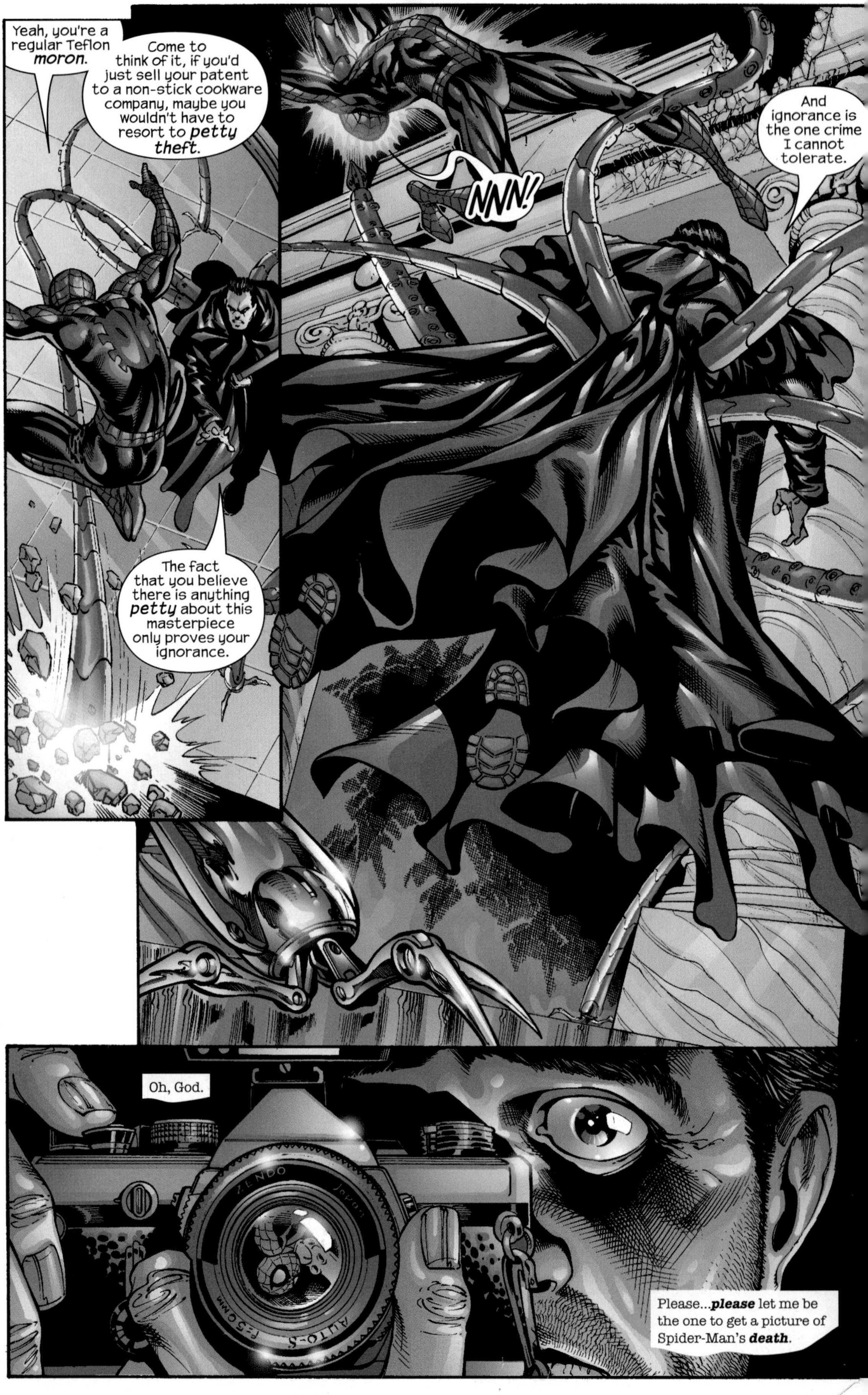
Yeah, you're a regular Teflon **moron**.
Come to think of it, if you'd just sell your patent to a non-stick cookware company, maybe you wouldn't have to resort to ***petty theft***.
NNN!
And ignorance is the one crime I cannot tolerate.
The fact that you believe there is anything ***petty*** about this masterpiece only proves your ignorance.
Oh, God.
Please...***please*** let me be the one to get a picture of Spider-Man's ***death***.

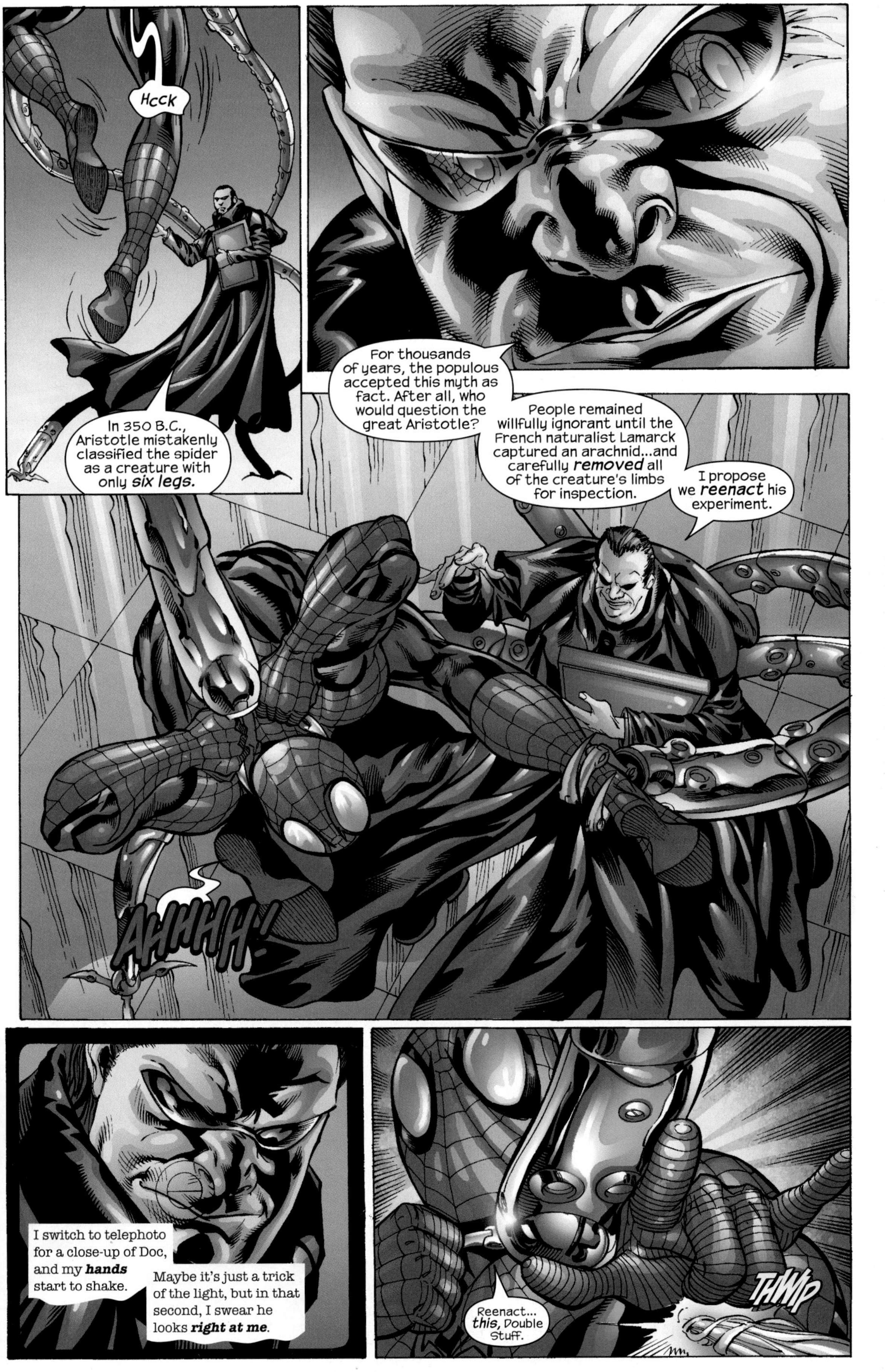
HCCK
In 350 B.C., Aristotle mistakenly classified the spider as a creature with only *six legs.*
For thousands of years, the populous accepted this myth as fact. After all, who would question the great Aristotle?
People remained willfully ignorant until the French naturalist Lamarck captured an arachnid...and carefully *removed* all of the creature's limbs for inspection.
I propose we *reenact* his experiment.
AHHHH!
I switch to telephoto for a close-up of Doc, and my *hands* start to shake.
Maybe it's just a trick of the light, but in that second, I swear he looks *right at me*.
Reenact... *this,* Double Stuff.
THWIP

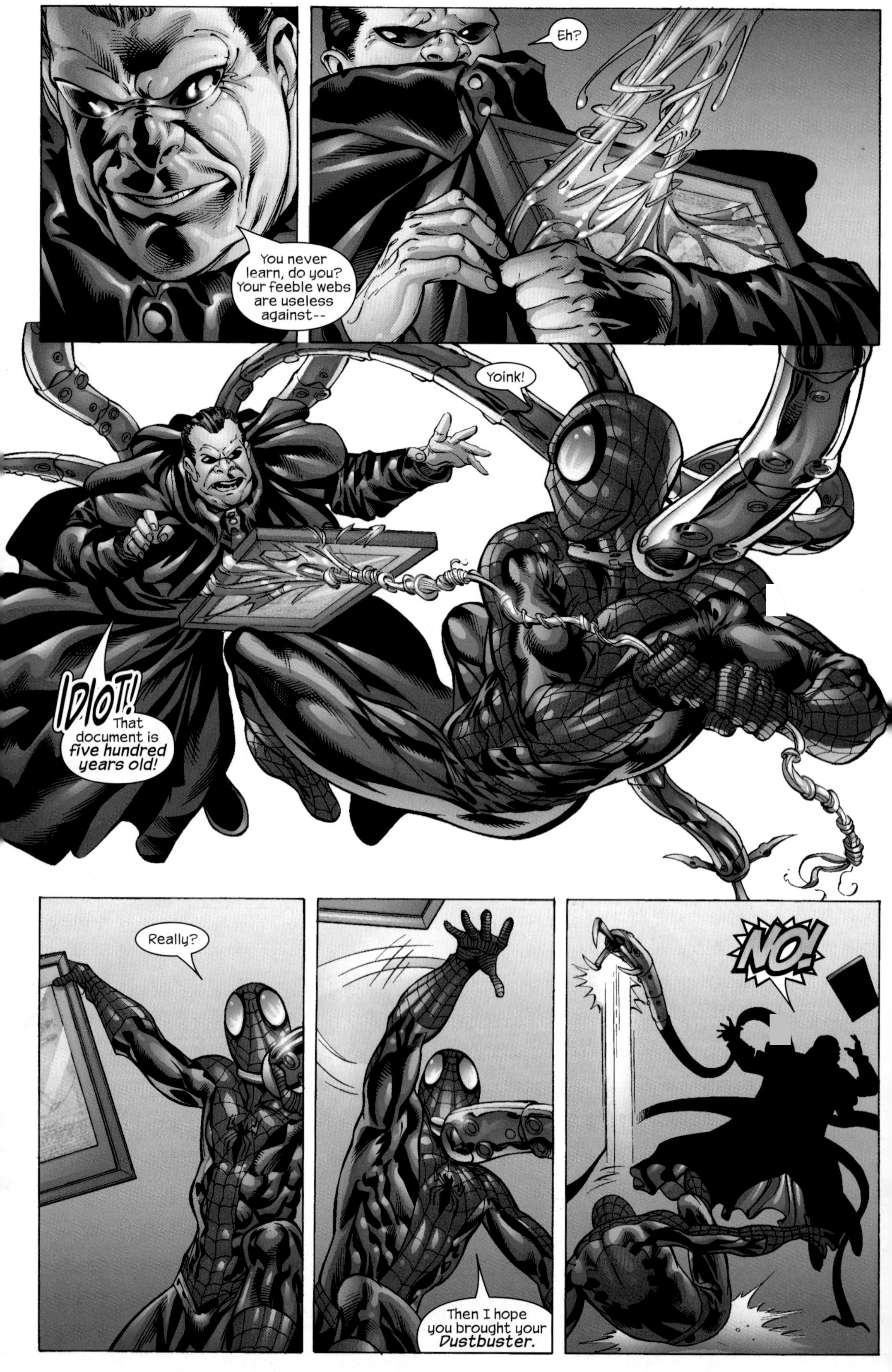
You never learn, do you? Your feeble webs are useless against--
Eh?
Yoink!
IDIOT! That document is five hundred years old!
Really?
Then I hope you brought your Dustbuster.
NO!

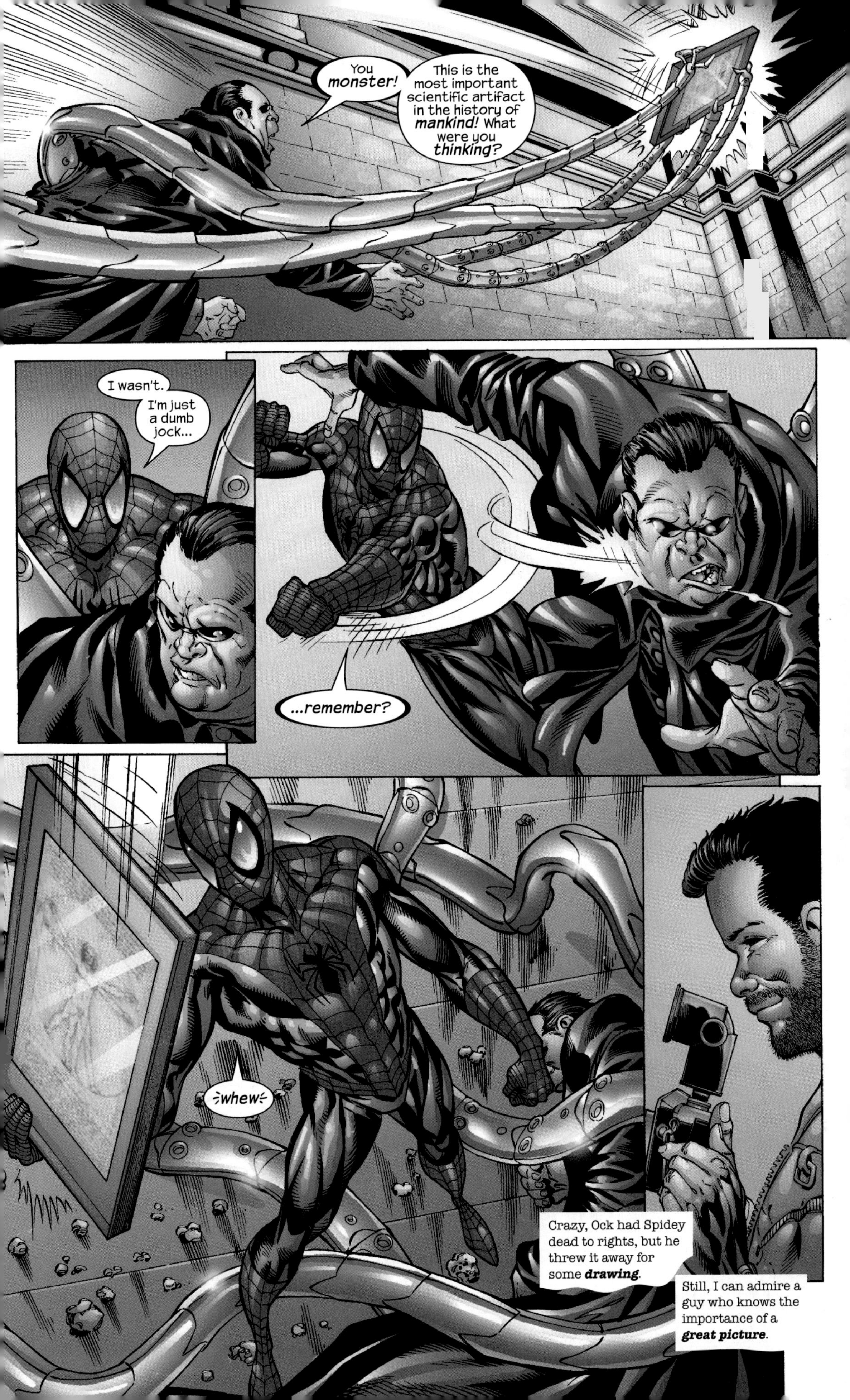
You monster!
This is the most important scientific artifact in the history of mankind! What were you thinking?
I wasn't.
I'm just a dumb jock...
...remember?
whew
Crazy, Ock had Spidey dead to rights, but he threw it away for some drawing.
Still, I can admire a guy who knows the importance of a great picture.

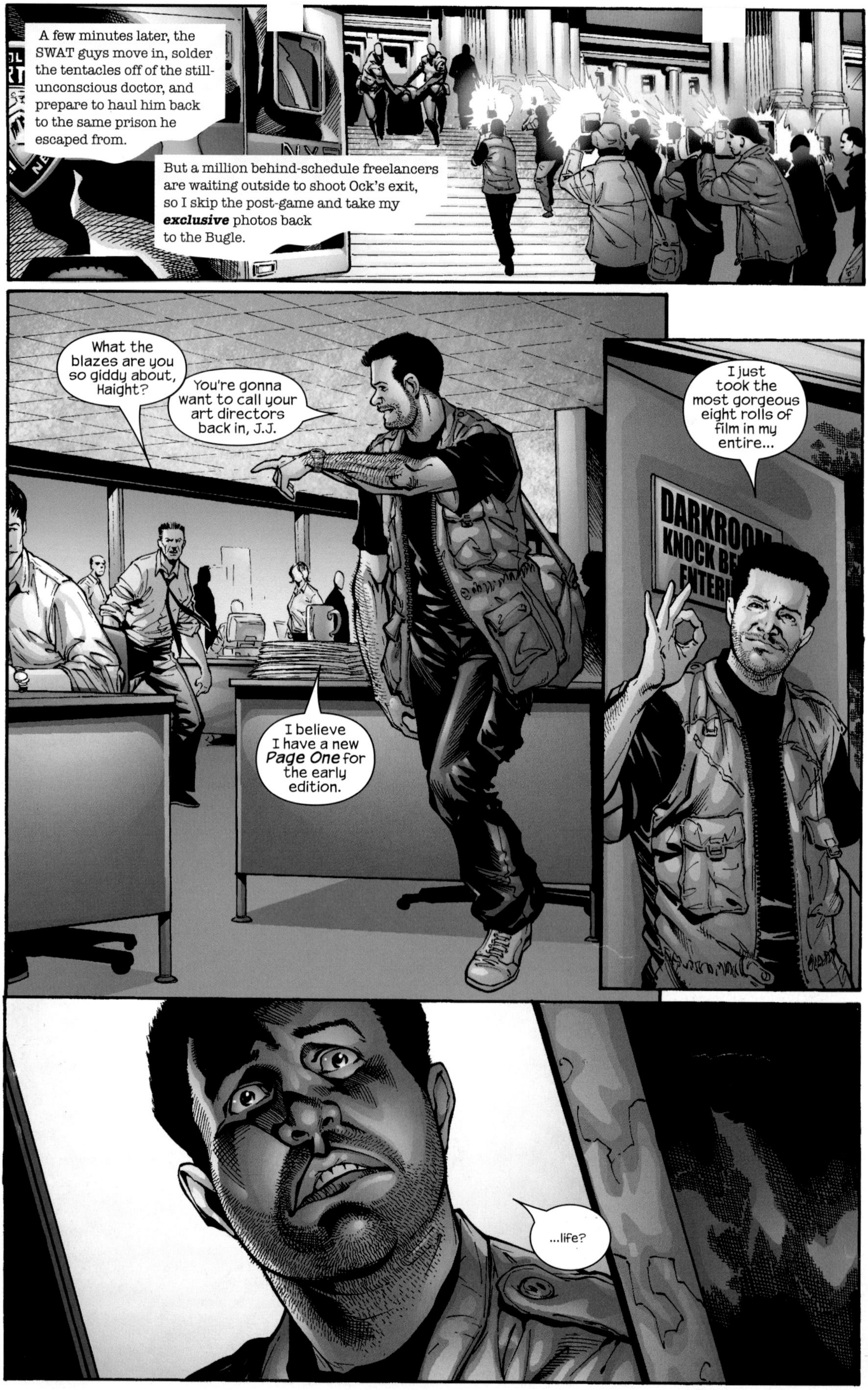
A few minutes later, the SWAT guys move in, solder the tentacles off of the still-unconscious doctor, and prepare to haul him back to the same prison he escaped from.
But a million behind-schedule freelancers are waiting outside to shoot Ock's exit, so I skip the post-game and take my *exclusive* photos back to the Bugle.
What the blazes are you so giddy about, Haight?
You're gonna want to call your art directors back in, J.J.
I believe I have a new *Page One* for the early edition.
I just took the most gorgeous eight rolls of film in my entire...
DARKROOM
...life?

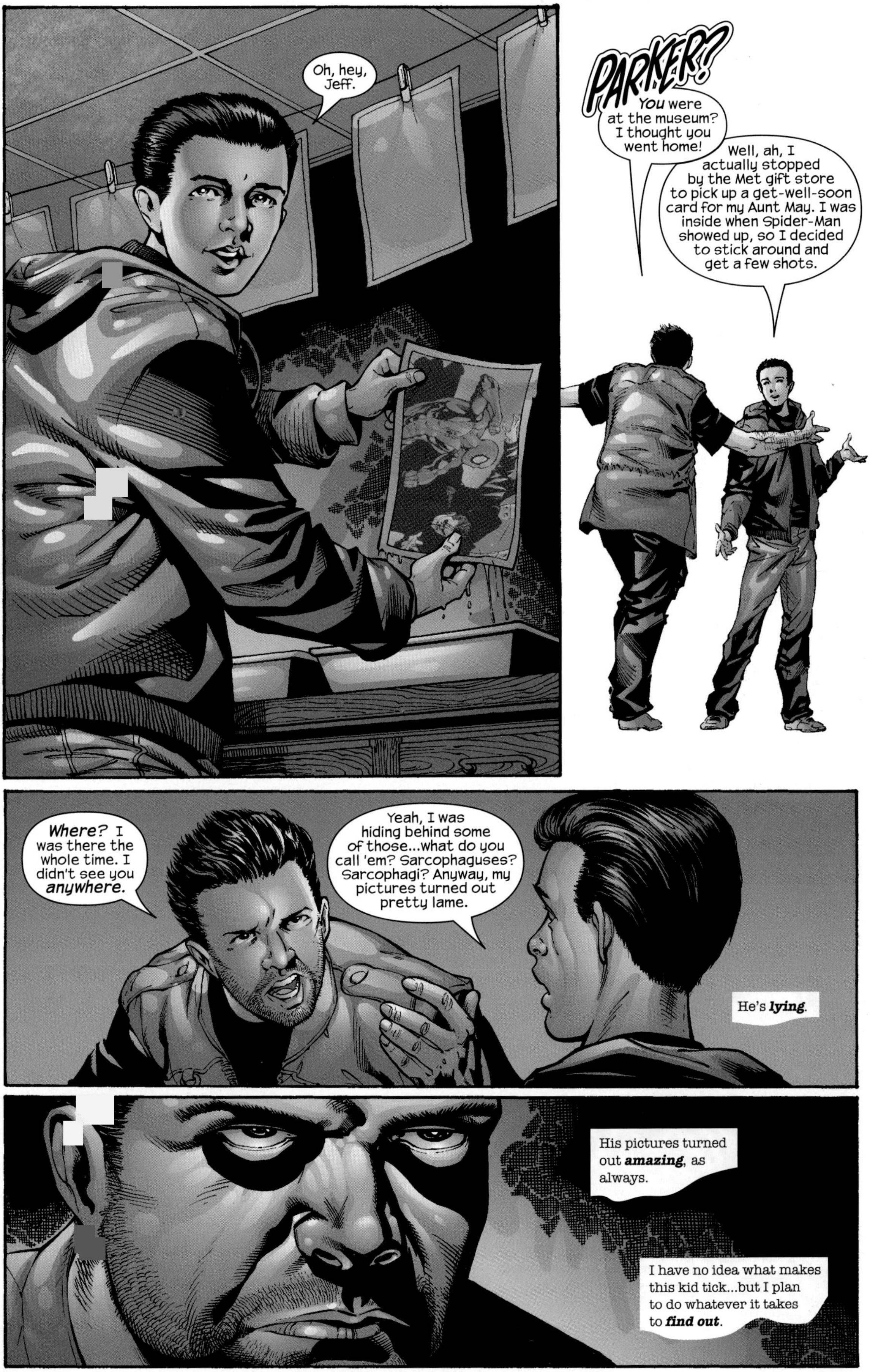
Oh, hey, Jeff.
PARKER?!
You were at the museum? I thought you went home!
Well, ah, I actually stopped by the Met gift store to pick up a get-well-soon card for my Aunt May. I was inside when Spider-Man showed up, so I decided to stick around and get a few shots.
Where? I was there the whole time. I didn't see you anywhere.
Yeah, I was hiding behind some of those...what do you call 'em? Sarcophaguses? Sarcophagi? Anyway, my pictures turned out pretty lame.
He's lying.
His pictures turned out amazing, as always.
I have no idea what makes this kid tick...but I plan to do whatever it takes to find out.

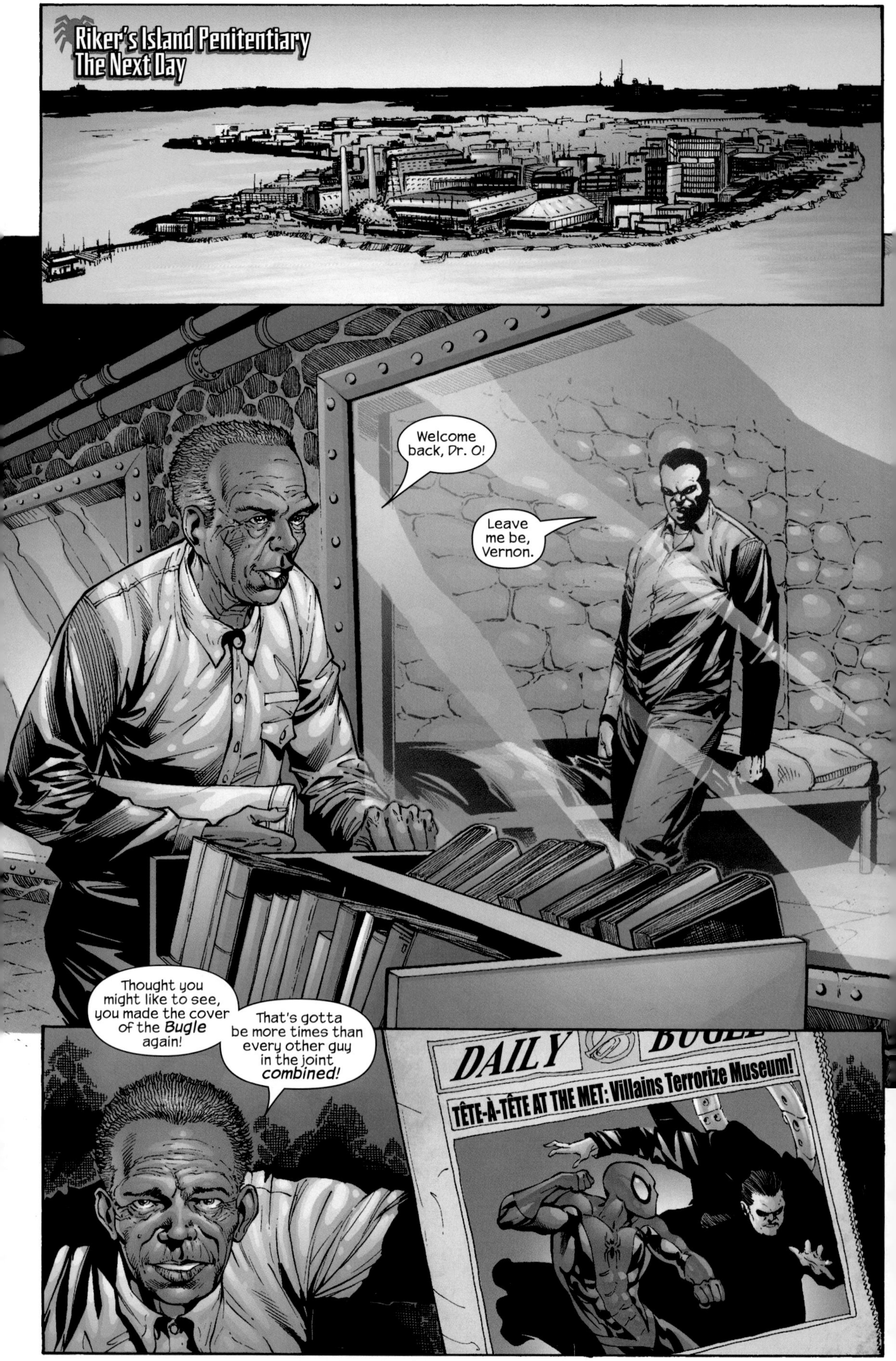
Riker's Island Penitentiary
The Next Day
Welcome back, Dr. O!
Leave me be, Vernon.
Thought you might like to see, you made the cover of the *Bugle* again!
That's gotta be more times than every other guy in the joint *combined!*
DAILY BUGLE
TÊTE-À-TÊTE AT THE MET: Villains Terrorize Museum!

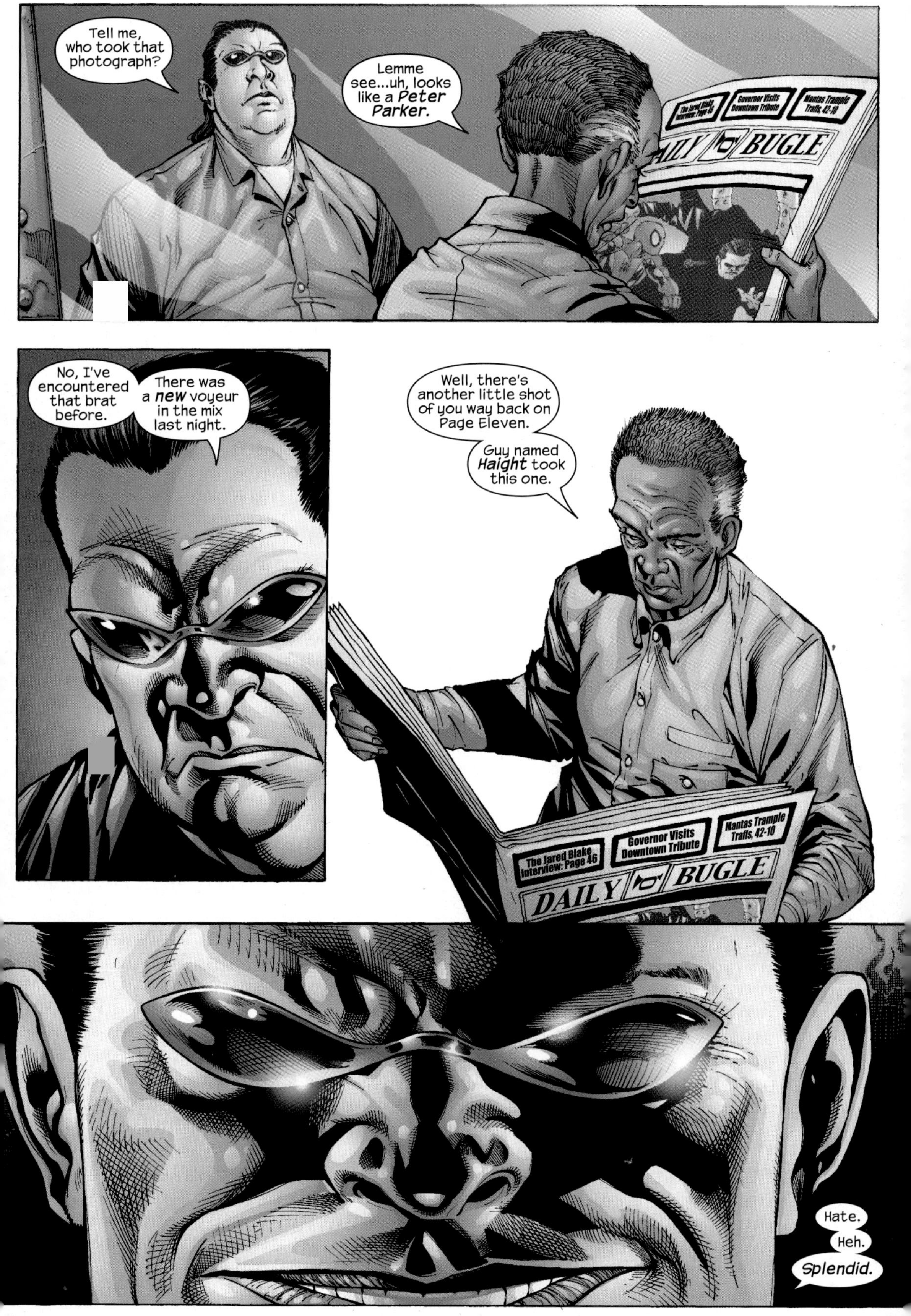
Tell me, who took that photograph?
Lemme see...uh, looks like a Peter Parker.
The Jared Blake Interview: Page 46
Governor Visits Downtown Tribute
Mantas Trample Traffs, 42-10
DAILY BUGLE
No, I've encountered that brat before.
There was a new voyeur in the mix last night.
Well, there's another little shot of you way back on Page Eleven.
Guy named Haight took this one.
The Jared Blake Interview: Page 46
Governor Visits Downtown Tribute
Mantas Trample Traffs, 42-10
DAILY BUGLE
Hate.
Heh.
Splendid.

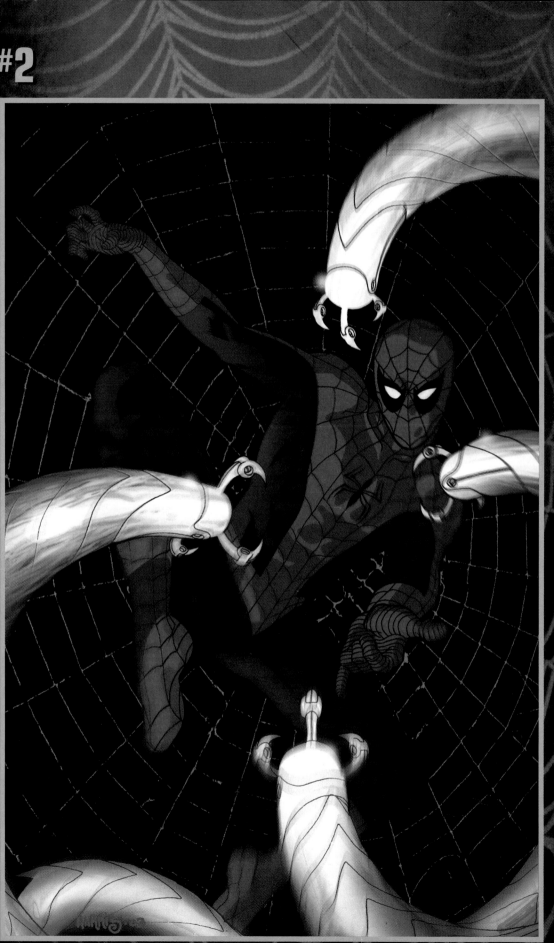

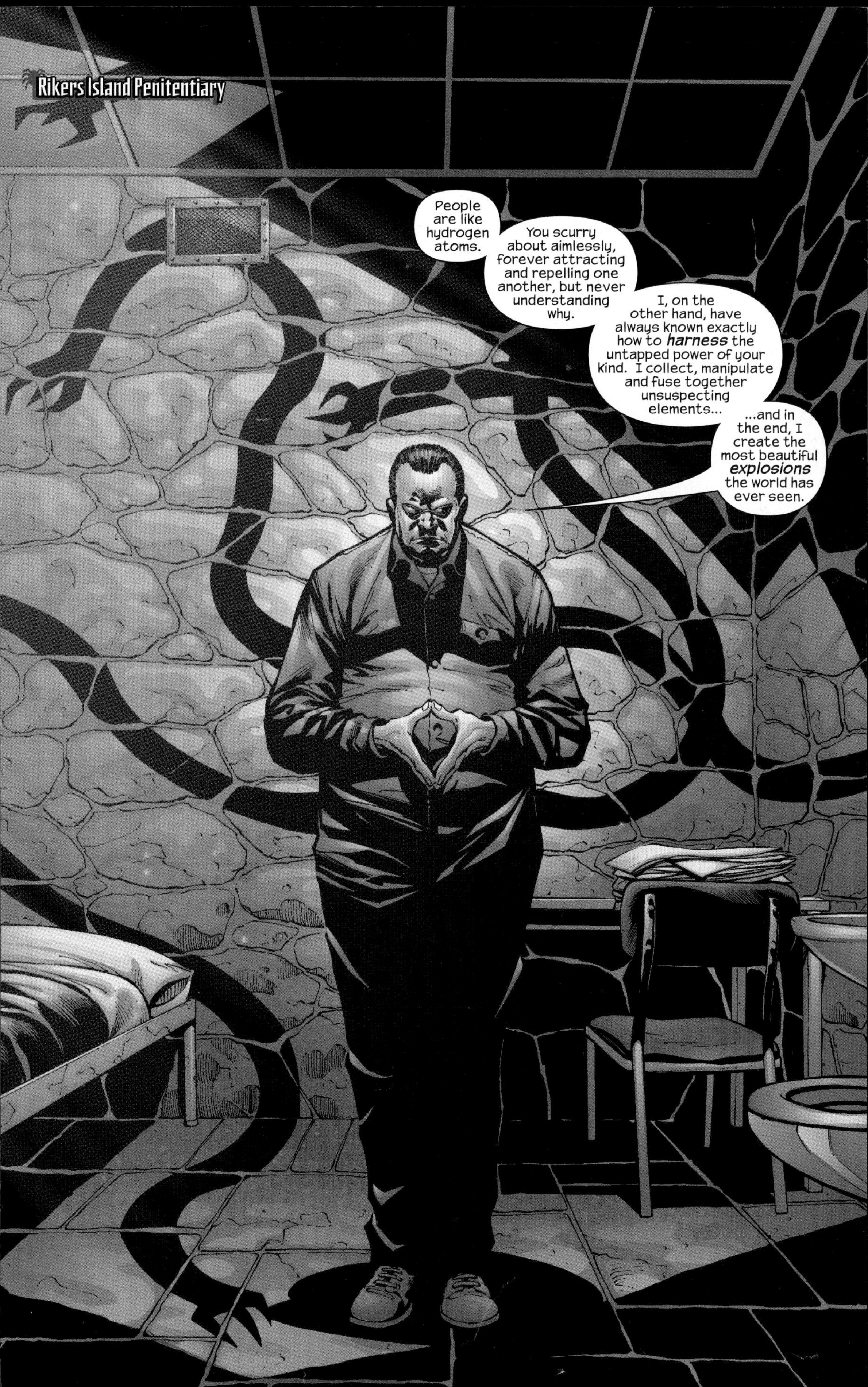
Rikers Island Penitentiary
People are like hydrogen atoms.
You scurry about aimlessly, forever attracting and repelling one another, but never understanding why.
I, on the other hand, have always known exactly how to *harness* the untapped power of your kind. I collect, manipulate and fuse together unsuspecting elements...
...and in the end, I create the most beautiful *explosions* the world has ever seen.

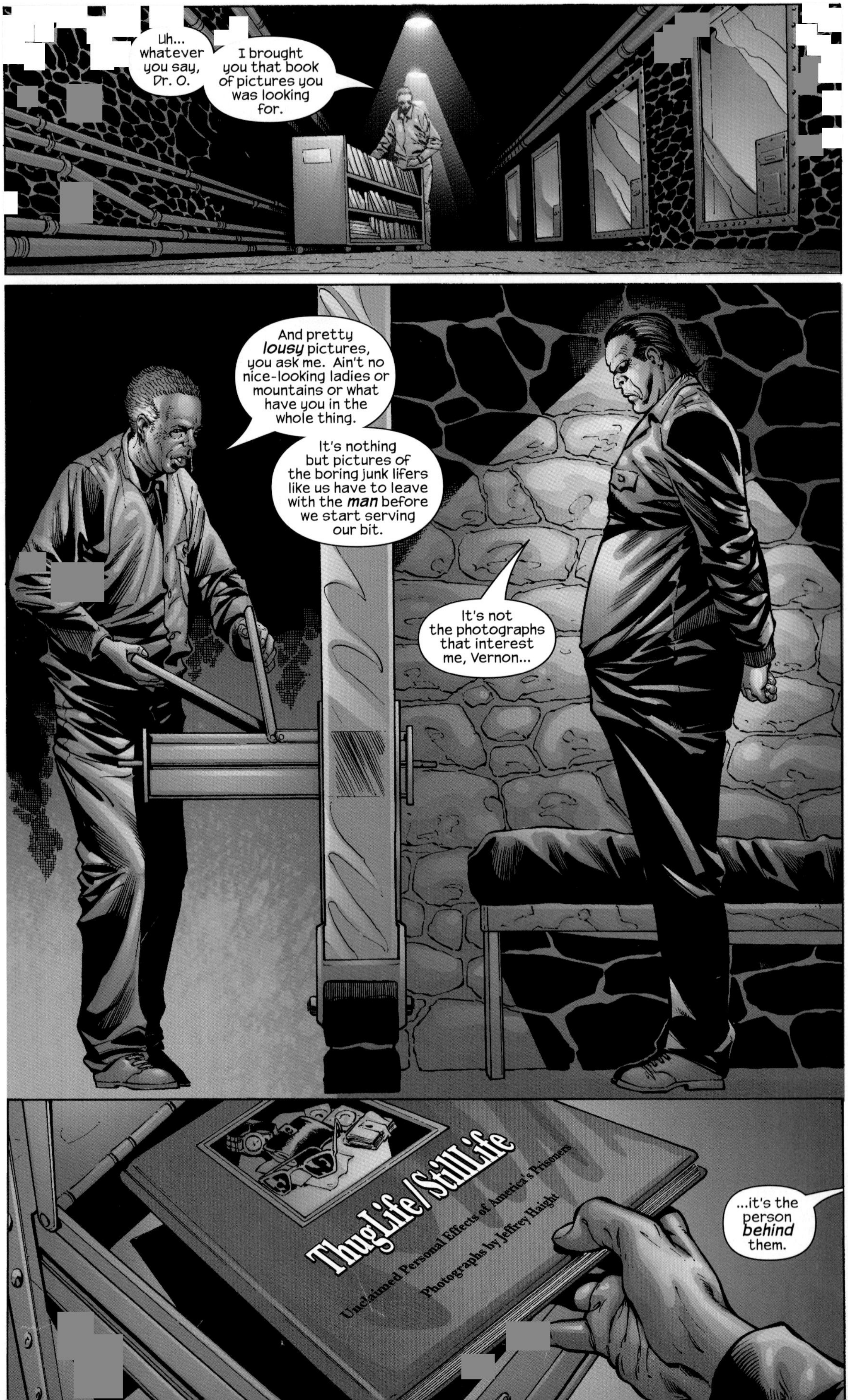
Uh... whatever you say, Dr. O.
I brought you that book of pictures you was looking for.
And pretty lousy pictures, you ask me. Ain't no nice-looking ladies or mountains or what have you in the whole thing.
It's nothing but pictures of the boring junk lifers like us have to leave with the man before we start serving our bit.
It's not the photographs that interest me, Vernon...
ThugLife/StillLife
Unclaimed Personal Effects of America's Prisoners
Photographs by Jeffrey Haight
...it's the person behind them.

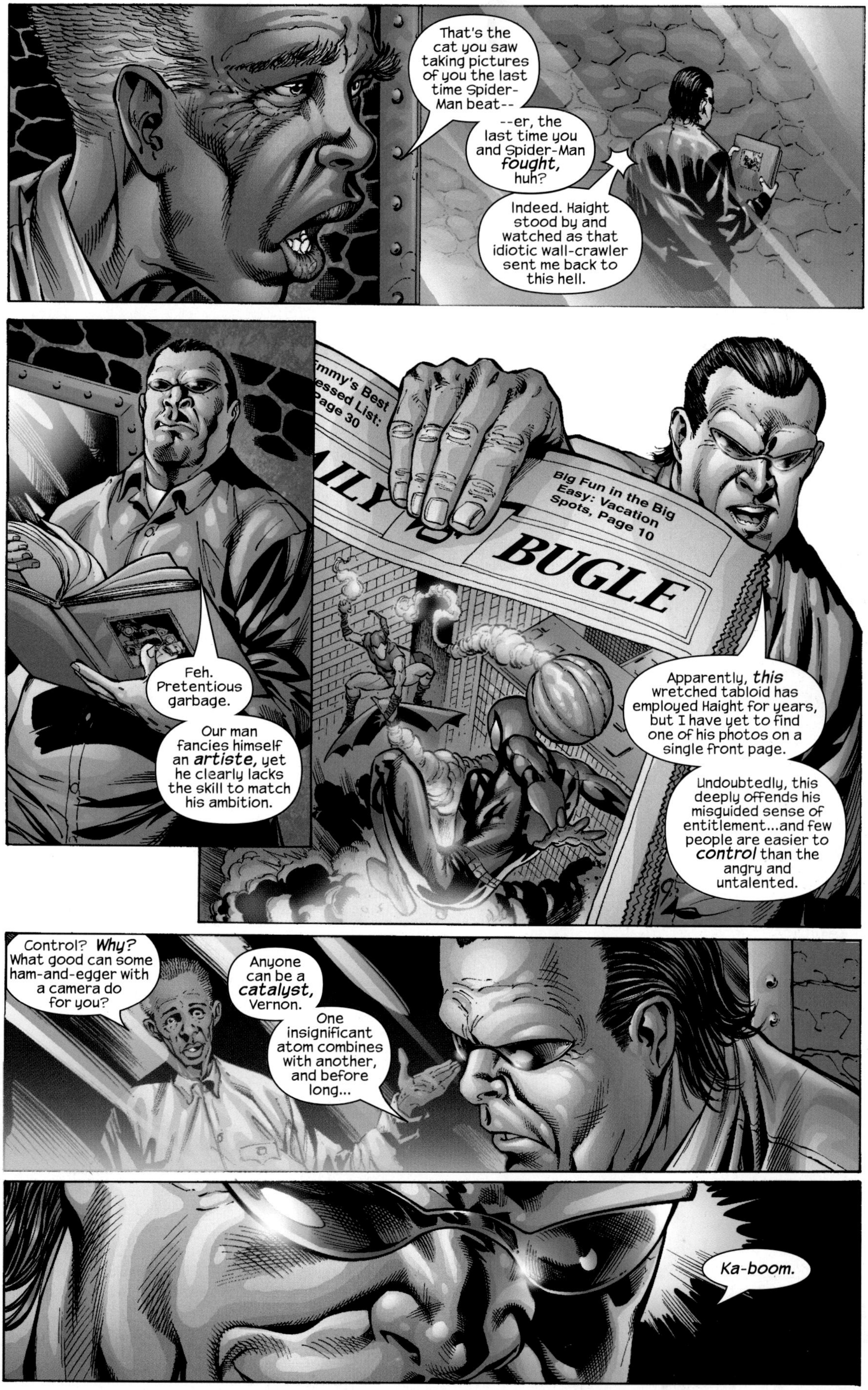

That's the cat you saw taking pictures of you the last time Spider-Man beat--
--er, the last time you and Spider-Man *fought,* huh?
Indeed. Haight stood by and watched as that idiotic wall-crawler sent me back to this hell.
Feh. Pretentious garbage.
Our man fancies himself an *artiste,* yet he clearly lacks the skill to match his ambition.
Big Fun in the Big Easy: Vacation Spots, Page 10
BUGLE
Apparently, *this* wretched tabloid has employed Haight for years, but I have yet to find one of his photos on a single front page.
Undoubtedly, this deeply offends his misguided sense of entitlement...and few people are easier to *control* than the angry and untalented.
Control? *Why?* What good can some ham-and-egger with a camera do for you?
Anyone can be a *catalyst,* Vernon.
One insignificant atom combines with another, and before long...
Ka-boom.

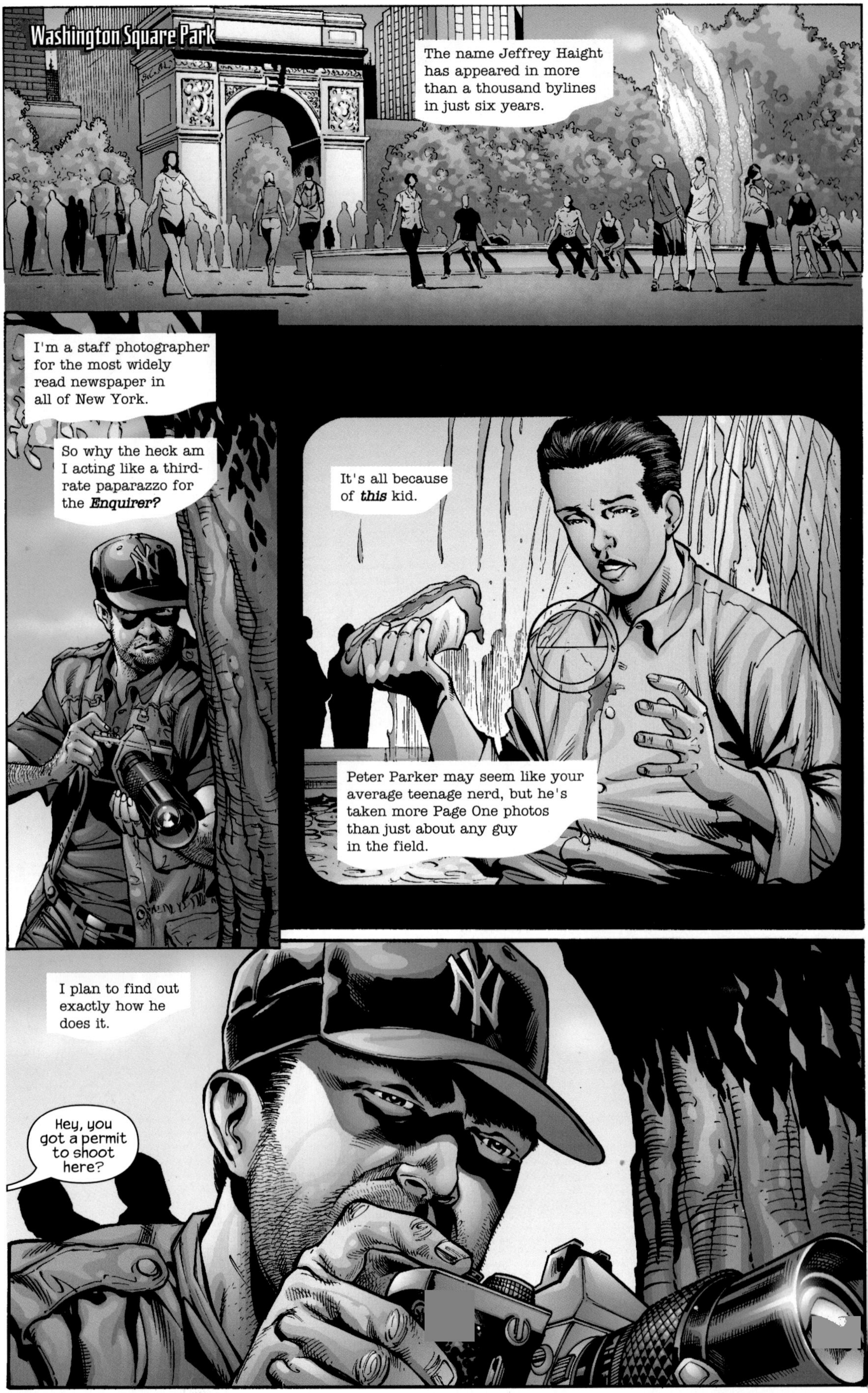
Washington Square Park
The name Jeffrey Haight has appeared in more than a thousand bylines in just six years.
I'm a staff photographer for the most widely read newspaper in all of New York.
So why the heck am I acting like a third-rate paparazzo for the *Enquirer?*
It's all because of ***this*** kid.
Peter Parker may seem like your average teenage nerd, but he's taken more Page One photos than just about any guy in the field.
I plan to find out exactly how he does it.
Hey, you got a permit to shoot here?

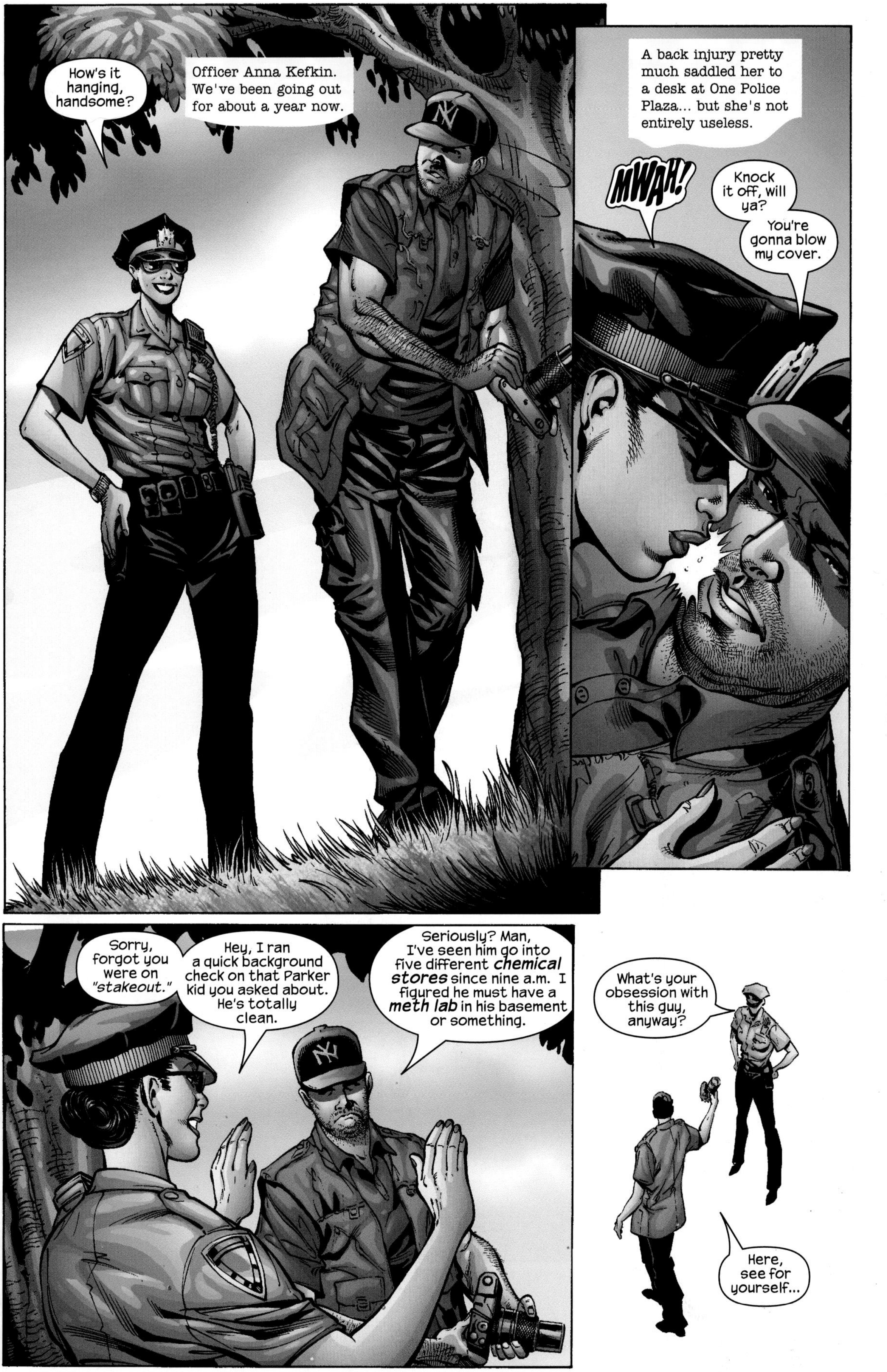
How's it hanging, handsome?
Officer Anna Kefkin. We've been going out for about a year now.
A back injury pretty much saddled her to a desk at One Police Plaza... but she's not entirely useless.
MWAH!
Knock it off, will ya?
You're gonna blow my cover.
Sorry, forgot you were on "stakeout."
Hey, I ran a quick background check on that Parker kid you asked about. He's totally clean.
Seriously? Man, I've seen him go into five different chemical stores since nine a.m. I figured he must have a meth lab in his basement or something.
What's your obsession with this guy, anyway?
Here, see for yourself...

Hm, little scrawny for my tastes.

Exactly.

Now take a look at the *chick* he's with.

Wow.

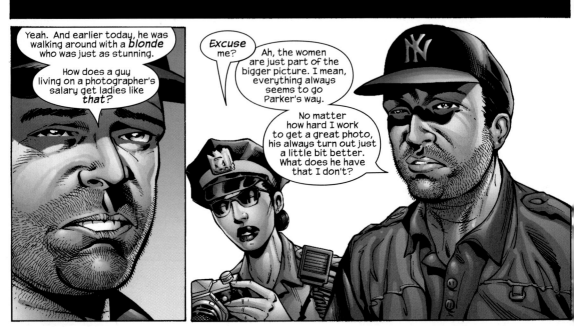

Yeah. And earlier today, he was walking around with a *blonde* who was just as stunning.

How does a guy living on a photographer's salary get ladies like *that*?

Excuse me?

Ah, the women are just part of the bigger picture. I mean, everything always seems to go Parker's way.

No matter how hard I work to get a great photo, his always turn out just a little bit better. What does he have that I don't?

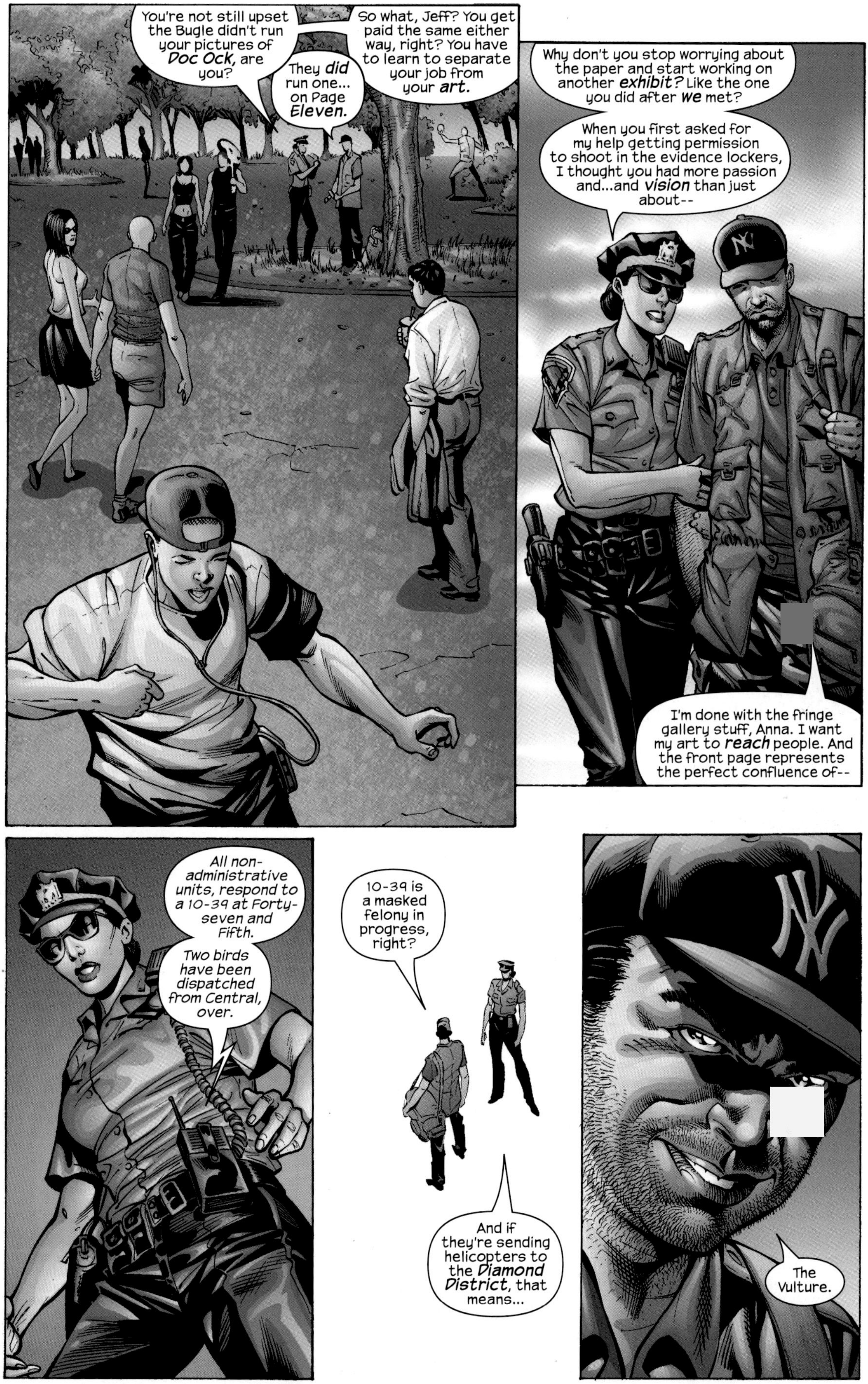
You're not still upset the Bugle didn't run your pictures of *Doc Ock,* are you?
They *did* run one... on Page *Eleven.*
So what, Jeff? You get paid the same either way, right? You have to learn to separate your job from your *art.*
Why don't you stop worrying about the paper and start working on another *exhibit?* Like the one you did after *we* met?
When you first asked for my help getting permission to shoot in the evidence lockers, I thought you had more passion and...and *vision* than just about--
I'm done with the fringe gallery stuff, Anna. I want my art to *reach* people. And the front page represents the perfect confluence of--
All non-administrative units, respond to a 10-39 at Forty-seven and Fifth.
Two birds have been dispatched from Central, over.
10-39 is a masked felony in progress, right?
And if they're sending helicopters to the *Diamond District*, that means...
The Vulture.

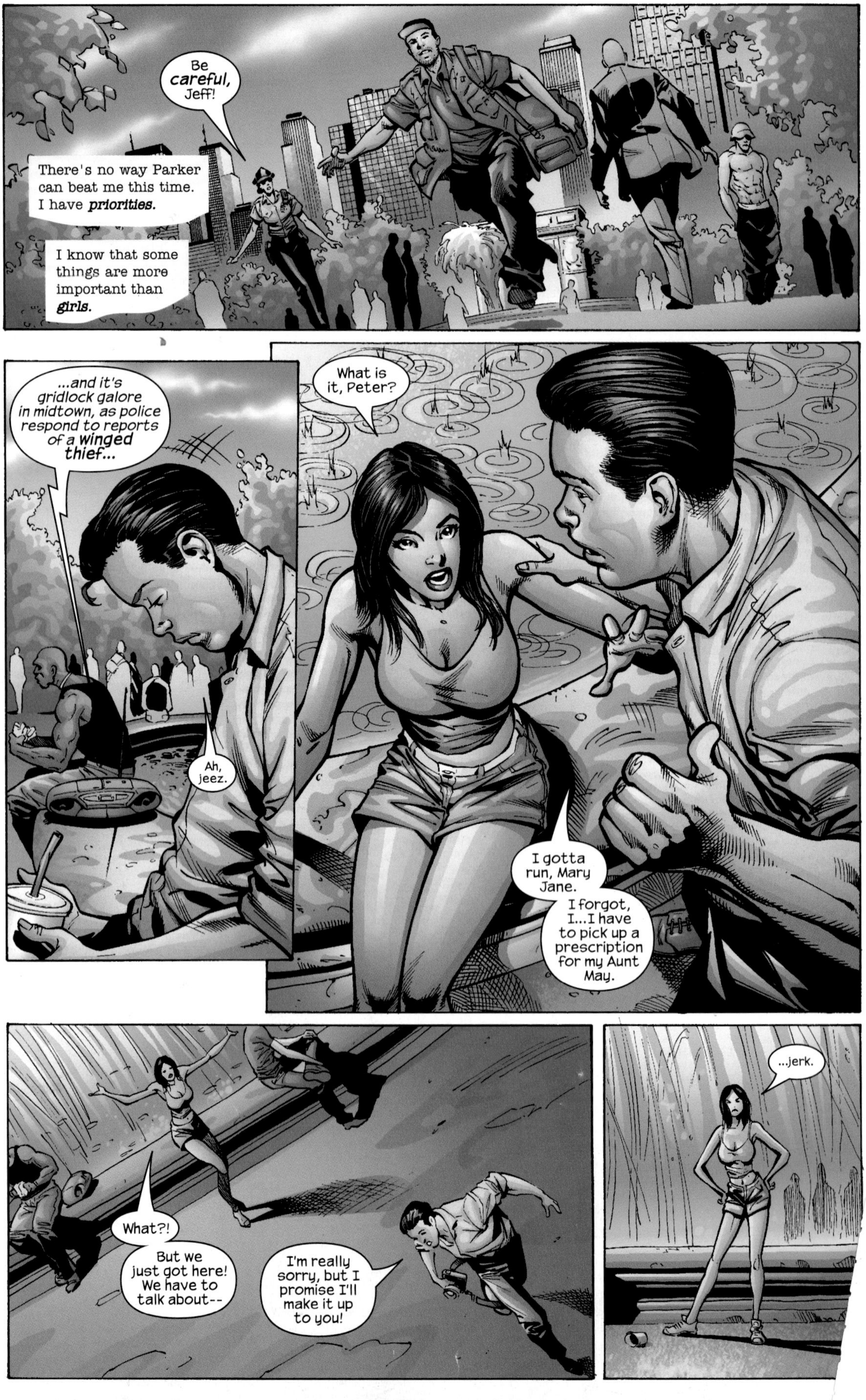
Be careful, Jeff!
There's no way Parker can beat me this time. I have priorities.
I know that some things are more important than girls.
...and it's gridlock galore in midtown, as police respond to reports of a winged thief...
Ah, jeez.
What is it, Peter?
I gotta run, Mary Jane.
I forgot, I...I have to pick up a prescription for my Aunt May.
What?!
But we just got here! We have to talk about--
I'm really sorry, but I promise I'll make it up to you!
...jerk.

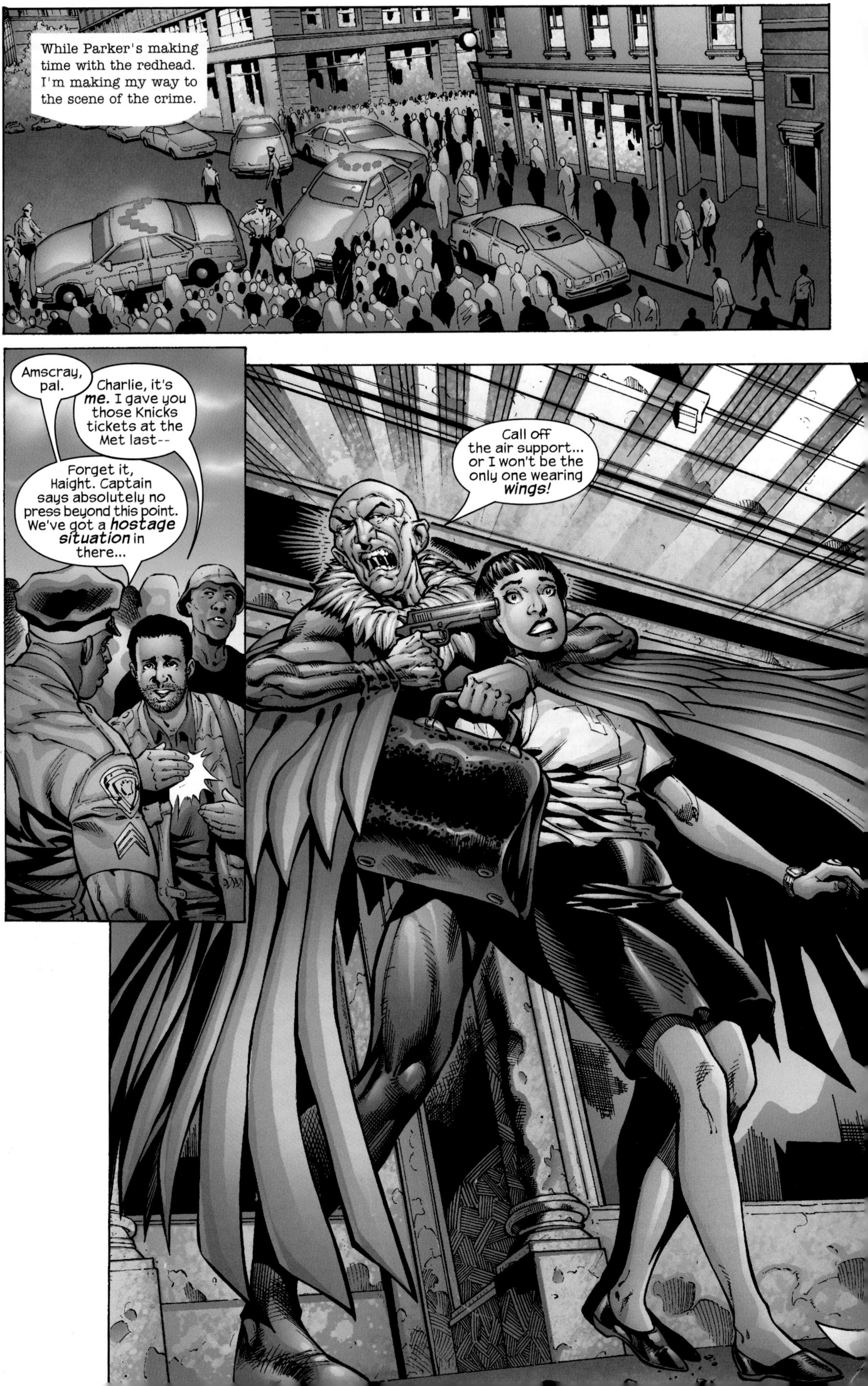
While Parker's making time with the redhead. I'm making my way to the scene of the crime.
Amscray, pal.
Charlie, it's *me.* I gave you those Knicks tickets at the Met last--
Forget it, Haight. Captain says absolutely no press beyond this point. We've got a ***hostage situation*** in there...
Call off the air support... or I won't be the only one wearing ***wings!***

"Hostage situation."

In the history of photojournalism, no two words have been more synonymous with *Pulitzer Prize.*

My professor back at NYU used to always say, *"Let your subject determine the composition of your photograph."*

That means I'm going to need a bird's-eye view...

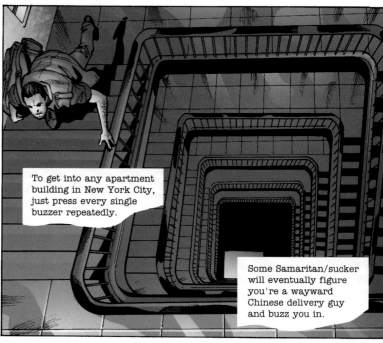

To get into any apartment building in New York City, just press every single buzzer repeatedly.

Some Samaritan/sucker will eventually figure you're a wayward Chinese delivery guy and buzz you in.

Two broken elevators and nine flights later...

Police! I need access to your fire escape!

Bull! Show me a badge, perv!

Fine! I'm... I'm with the *Bugle.* I'll give you a hundred dollars if you let me in!

TWO hundred!

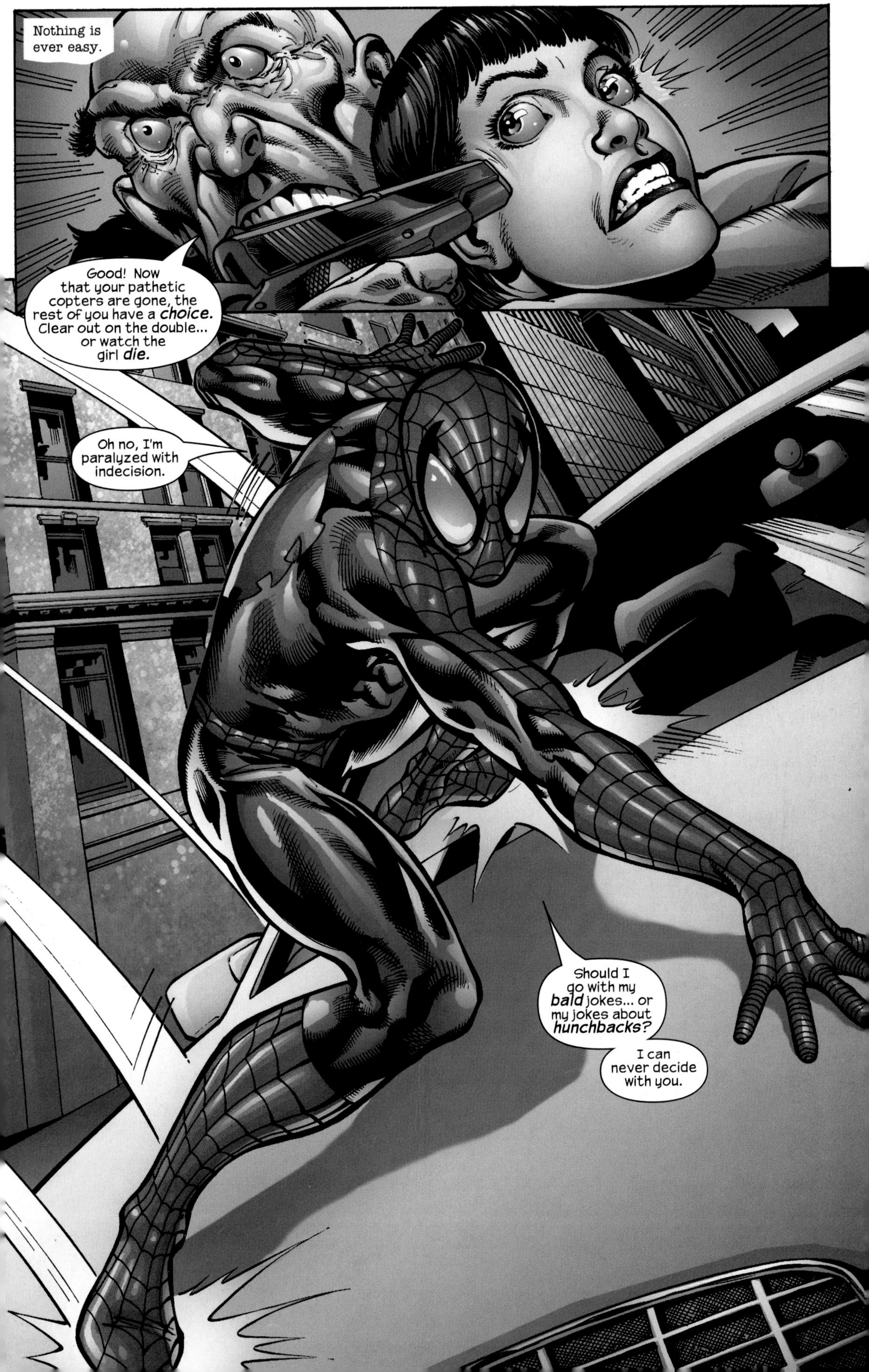
Nothing is ever easy.
Good! Now that your pathetic copters are gone, the rest of you have a *choice.* Clear out on the double... or watch the girl *die.*
Oh no, I'm paralyzed with indecision.
Should I go with my *bald* jokes... or my jokes about *hunchbacks?*
I can never decide with you.

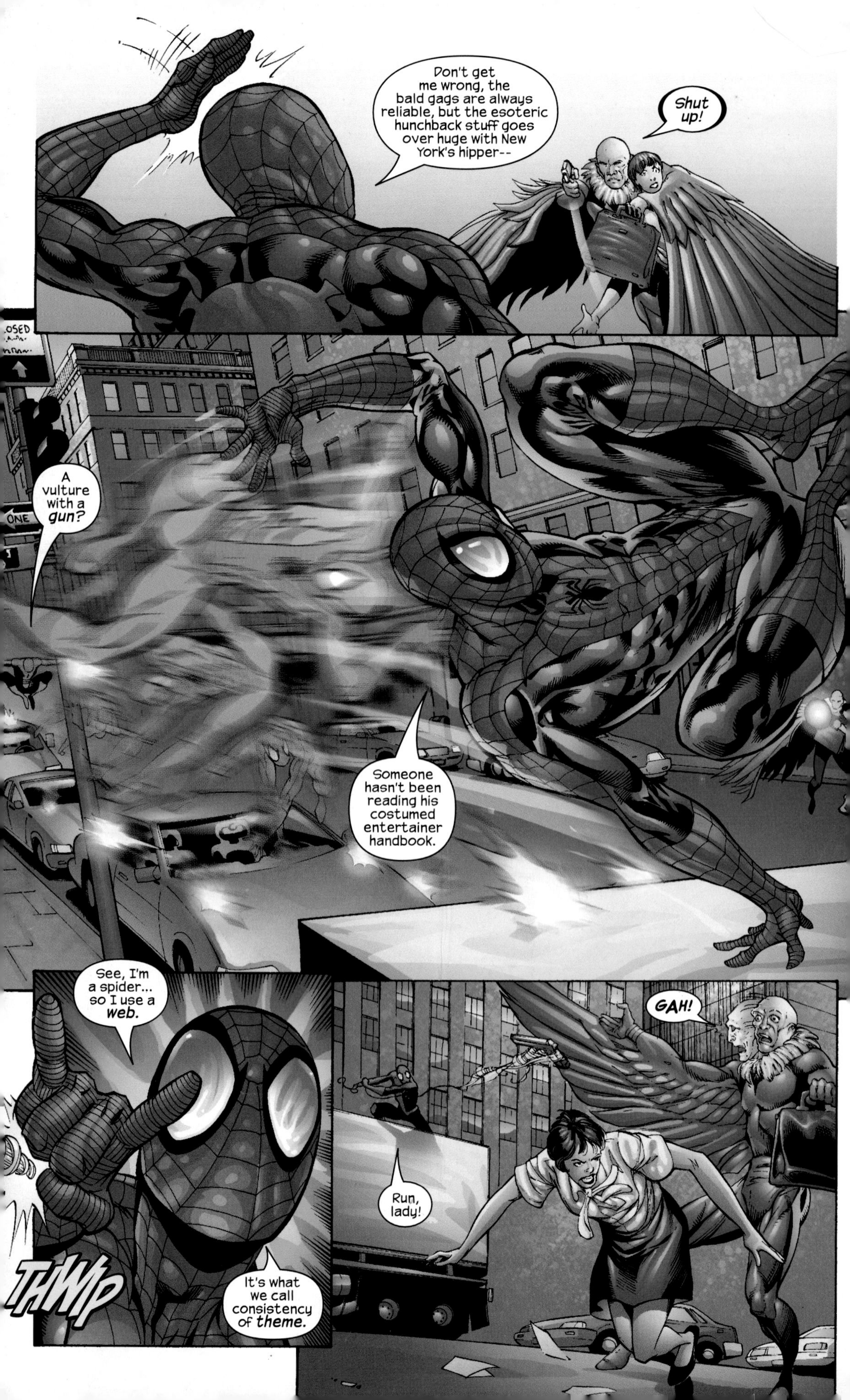

Don't get me wrong, the bald gags are always reliable, but the esoteric hunchback stuff goes over huge with New York's hipper--
Shut up!
A vulture with a gun?
Someone hasn't been reading his costumed entertainer handbook.
See, I'm a spider... so I use a web.
THWIP
It's what we call consistency of theme.
GAH!
Run, lady!

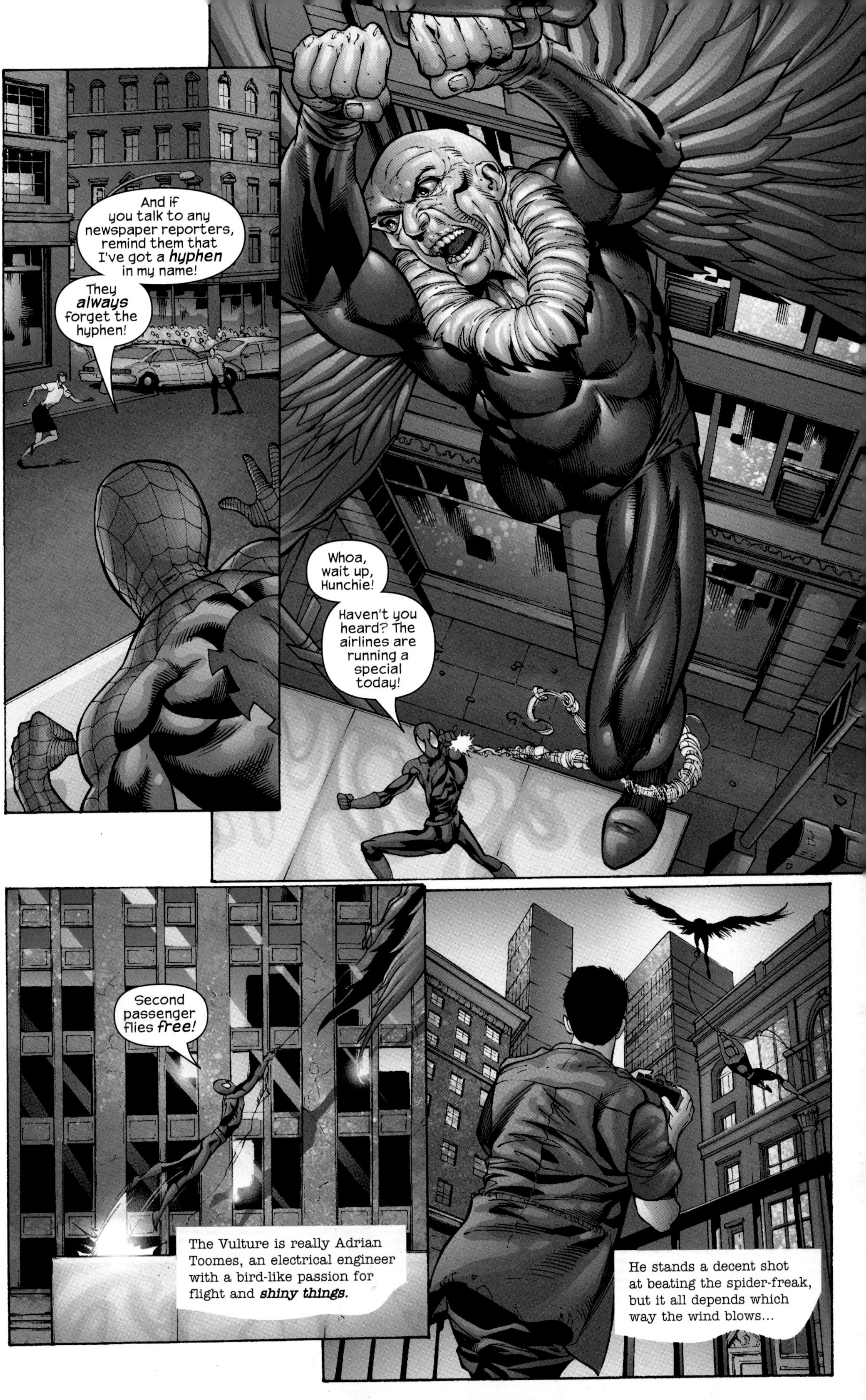

And if you talk to any newspaper reporters, remind them that I've got a **hyphen** in my name!
They **always** forget the hyphen!
Whoa, wait up, Hunchie!
Haven't you heard? The airlines are running a special today!
Second passenger flies **free!**
The Vulture is really Adrian Toomes, an electrical engineer with a bird-like passion for flight and **shiny things.**
He stands a decent shot at beating the spider-freak, but it all depends which way the wind blows...

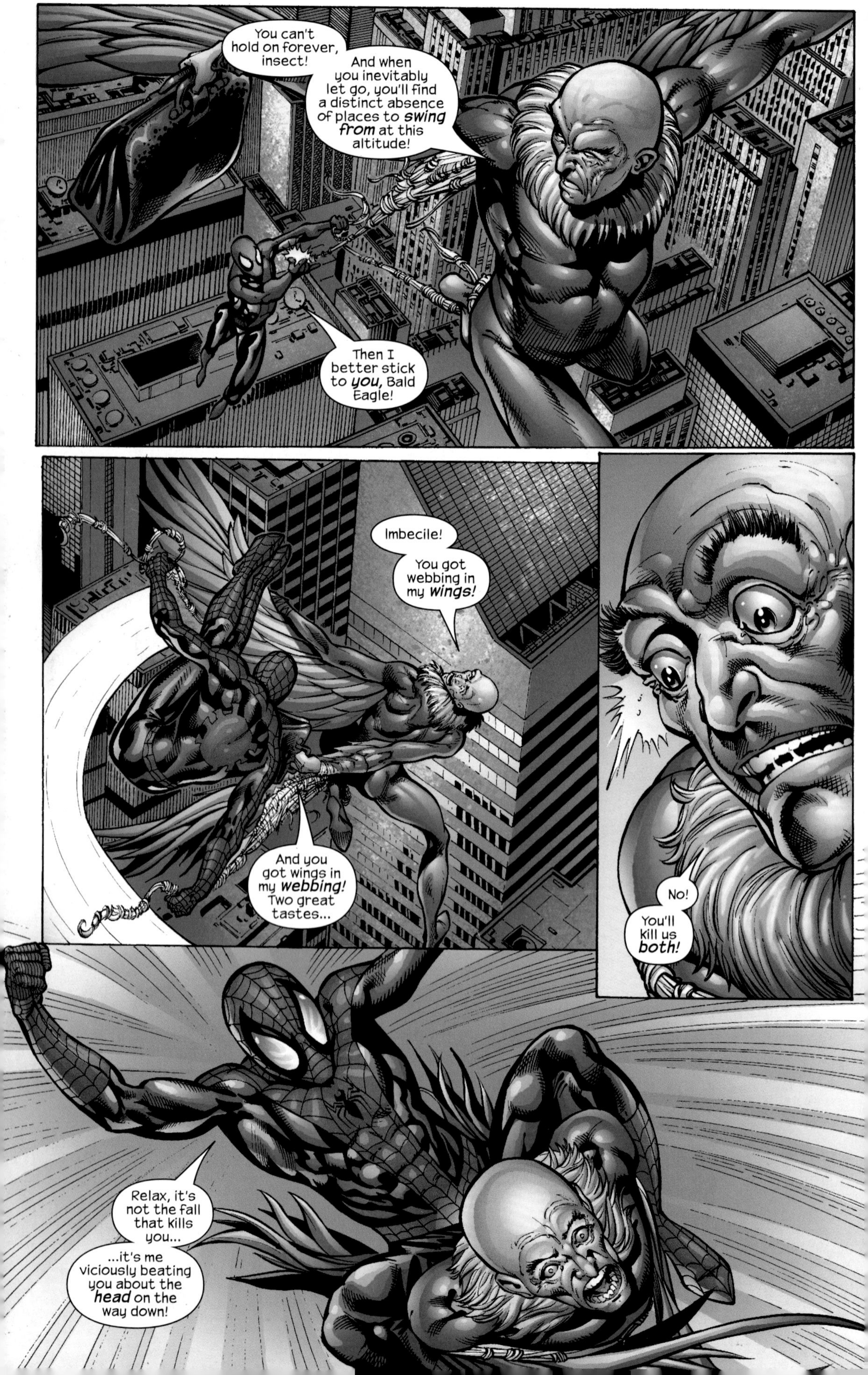

You can't hold on forever, insect!
And when you inevitably let go, you'll find a distinct absence of places to swing from at this altitude!
Then I better stick to you, Bald Eagle!
Imbecile!
You got webbing in my wings!
And you got wings in my webbing! Two great tastes...
No!
You'll kill us both!
Relax, it's not the fall that kills you...
...it's me viciously beating you about the head on the way down!

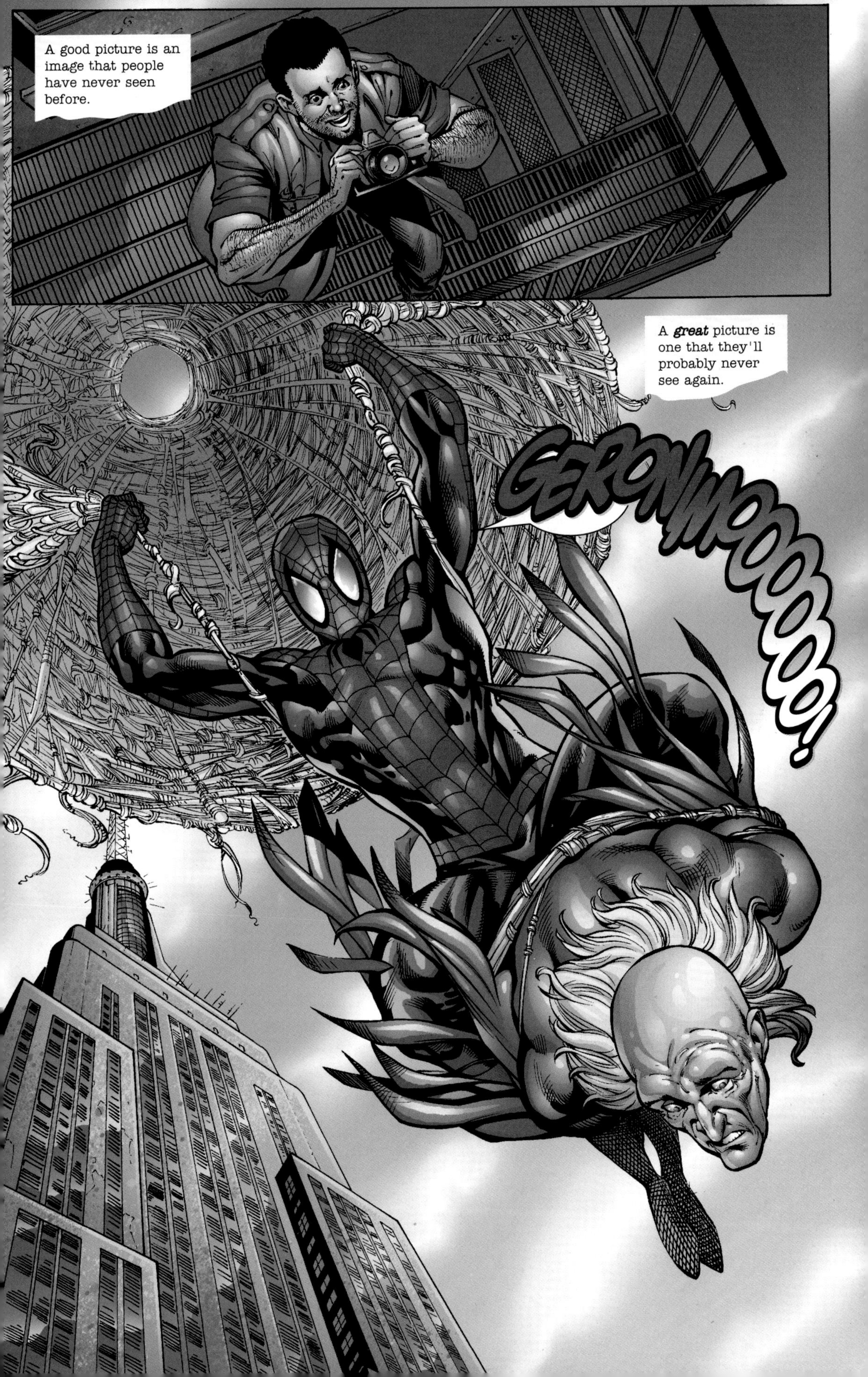
A good picture is an image that people have never seen before.
A *great* picture is one that they'll probably never see again.
GERONIMOOOOOOO!

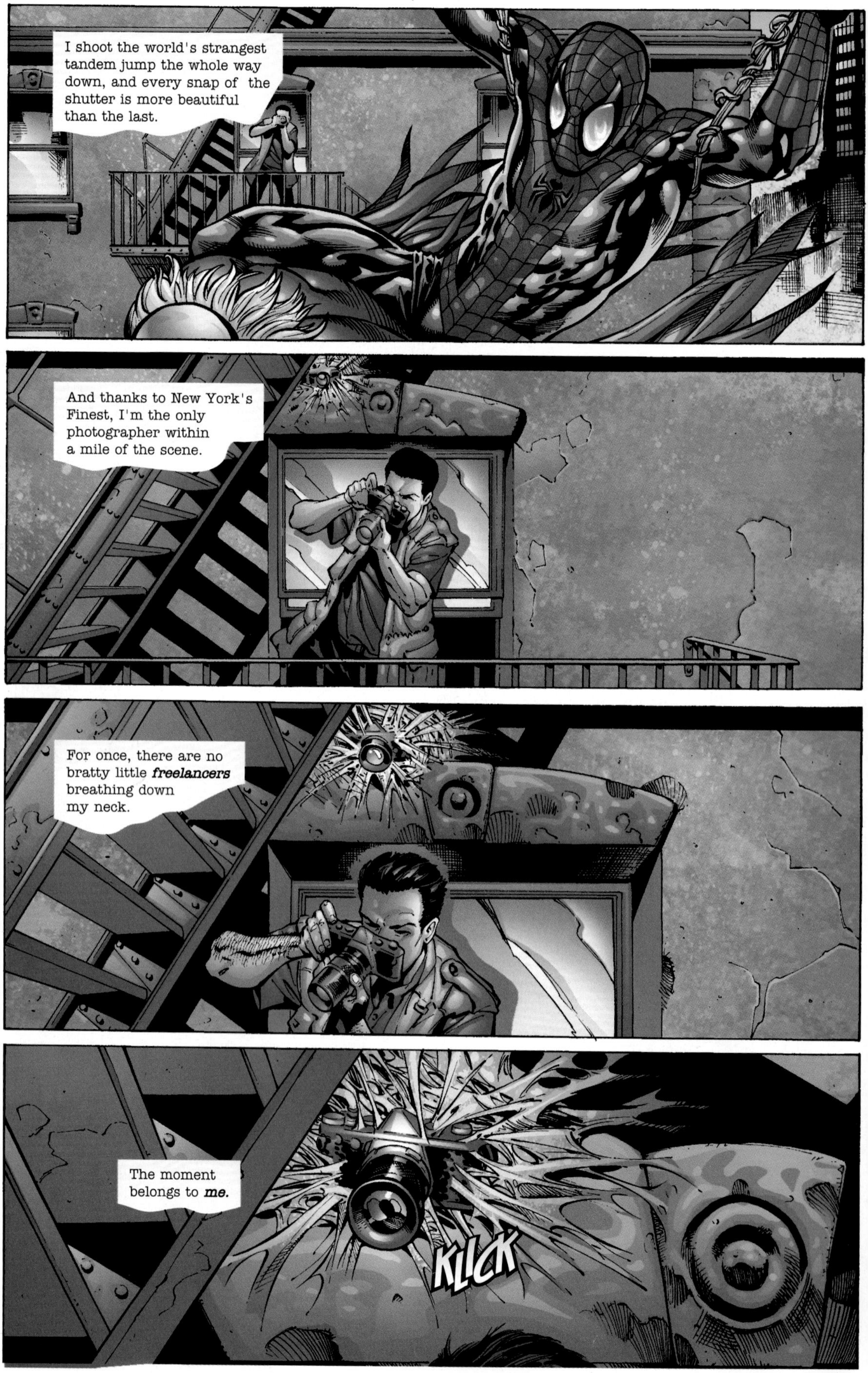
I shoot the world's strangest tandem jump the whole way down, and every snap of the shutter is more beautiful than the last.
And thanks to New York's Finest, I'm the only photographer within a mile of the scene.
For once, there are no bratty little *freelancers* breathing down my neck.
The moment belongs to *me.*
KLICK

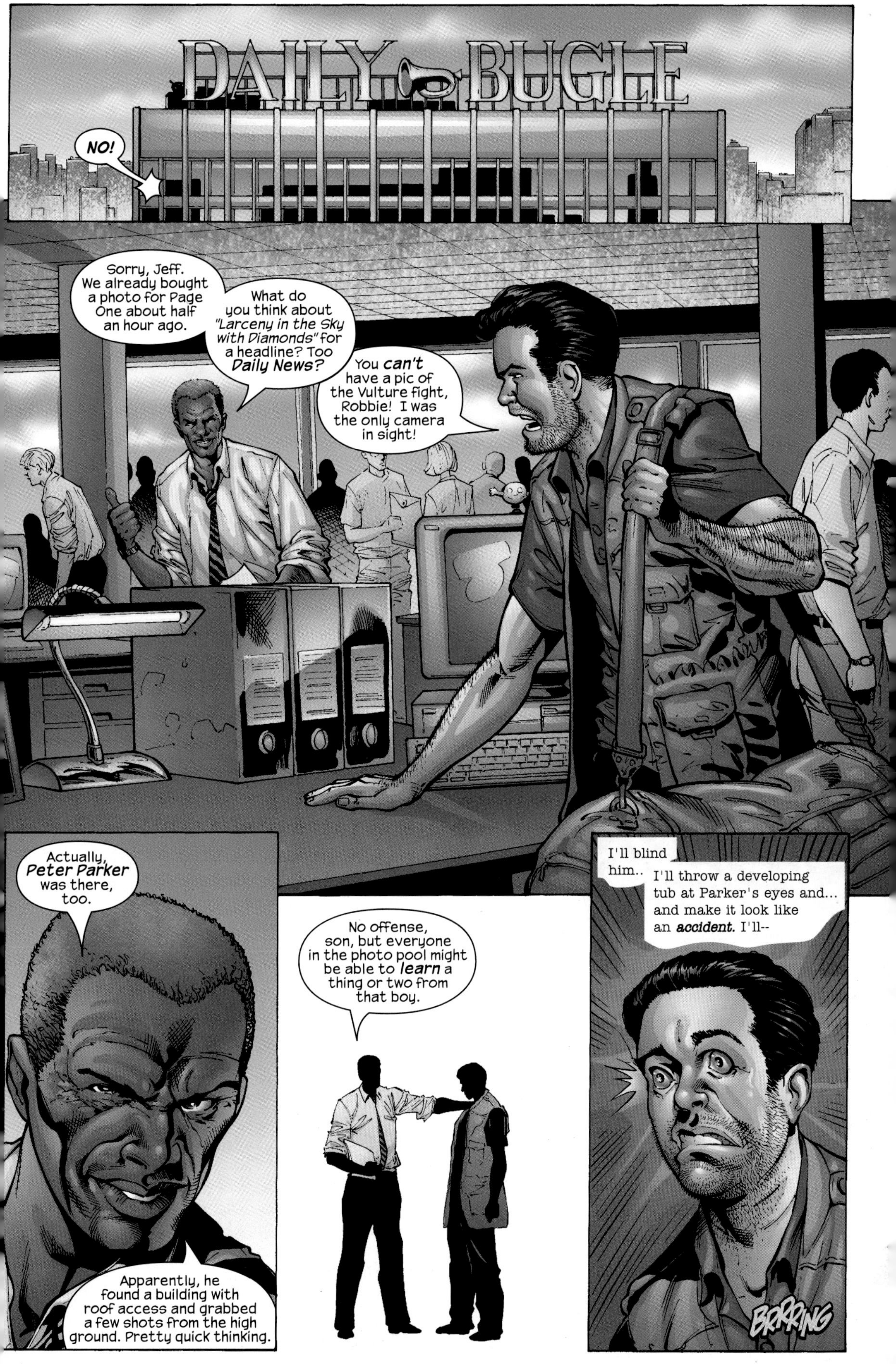
DAILY BUGLE
NO!
Sorry, Jeff. We already bought a photo for Page One about half an hour ago.
What do you think about "Larceny in the Sky with Diamonds" for a headline? Too Daily News?
You can't have a pic of the Vulture fight, Robbie! I was the only camera in sight!
Actually, Peter Parker was there, too.
Apparently, he found a building with roof access and grabbed a few shots from the high ground. Pretty quick thinking.
No offense, son, but everyone in the photo pool might be able to learn a thing or two from that boy.
I'll blind him..
I'll throw a developing tub at Parker's eyes and... and make it look like an accident. I'll--
BRRRING

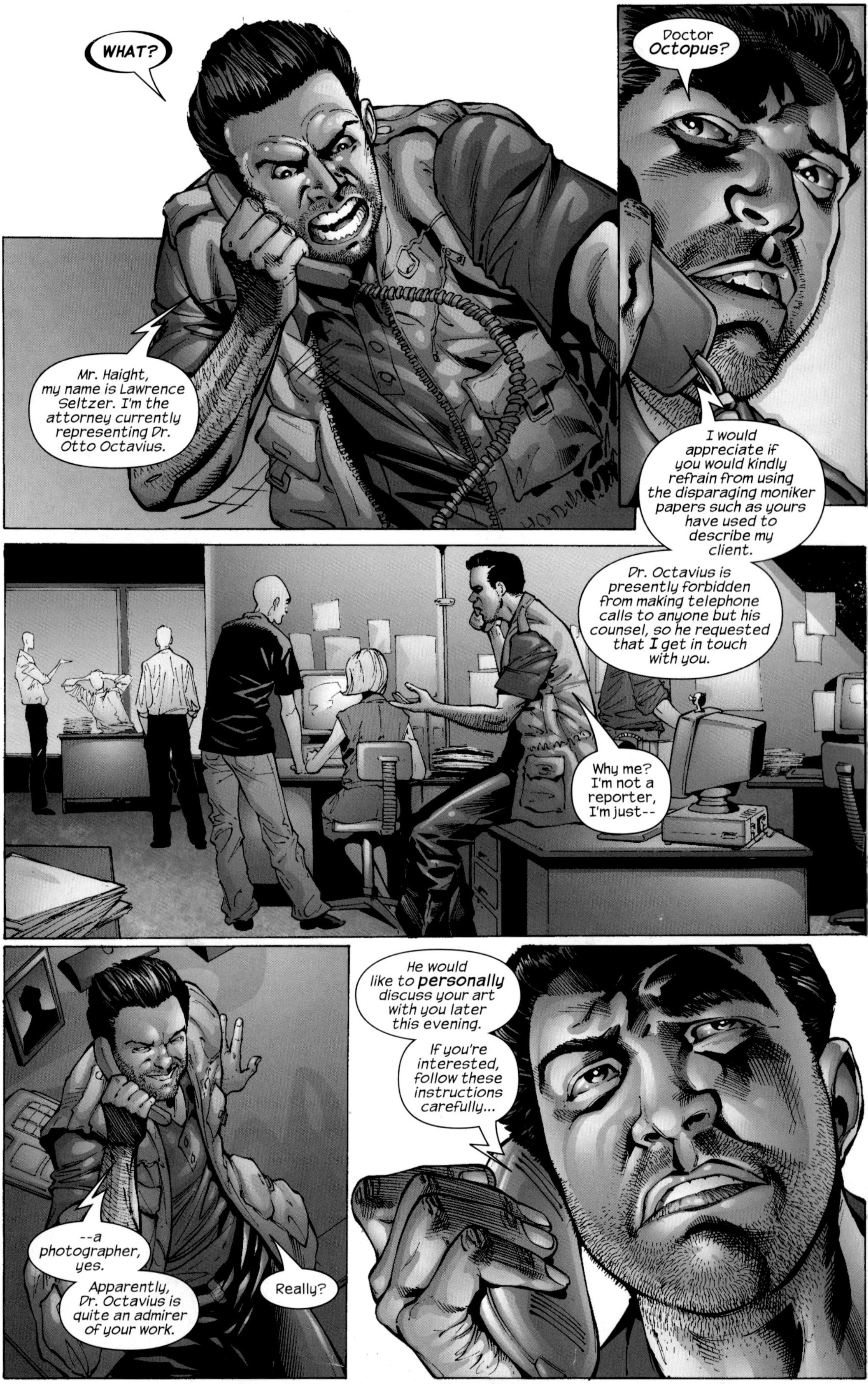
WHAT?
Doctor Octopus?
Mr. Haight, my name is Lawrence Seltzer. I'm the attorney currently representing Dr. Otto Octavius.
I would appreciate if you would kindly refrain from using the disparaging moniker papers such as yours have used to describe my client.
Dr. Octavius is presently forbidden from making telephone calls to anyone but his counsel, so he requested that I get in touch with you.
Why me? I'm not a reporter, I'm just--
--a photographer, yes.
Apparently, Dr. Octavius is quite an admirer of your work.
Really?
He would like to personally discuss your art with you later this evening.
If you're interested, follow these instructions carefully...

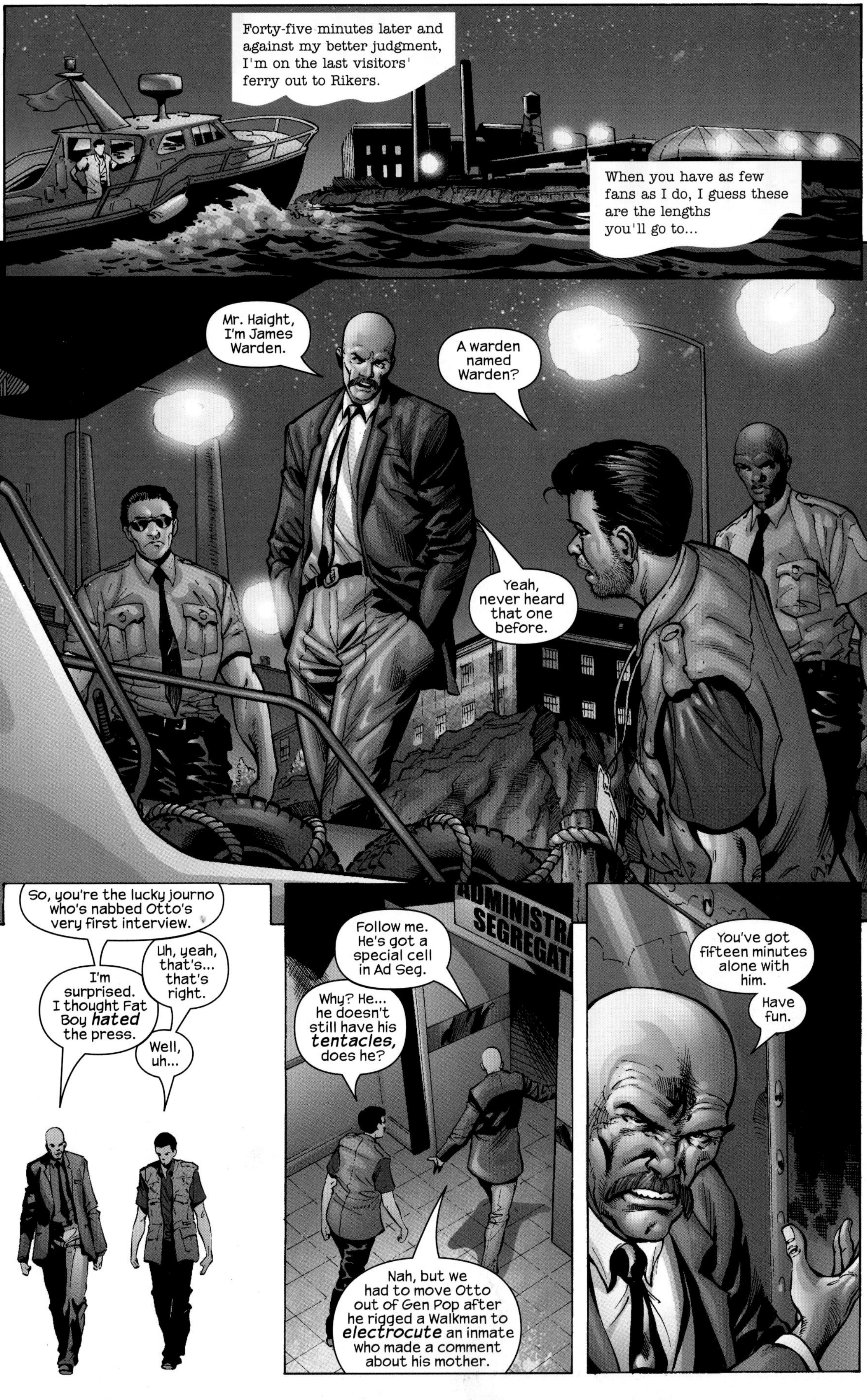

Forty-five minutes later and against my better judgment, I'm on the last visitors' ferry out to Rikers.
When you have as few fans as I do, I guess these are the lengths you'll go to...
Mr. Haight, I'm James Warden.
A warden named Warden?
Yeah, never heard that one before.
So, you're the lucky journo who's nabbed Otto's very first interview.
I'm surprised. I thought Fat Boy *hated* the press.
Uh, yeah, that's... that's right.
Well, uh...
ADMINISTRA
SEGREGATI
Follow me. He's got a special cell in Ad Seg.
Why? He... he doesn't still have his *tentacles,* does he?
Nah, but we had to move Otto out of Gen Pop after he rigged a Walkman to *electrocute* an inmate who made a comment about his mother.
You've got fifteen minutes alone with him.
Have fun.

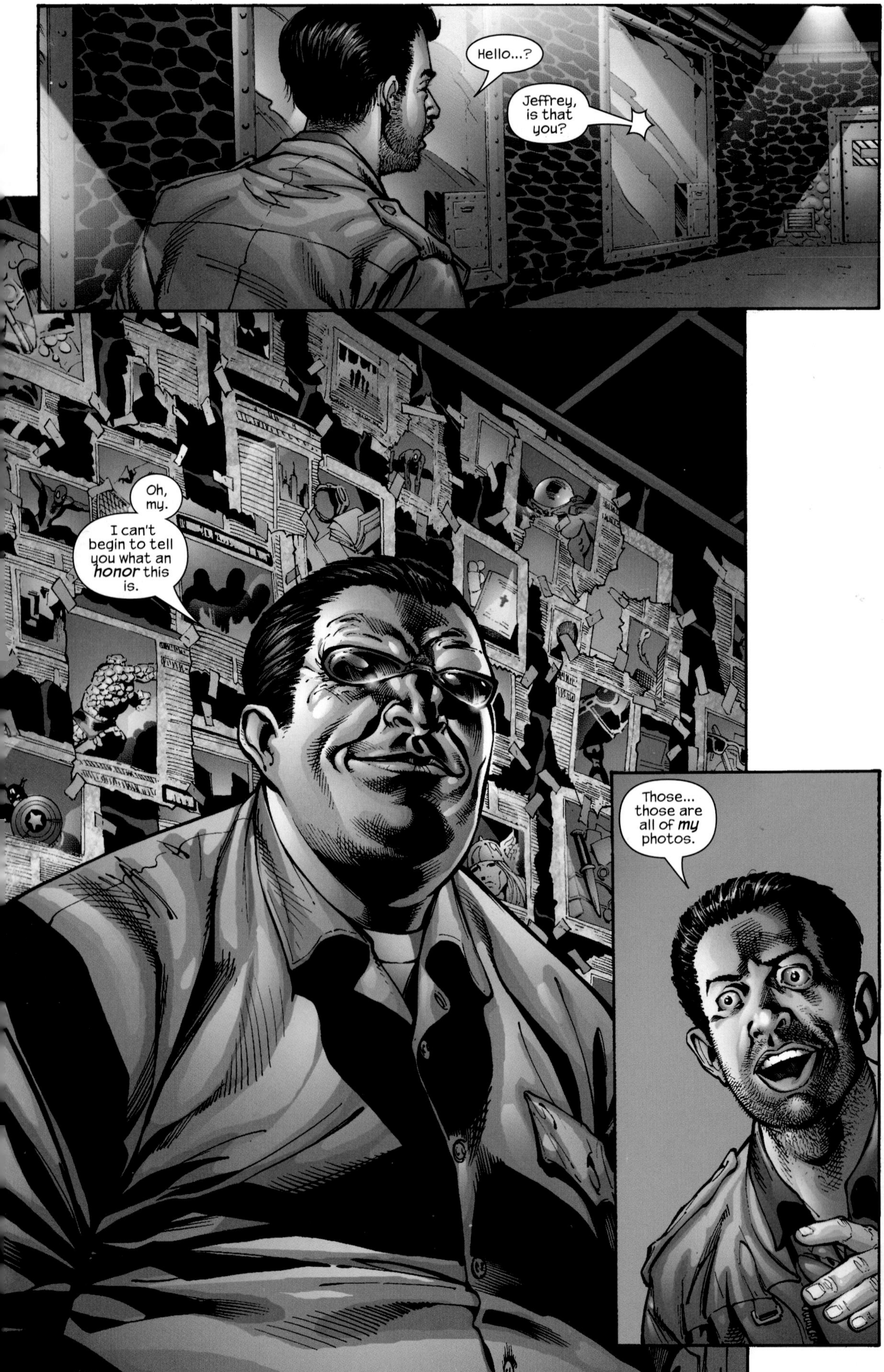
Hello...?
Jeffrey, is that you?
Oh, my.
I can't begin to tell you what an *honor* this is.
Those... those are all of *my* photos.

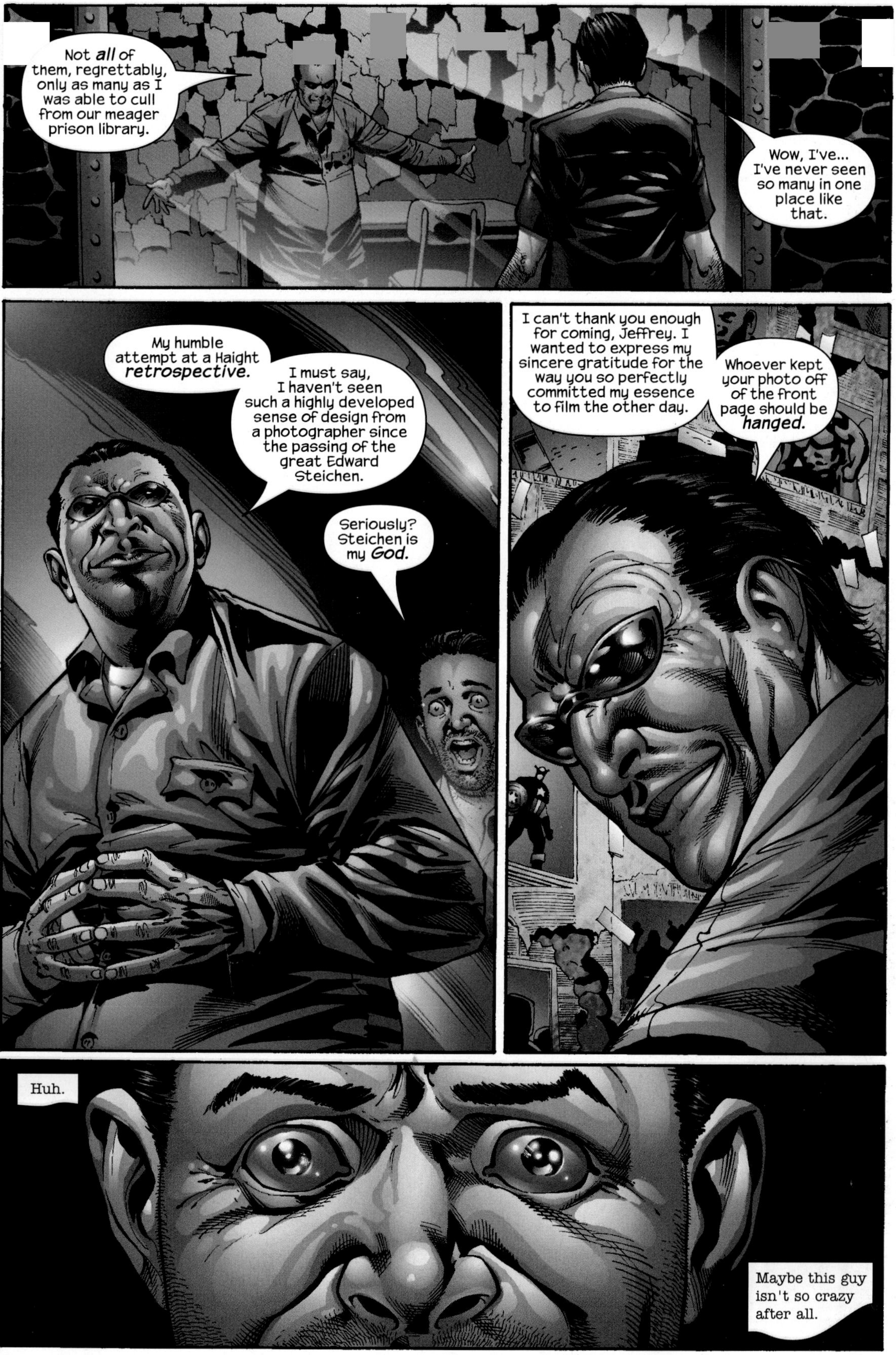

Not *all* of them, regrettably, only as many as I was able to cull from our meager prison library.
Wow, I've... I've never seen so many in one place like that.
My humble attempt at a Haight *retrospective.*
I must say, I haven't seen such a highly developed sense of design from a photographer since the passing of the great Edward Steichen.
Seriously? Steichen is my *God.*
I can't thank you enough for coming, Jeffrey. I wanted to express my sincere gratitude for the way you so perfectly committed my essence to film the other day.
Whoever kept your photo off of the front page should be *hanged.*
Huh.
Maybe this guy isn't so crazy after all.

#3

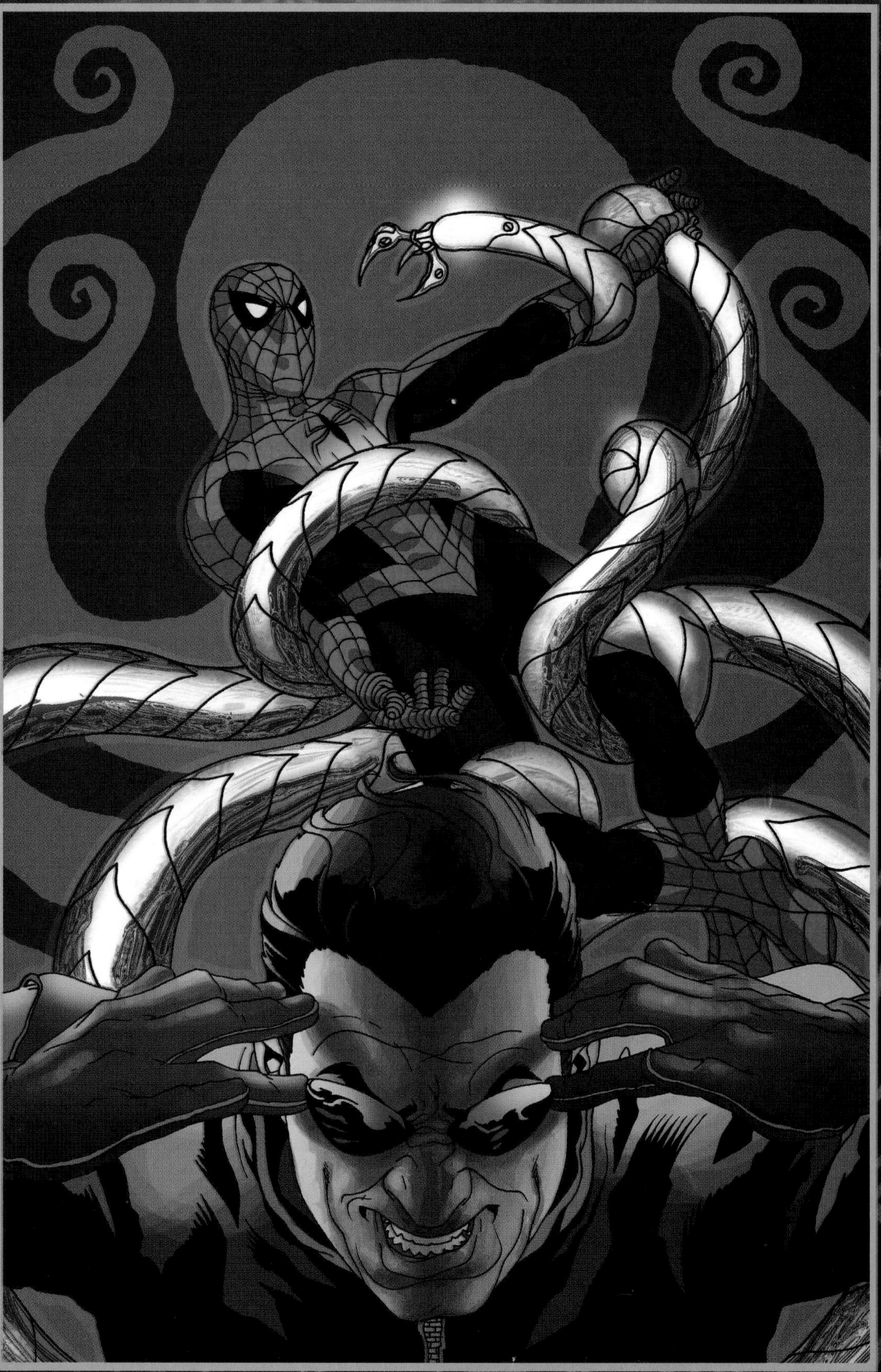

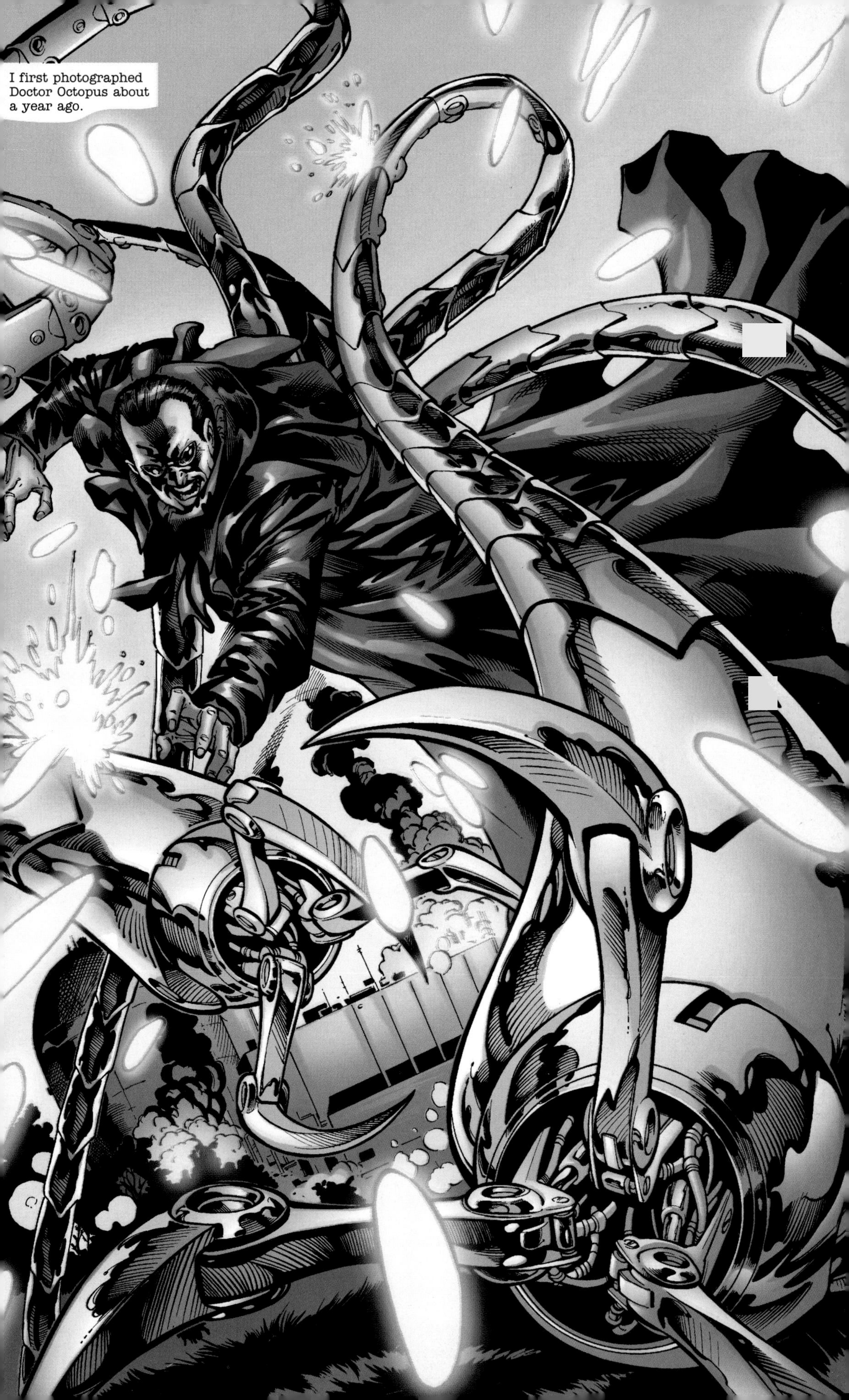
I first photographed Doctor Octopus about a year ago.

An entire division of the National Guard had interrupted his attempt to steal weapons-grade plutonium from Indian Point.

They lasted about thirty seconds.

Ever since that day, I've wondered what could have turned an ordinary guy into something so...*other.*

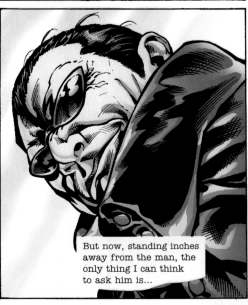

But now, standing inches away from the man, the only thing I can think to ask him is...

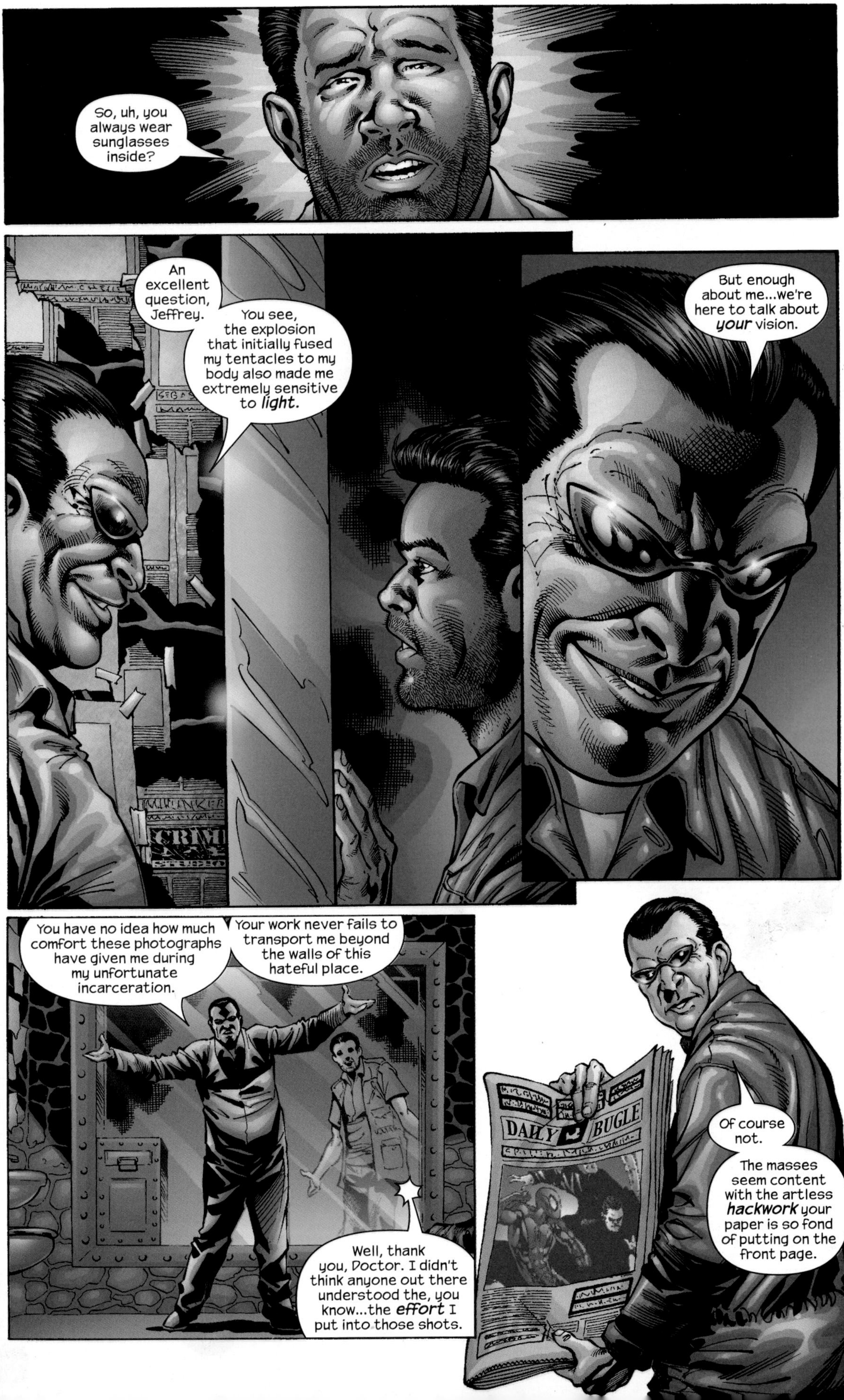
So, uh, you always wear sunglasses inside?
An excellent question, Jeffrey.
You see, the explosion that initially fused my tentacles to my body also made me extremely sensitive to *light.*
But enough about me...we're here to talk about *your* vision.
You have no idea how much comfort these photographs have given me during my unfortunate incarceration.
Your work never fails to transport me beyond the walls of this hateful place.
Well, thank you, Doctor. I didn't think anyone out there understood the, you know...the *effort* I put into those shots.
DAILY BUGLE
Of course not.
The masses seem content with the artless *hackwork* your paper is so fond of putting on the front page.

Yeah, that's Peter Parker's stuff. He's...

I'm not exactly a *fan*.

You're too kind. This Parker clearly lacks an *ounce* of talent. From what I can discern, he's simply always in the right place at the right time.

And something tells me that's not an *accident*.

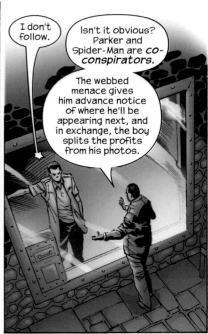

I don't follow.

Isn't it obvious? Parker and Spider-Man are *co-conspirators*.

The webbed menace gives him advance notice of where he'll be appearing next, and in exchange, the boy splits the profits from his photos.

Huh. That actually explains *a lot*.

If only I had uncovered the situation sooner, perhaps I could have *done* something about your unscrupulous competition.

Ah, well. "If wishes were fishes," as my dear mother used to say.

Thank you again for coming, Jeffrey. I wish you nothing but the best with your career.

Wait, that's *it*? You really brought me out here just to...to compliment my *work*?

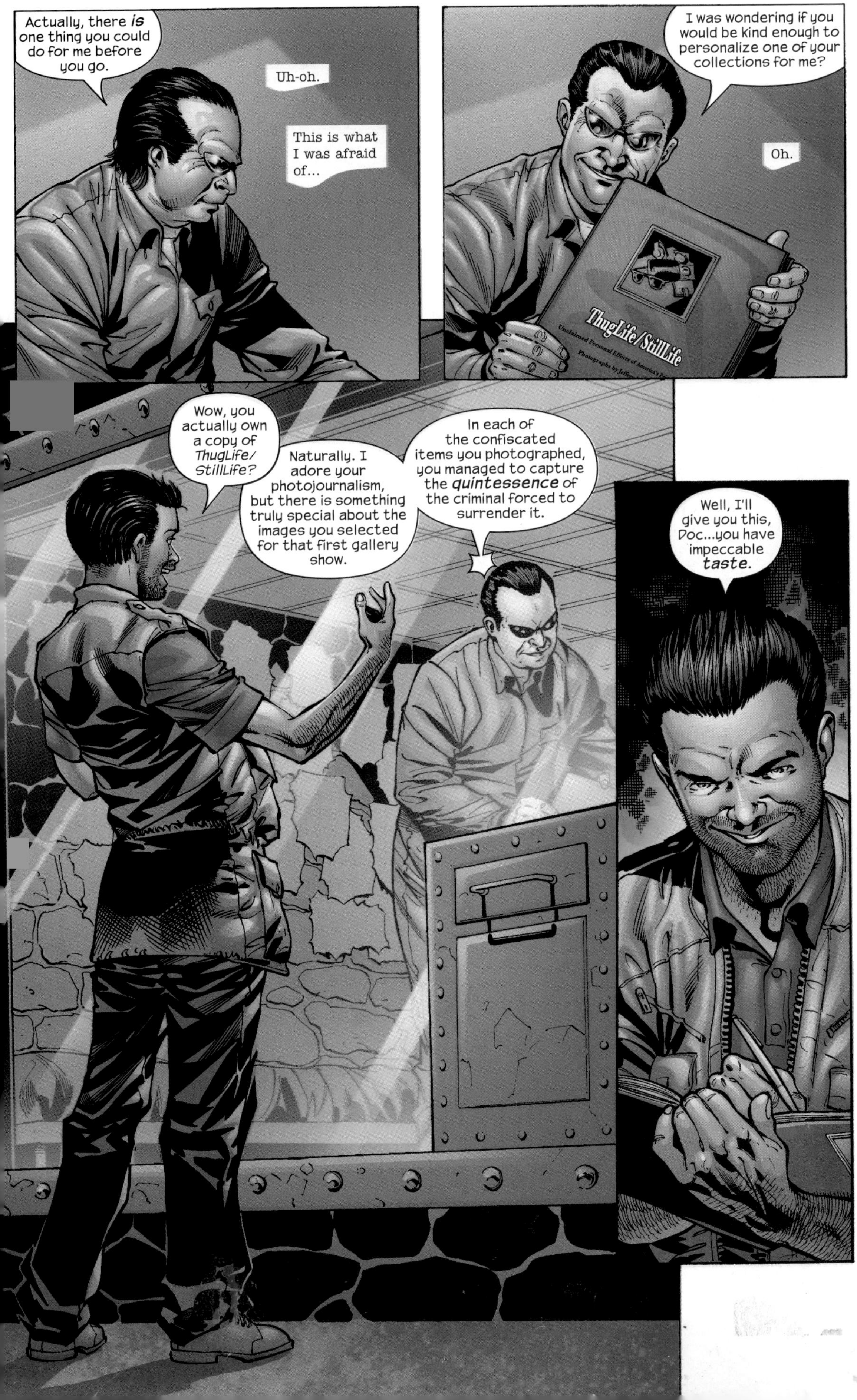
Actually, there *is* one thing you could do for me before you go.
Uh-oh.
This is what I was afraid of...
I was wondering if you would be kind enough to personalize one of your collections for me?
Oh.
ThugLife/StillLife
Wow, you actually own a copy of *ThugLife/ StillLife?*
Naturally. I adore your photojournalism, but there is something truly special about the images you selected for that first gallery show.
In each of the confiscated items you photographed, you managed to capture the ***quintessence*** of the criminal forced to surrender it.
Well, I'll give you this, Doc...you have impeccable ***taste.***

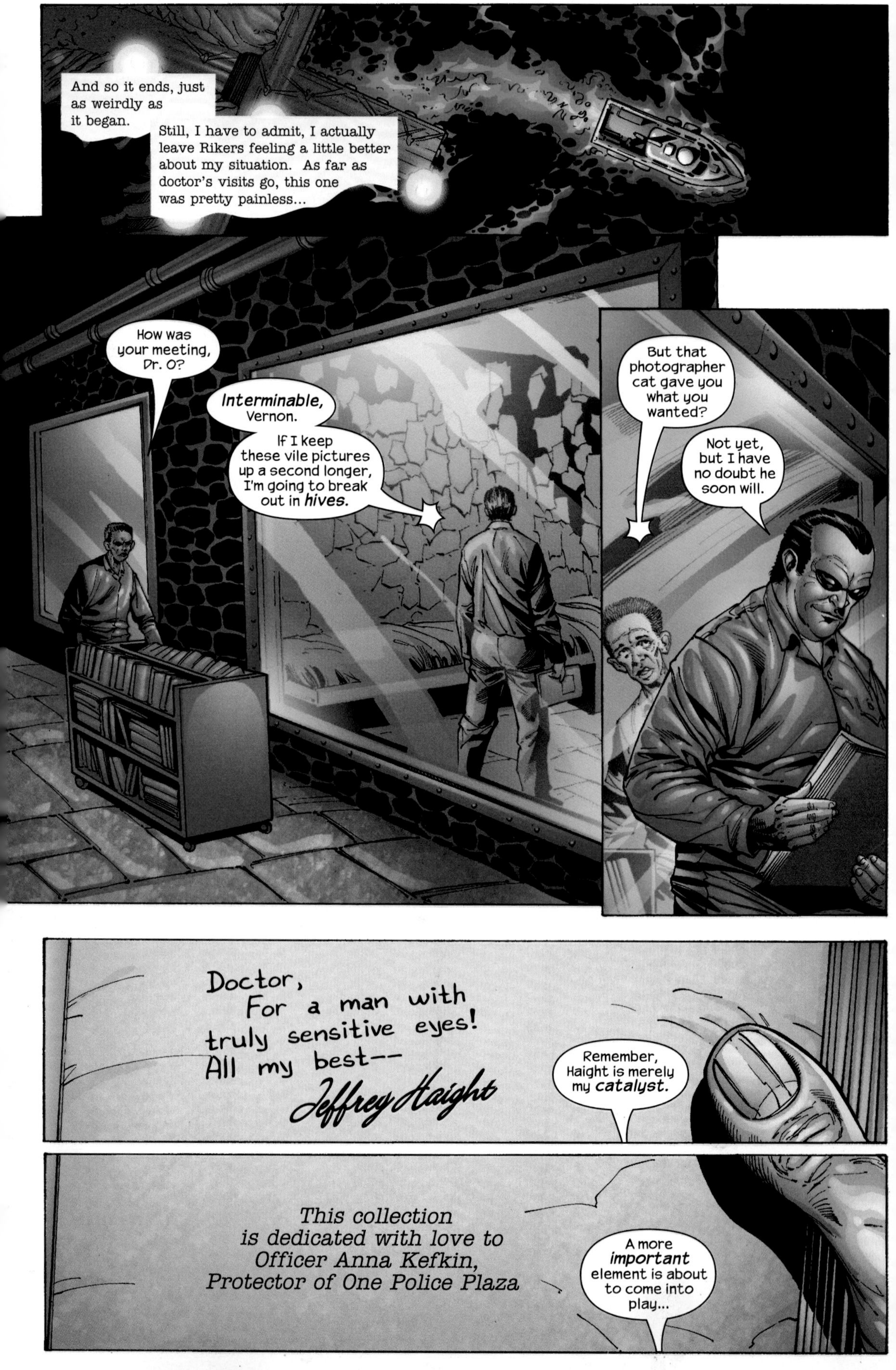
And so it ends, just as weirdly as it began.
Still, I have to admit, I actually leave Rikers feeling a little better about my situation. As far as doctor's visits go, this one was pretty painless...
How was your meeting, Dr. O?
Interminable, Vernon.
If I keep these vile pictures up a second longer, I'm going to break out in hives.
But that photographer cat gave you what you wanted?
Not yet, but I have no doubt he soon will.
Doctor, For a man with truly sensitive eyes! All my best-- Jeffrey Haight
Remember, Haight is merely my catalyst.
This collection is dedicated with love to Officer Anna Kefkin, Protector of One Police Plaza
A more important element is about to come into play...

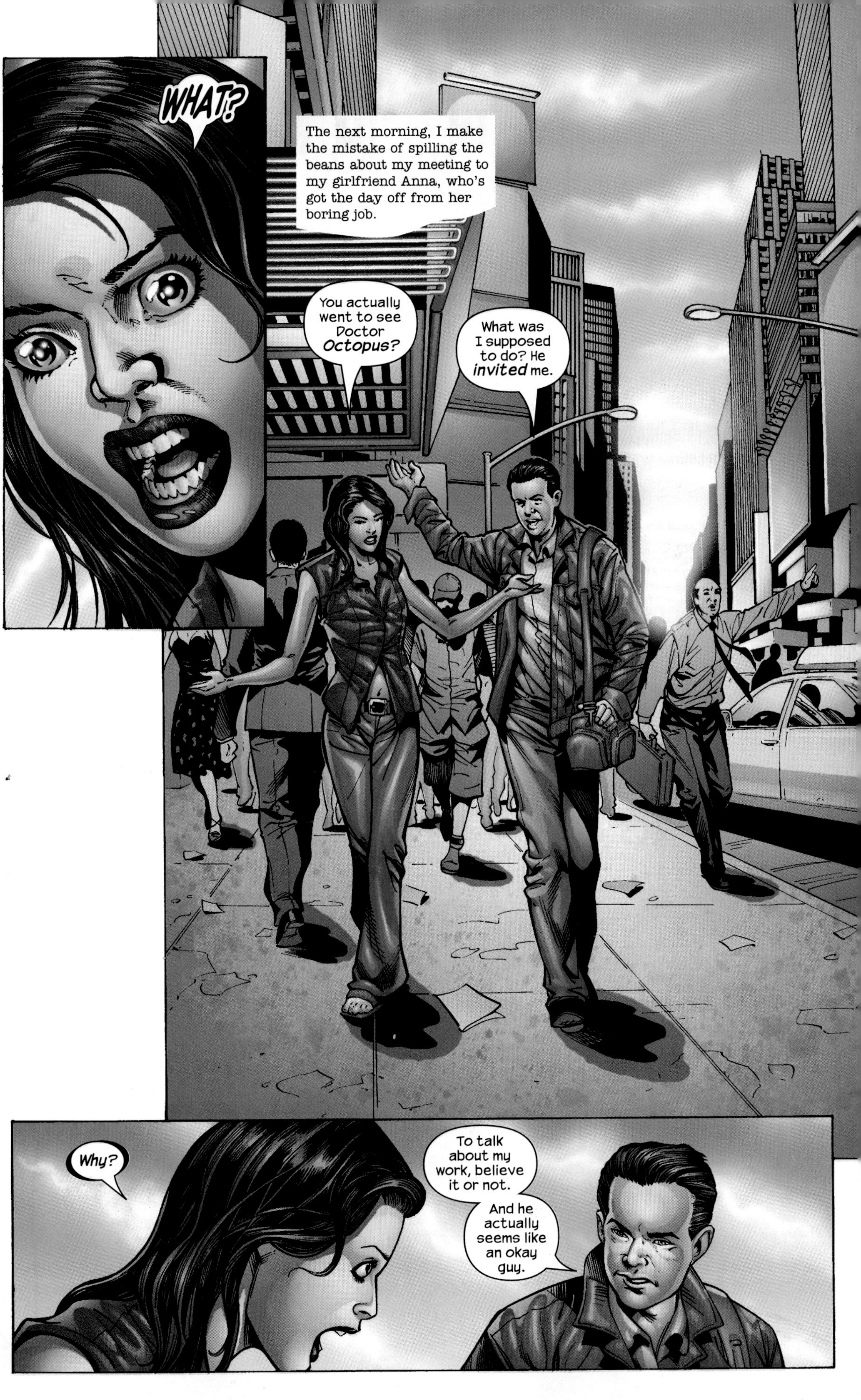
WHAT?
The next morning, I make the mistake of spilling the beans about my meeting to my girlfriend Anna, who's got the day off from her boring job.
You actually went to see Doctor *Octopus?*
What was I supposed to do? He *invited* me.
Why?
To talk about my work, believe it or not.
And he actually seems like an okay guy.

Are you *high?* He's a mass murderer!

So was Hitler, but that doesn't mean he doesn't know anything about *art.*

Hitler was a *terrible* artist!

Oh, he couldn't paint to save his life, but he had an excellent eye. He helped design the original VW bug, you know. Anyway, you can hardly compare what Dr. Octavius has done to--

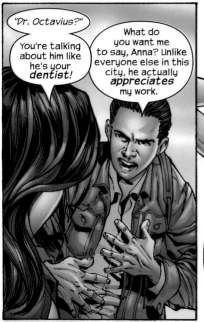

"Dr. Octavius?" You're talking about him like he's your *dentist!*

What do you want me to say, Anna? Unlike everyone else in this city, he actually *appreciates* my work.

God, when did you get so *needy?*

When we first met, I let you into the evidence rooms at work--I put my *job* on the line--because you made me *believe* in you. You believed in *yourself.*

But this ridiculous obsession with landing the front page has turned you into some kind of--

Help! They're *coming!*

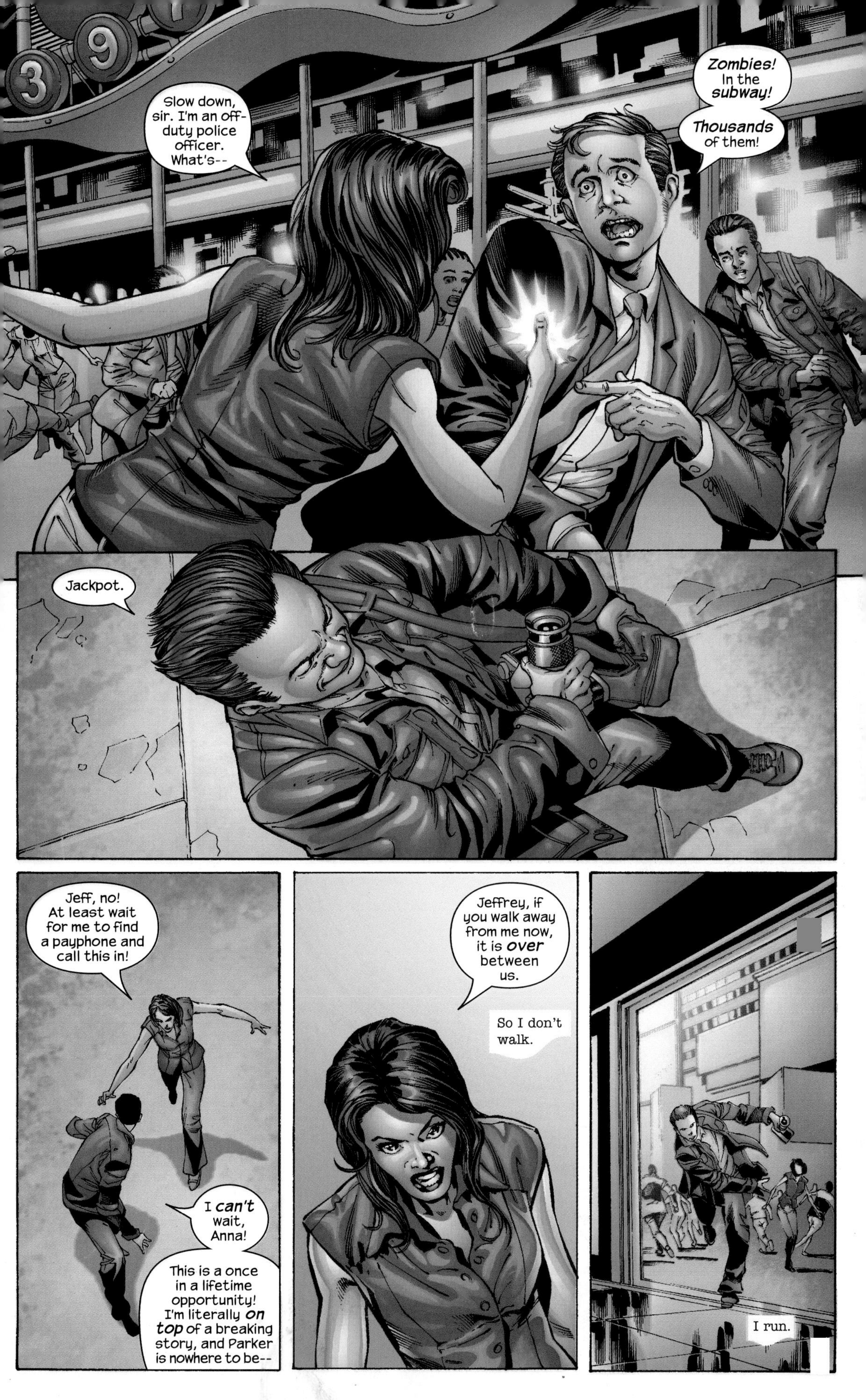
Slow down, sir. I'm an off-duty police officer. What's--
Zombies! In the subway!
Thousands of them!
Jackpot.
Jeff, no! At least wait for me to find a payphone and call this in!
I can't wait, Anna!
This is a once in a lifetime opportunity! I'm literally on top of a breaking story, and Parker is nowhere to be--
Jeffrey, if you walk away from me now, it is over between us.
So I don't walk.
I run.

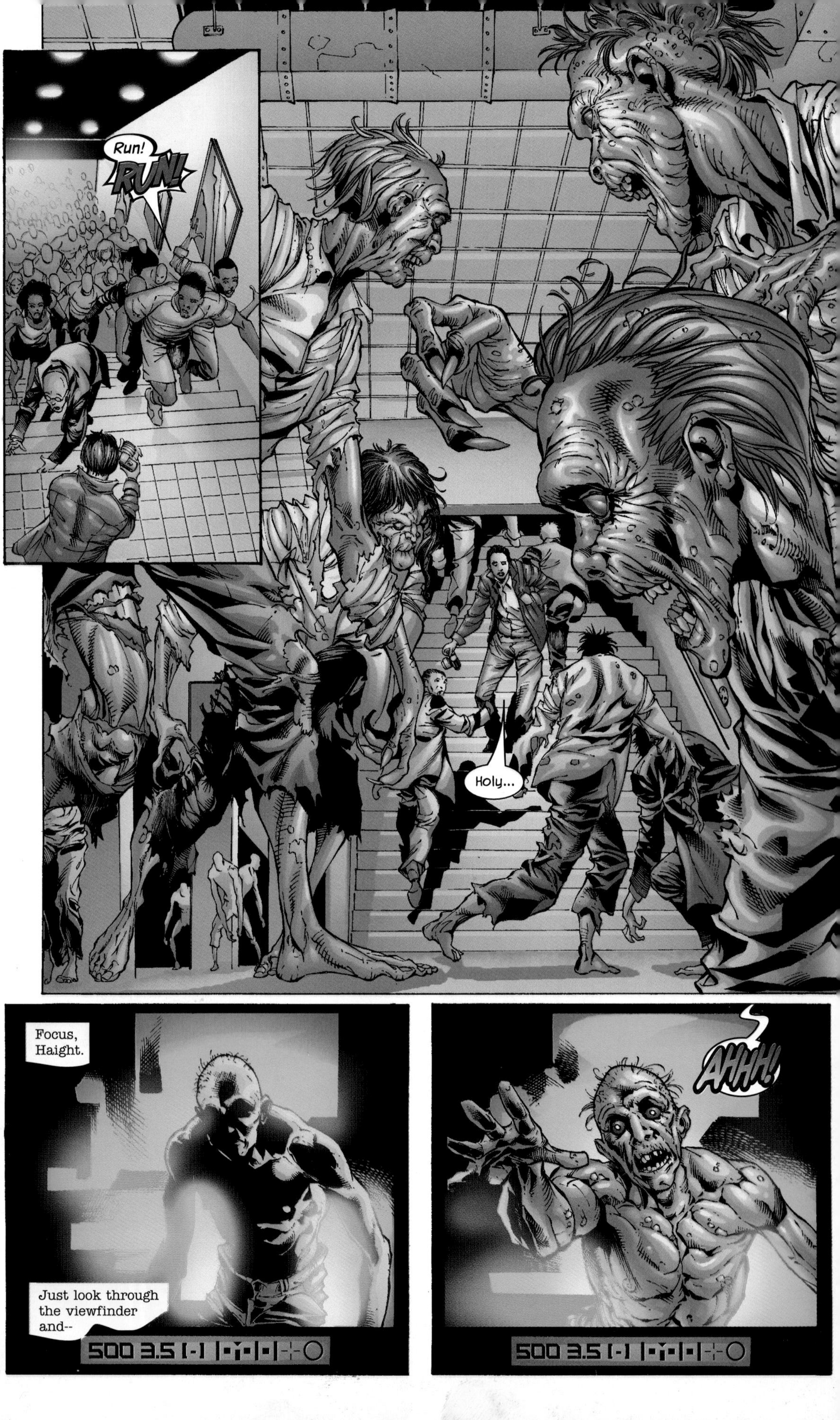

Run!
RUN!
Holy...
Focus, Haight.
Just look through the viewfinder and--
500 3.5
AHHH!
500 3.5

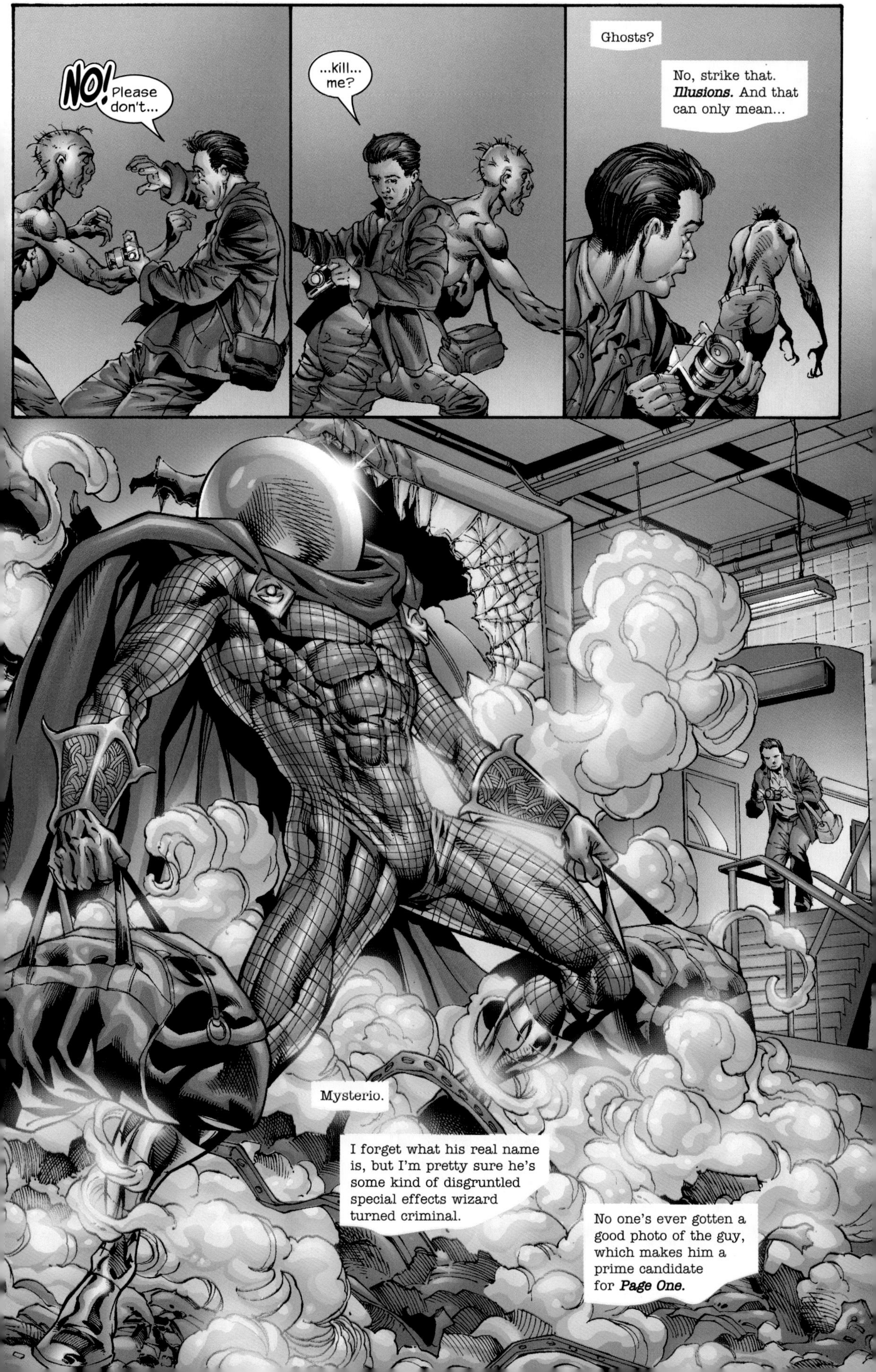
NO!
Please don't...
...kill... me?
Ghosts?
No, strike that. ***Illusions.*** And that can only mean...
Mysterio.
I forget what his real name is, but I'm pretty sure he's some kind of disgruntled special effects wizard turned criminal.
No one's ever gotten a good photo of the guy, which makes him a prime candidate for ***Page One.***

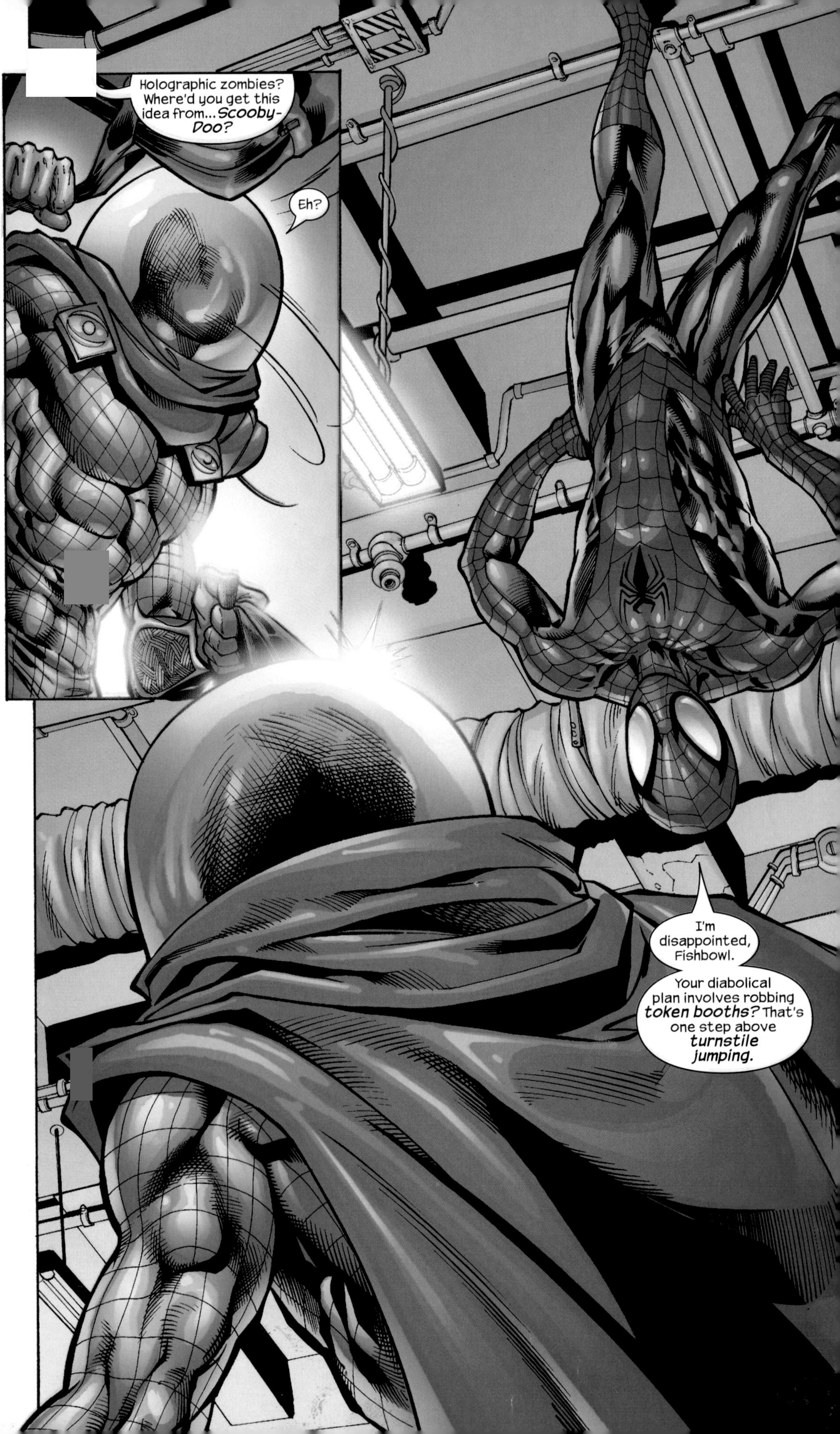
Holographic zombies? Where'd you get this idea from... Scooby-Doo?
Eh?
I'm disappointed, Fishbowl.
Your diabolical plan involves robbing token booths? That's one step above turnstile jumping.

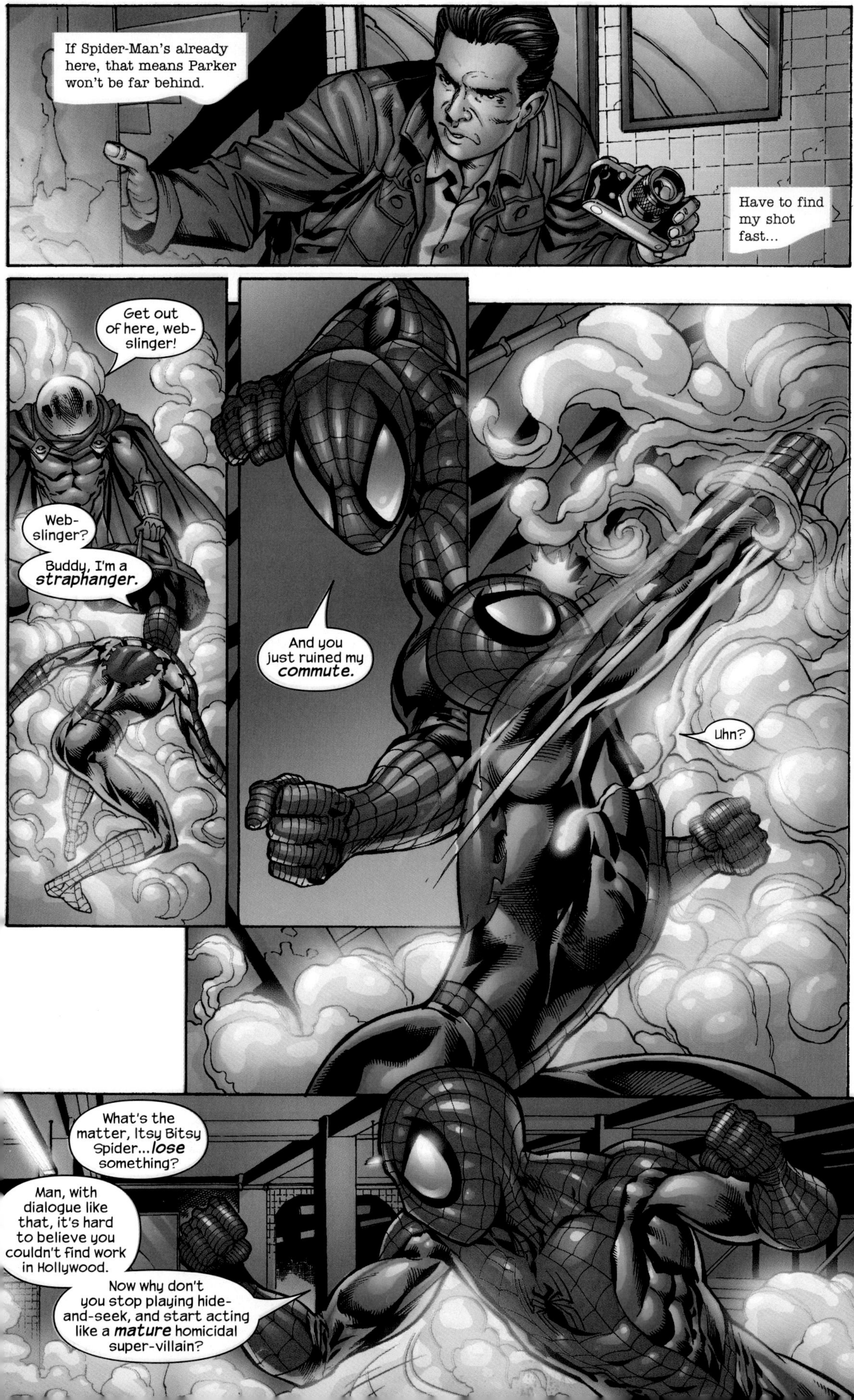

If Spider-Man's already here, that means Parker won't be far behind.
Have to find my shot fast...
Get out of here, web-slinger!
Web-slinger?
Buddy, I'm a *straphanger.*
And you just ruined my *commute.*
Uhn?
What's the matter, Itsy Bitsy Spider...*lose* something?
Man, with dialogue like that, it's hard to believe you couldn't find work in Hollywood.
Now why don't you stop playing hide-and-seek, and start acting like a *mature* homicidal super-villain?

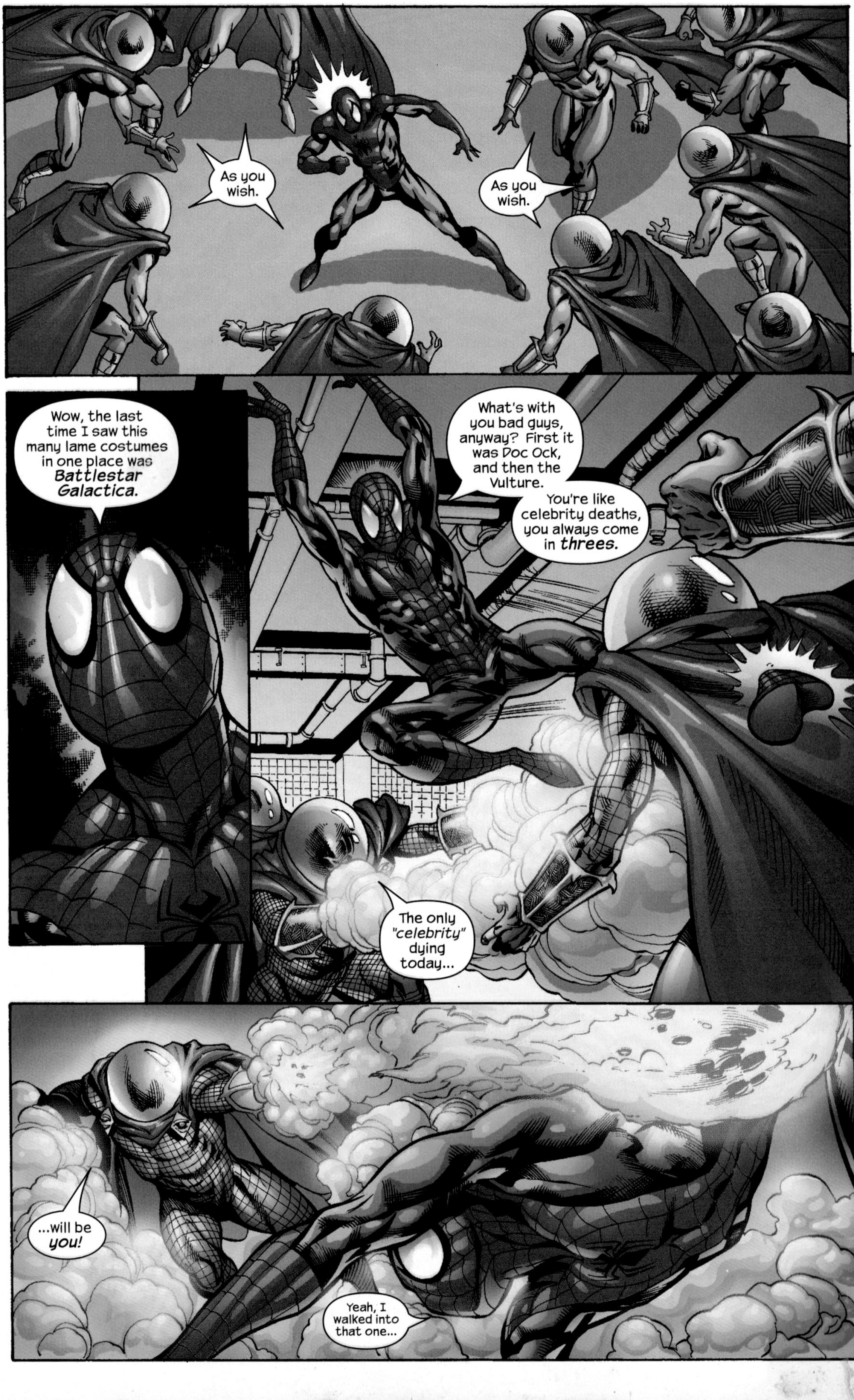
As you wish.
As you wish.
Wow, the last time I saw this many lame costumes in one place was *Battlestar Galactica.*
What's with you bad guys, anyway? First it was Doc Ock, and then the Vulture.
You're like celebrity deaths, you always come in *threes.*
The only *"celebrity"* dying today...
...will be *you!*
Yeah, I walked into that one...

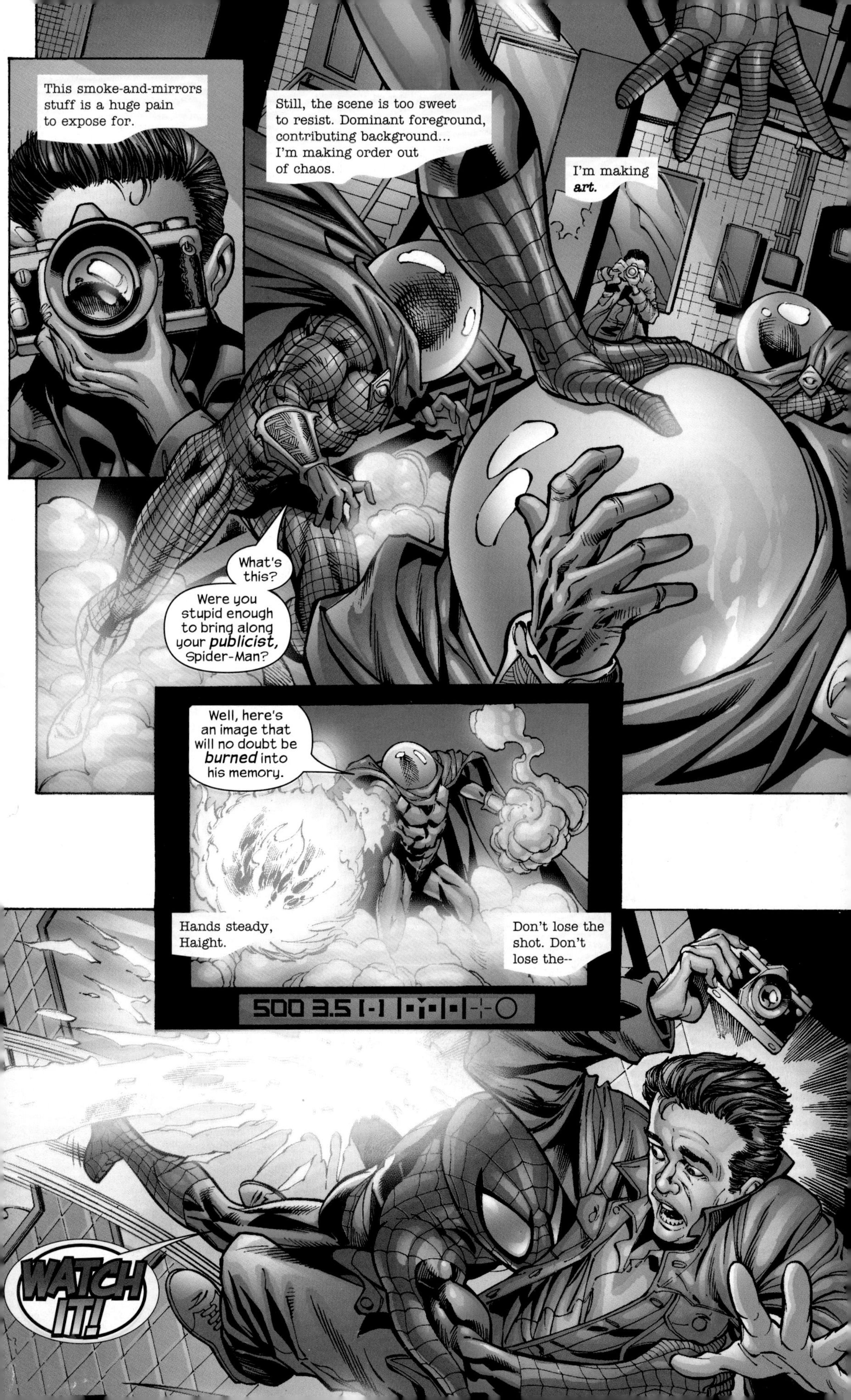
This smoke-and-mirrors stuff is a huge pain to expose for.
Still, the scene is too sweet to resist. Dominant foreground, contributing background... I'm making order out of chaos.
I'm making **art**.
What's this?
Were you stupid enough to bring along your **publicist,** Spider-Man?
Well, here's an image that will no doubt be **burned** into his memory.
Hands steady, Haight.
Don't lose the shot. Don't lose the--
500 3.5
WATCH IT!

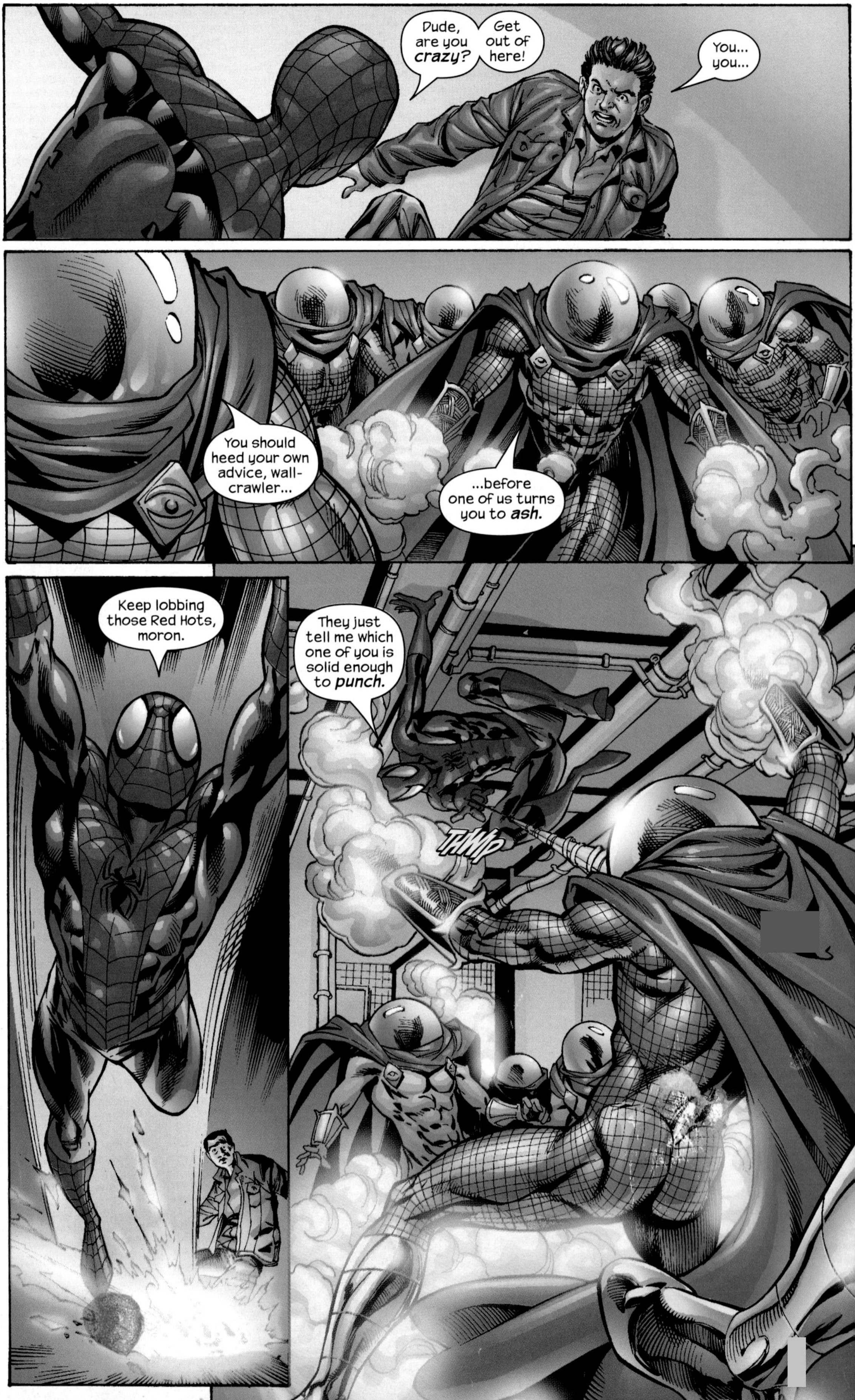
Dude, are you crazy?
Get out of here!
You... you...
You should heed your own advice, wall-crawler...
...before one of us turns you to ash.
Keep lobbing those Red Hots, moron.
They just tell me which one of you is solid enough to punch.
THWIP

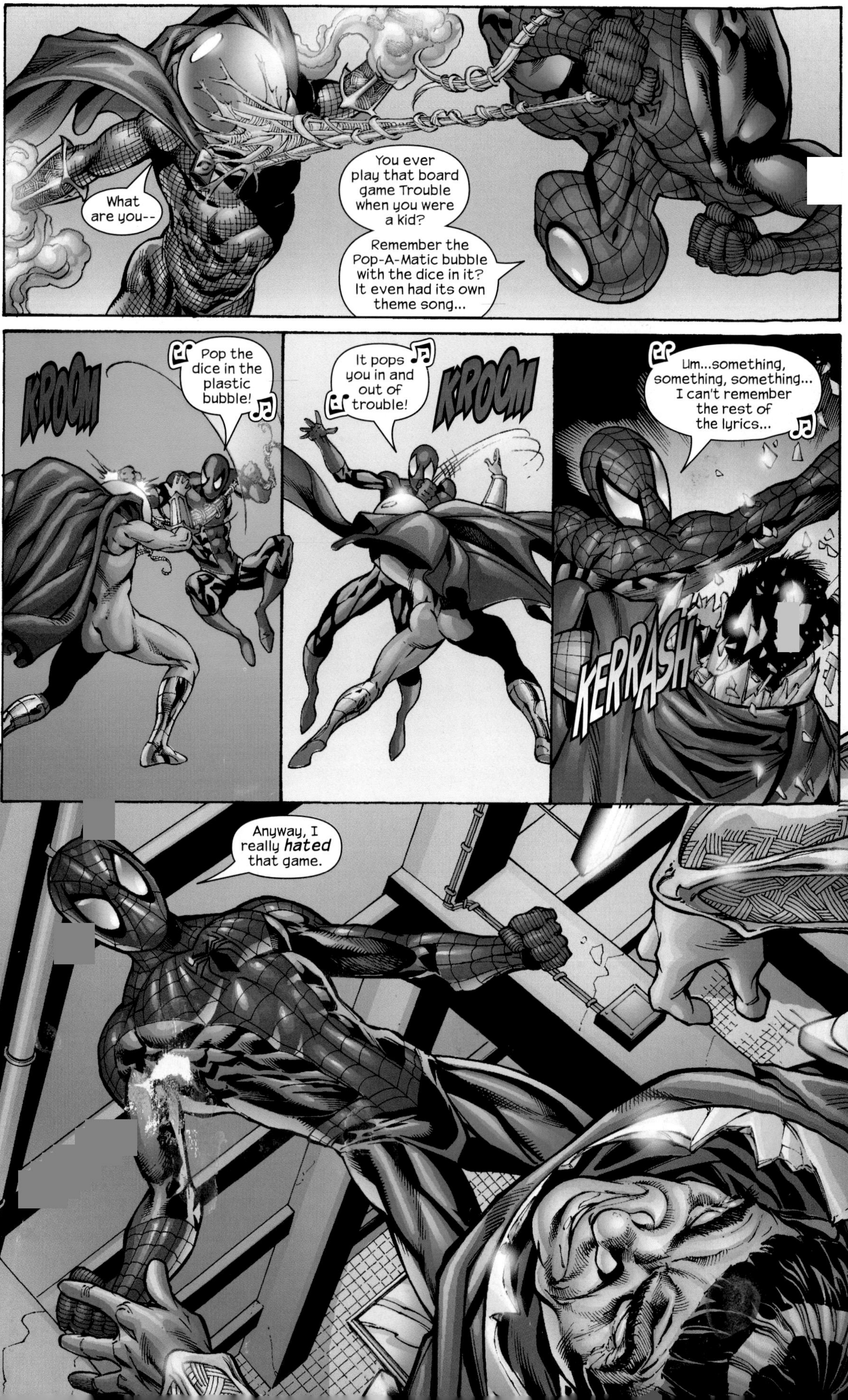
What are you--
You ever play that board game Trouble when you were a kid?
Remember the Pop-A-Matic bubble with the dice in it? It even had its own theme song...
KROOM
Pop the dice in the plastic bubble!
It pops you in and out of trouble!
KROOM
Um...something, something, something... I can't remember the rest of the lyrics...
KERRASH
Anyway, I really ***hated*** that game.

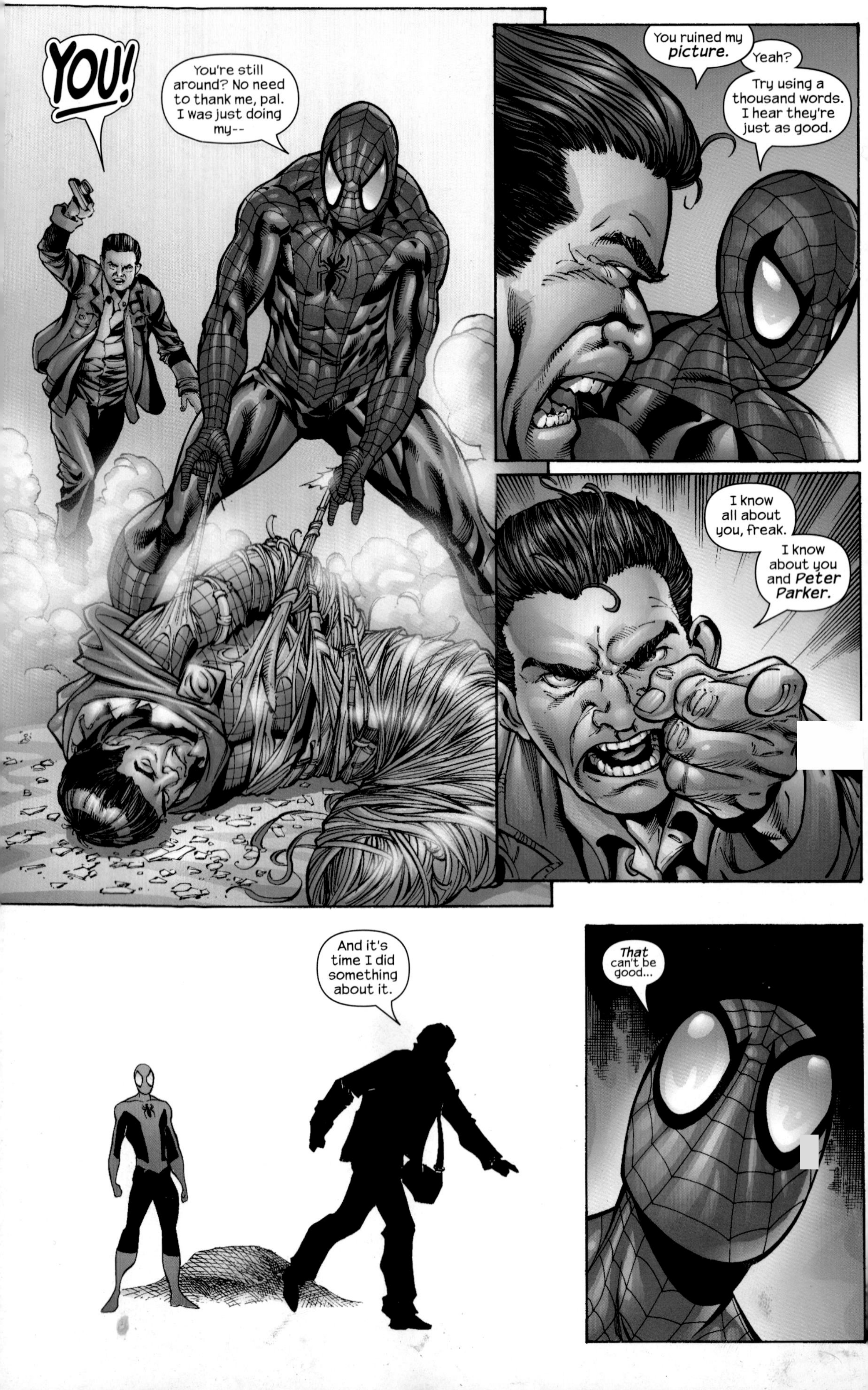

YOU!
You're still around? No need to thank me, pal. I was just doing my--
You ruined my *picture.*
Yeah?
Try using a thousand words. I hear they're just as good.
I know all about you, freak.
I know about you and *Peter Parker.*
And it's time I did something about it.
That can't be good...

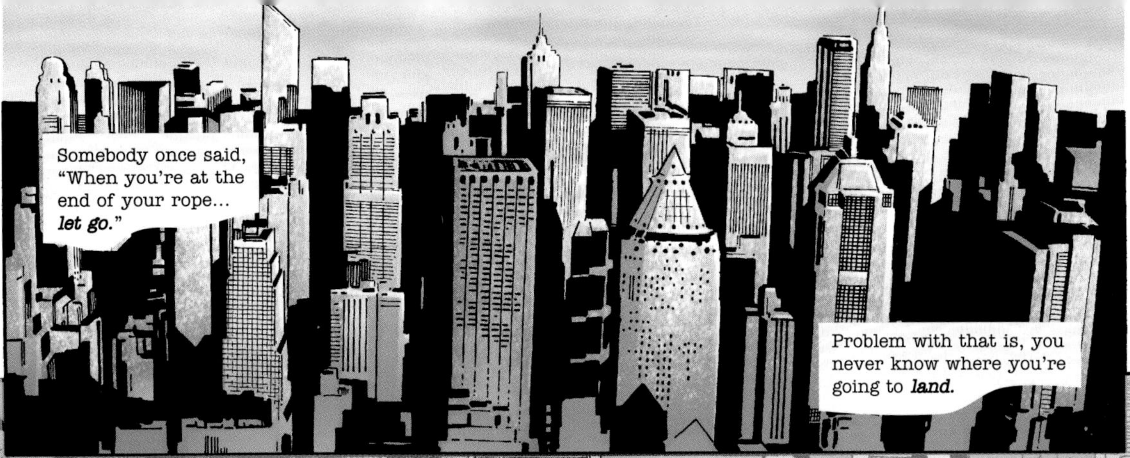
Somebody once said, "When you're at the end of your rope... *let go.*"
Problem with that is, you never know where you're going to *land.*

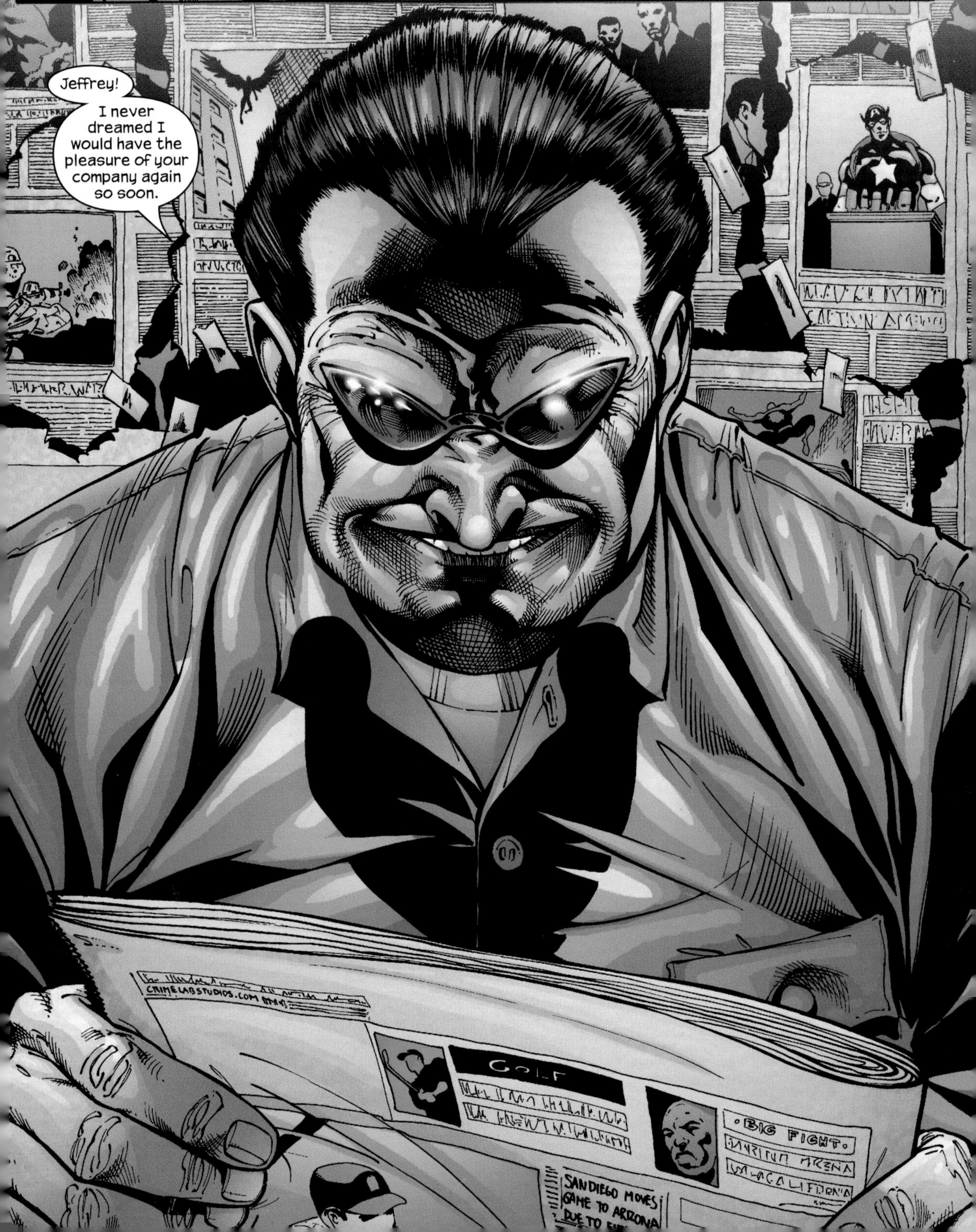
Jeffrey!
I never dreamed I would have the pleasure of your company again so soon.

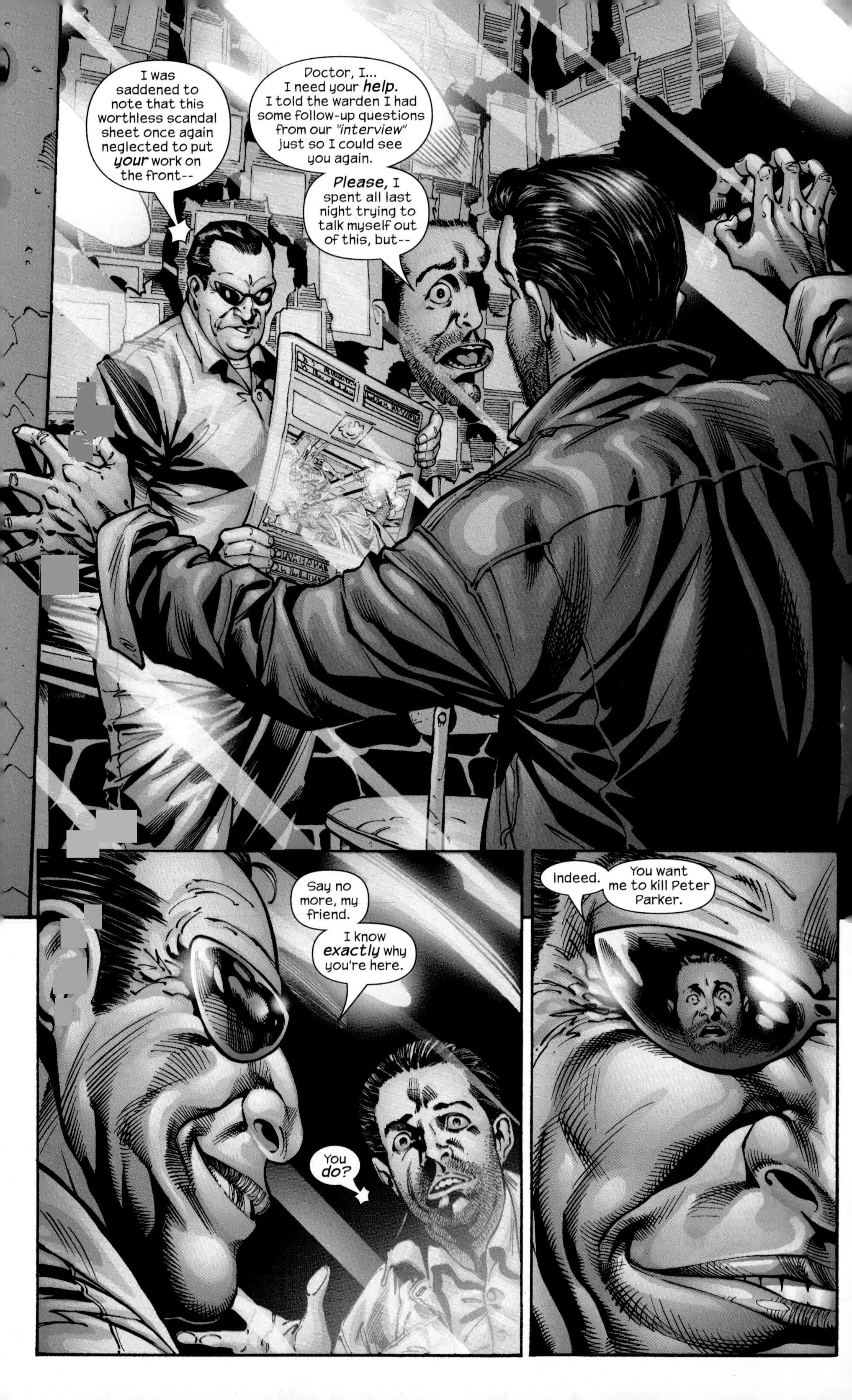
I was saddened to note that this worthless scandal sheet once again neglected to put *your* work on the front--
Doctor, I... I need your *help.* I told the warden I had some follow-up questions from our "*interview*" just so I could see you again.
Please, I spent all last night trying to talk myself out of this, but--
Say no more, my friend.
I know *exactly* why you're here.
You *do?*
Indeed.
You want me to kill Peter Parker.

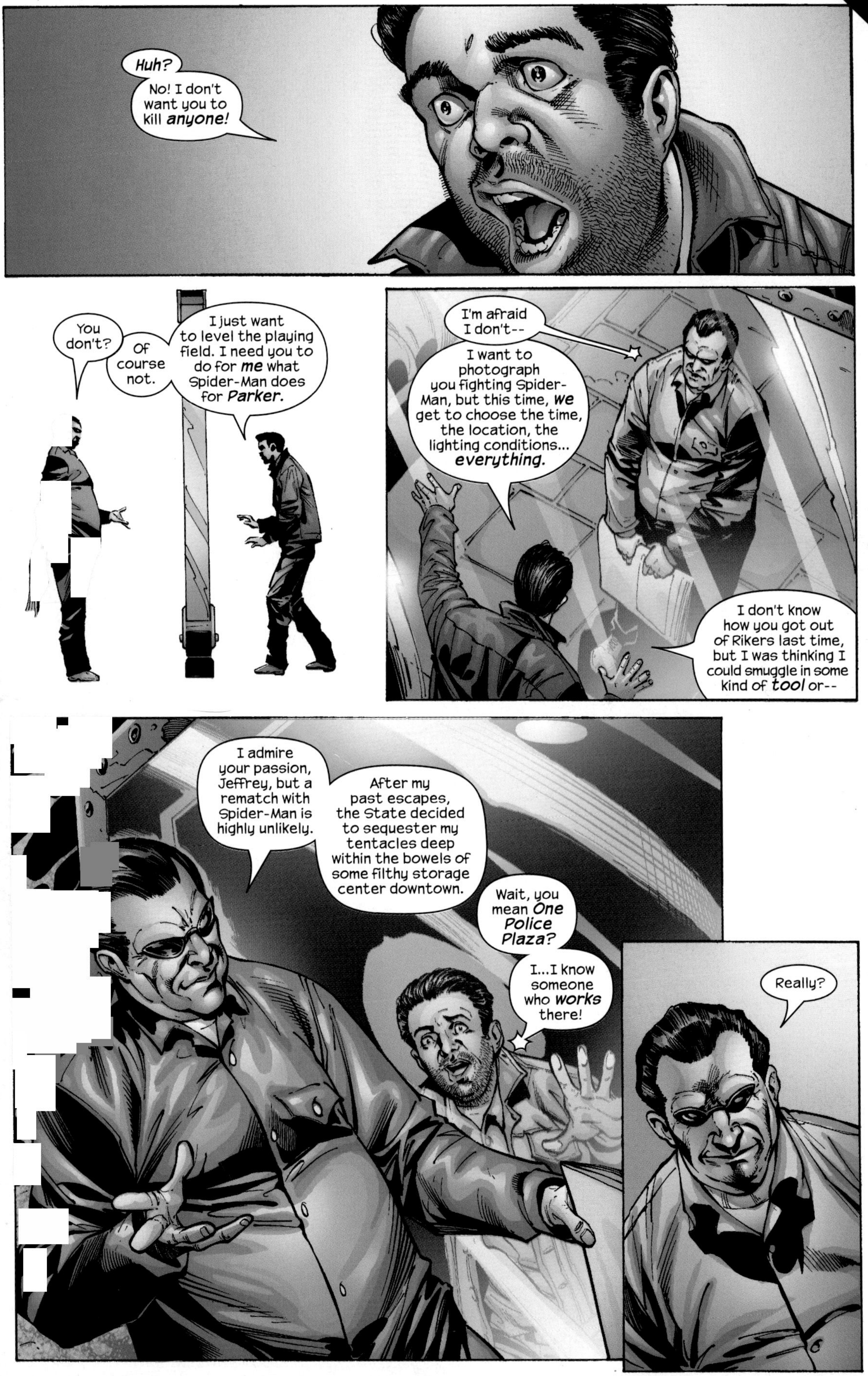
Huh?
No! I don't want you to kill anyone!
You don't?
Of course not.
I just want to level the playing field. I need you to do for me what Spider-Man does for Parker.
I'm afraid I don't--
I want to photograph you fighting Spider-Man, but this time, we get to choose the time, the location, the lighting conditions... everything.
I don't know how you got out of Rikers last time, but I was thinking I could smuggle in some kind of tool or--
I admire your passion, Jeffrey, but a rematch with Spider-Man is highly unlikely.
After my past escapes, the State decided to sequester my tentacles deep within the bowels of some filthy storage center downtown.
Wait, you mean One Police Plaza?
I...I know someone who works there!
Really?

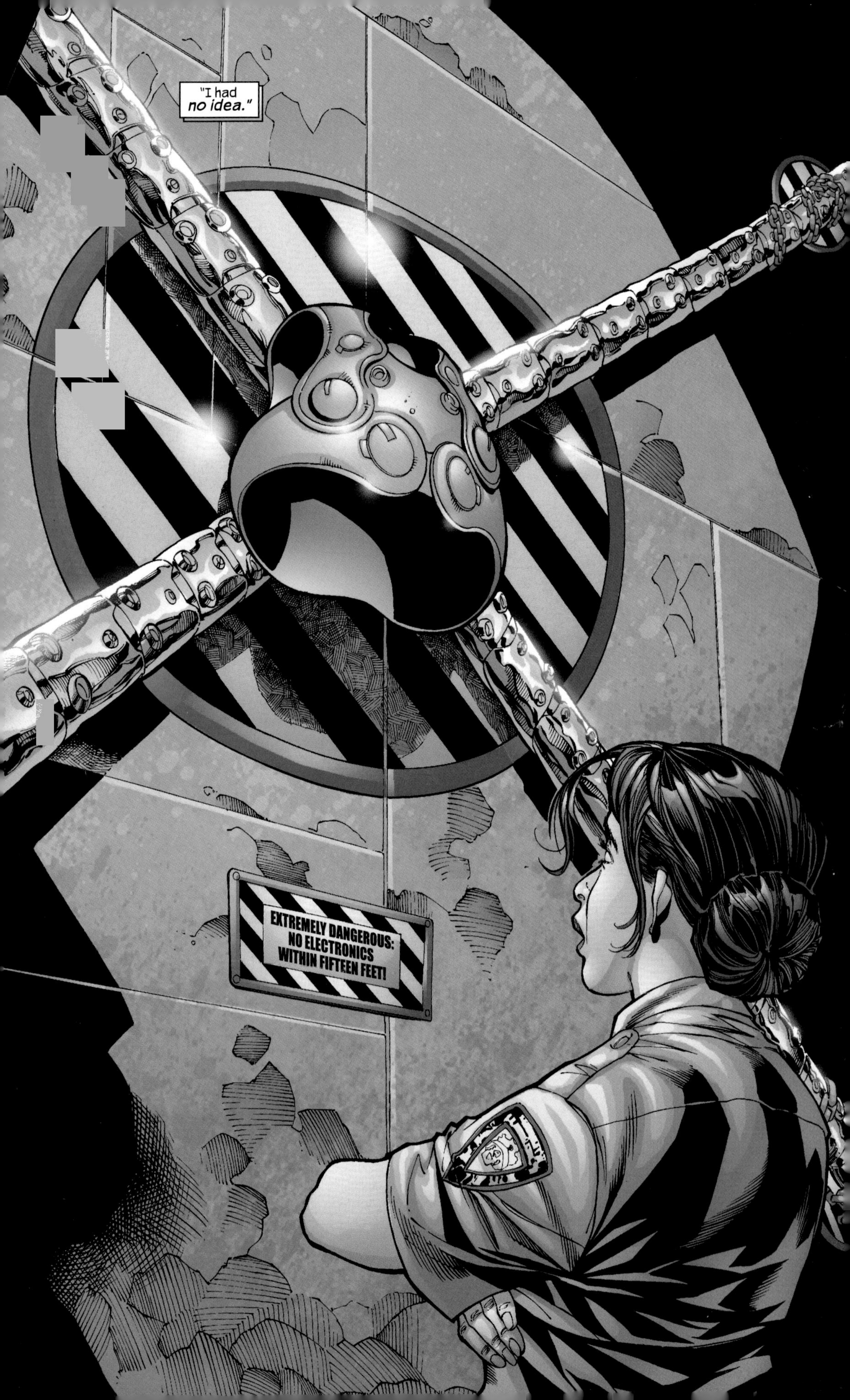
"I had no idea."
EXTREMELY DANGEROUS: NO ELECTRONICS WITHIN FIFTEEN FEET!

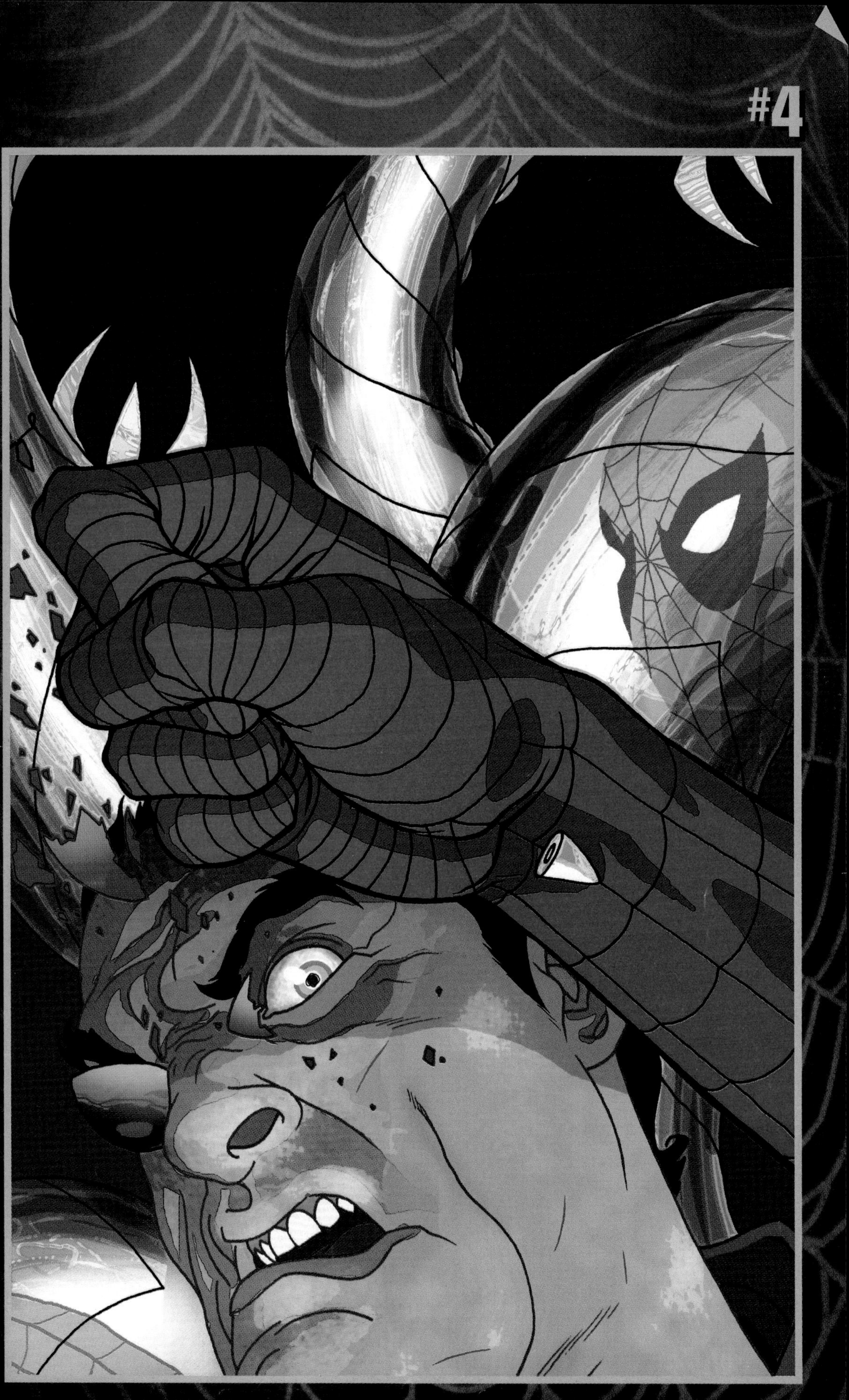
#4

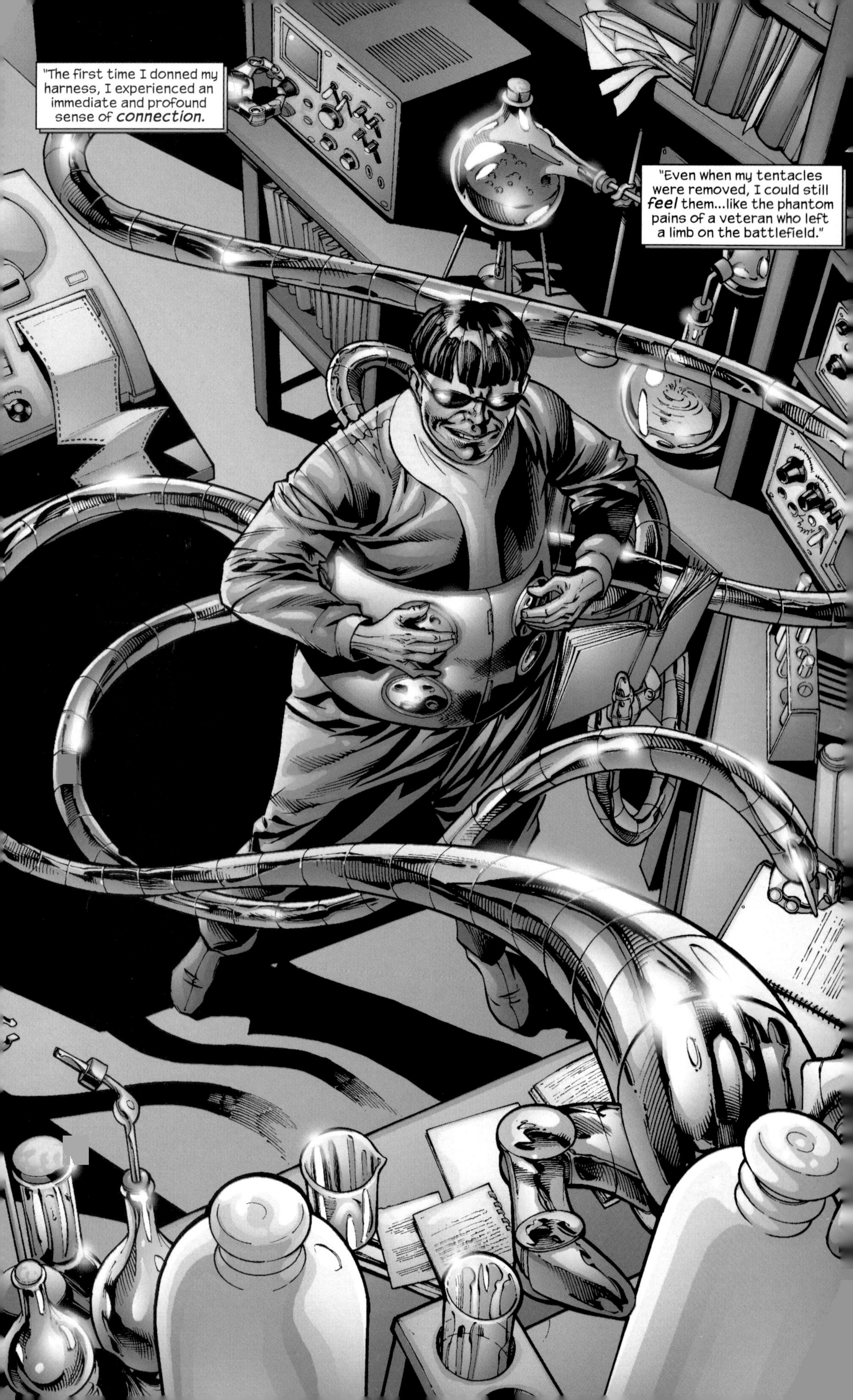
"The first time I donned my harness, I experienced an immediate and profound sense of *connection.*
"Even when my tentacles were removed, I could still *feel* them...like the phantom pains of a veteran who left a limb on the battlefield."

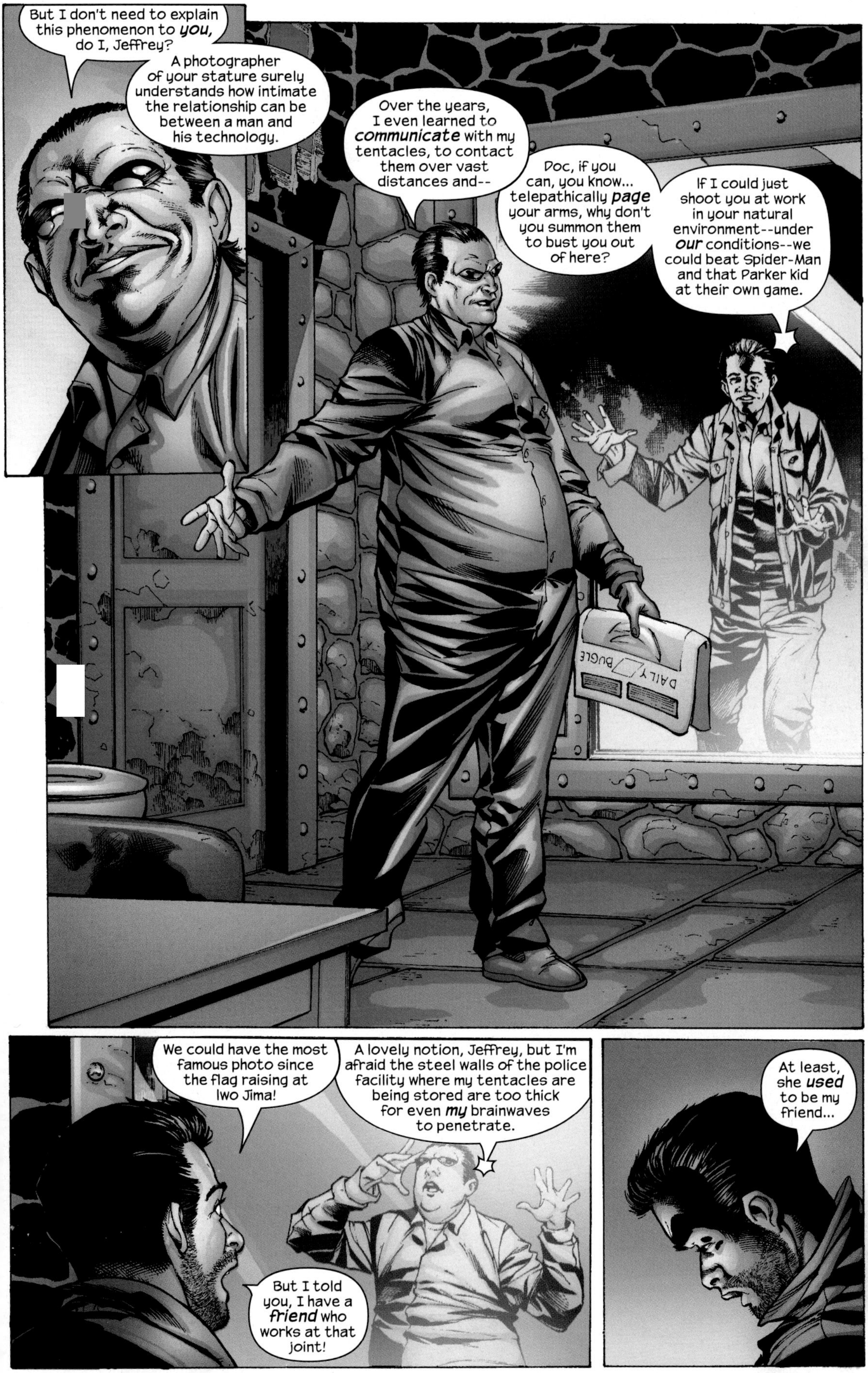
But I don't need to explain this phenomenon to *you,* do I, Jeffrey?
A photographer of your stature surely understands how intimate the relationship can be between a man and his technology.
Over the years, I even learned to *communicate* with my tentacles, to contact them over vast distances and--
Doc, if you can, you know... telepathically *page* your arms, why don't you summon them to bust you out of here?
If I could just shoot you at work in your natural environment--under *our* conditions--we could beat Spider-Man and that Parker kid at their own game.
We could have the most famous photo since the flag raising at Iwo Jima!
A lovely notion, Jeffrey, but I'm afraid the steel walls of the police facility where my tentacles are being stored are too thick for even *my* brainwaves to penetrate.
But I told you, I have a *friend* who works at that joint!
At least, she *used* to be my friend...

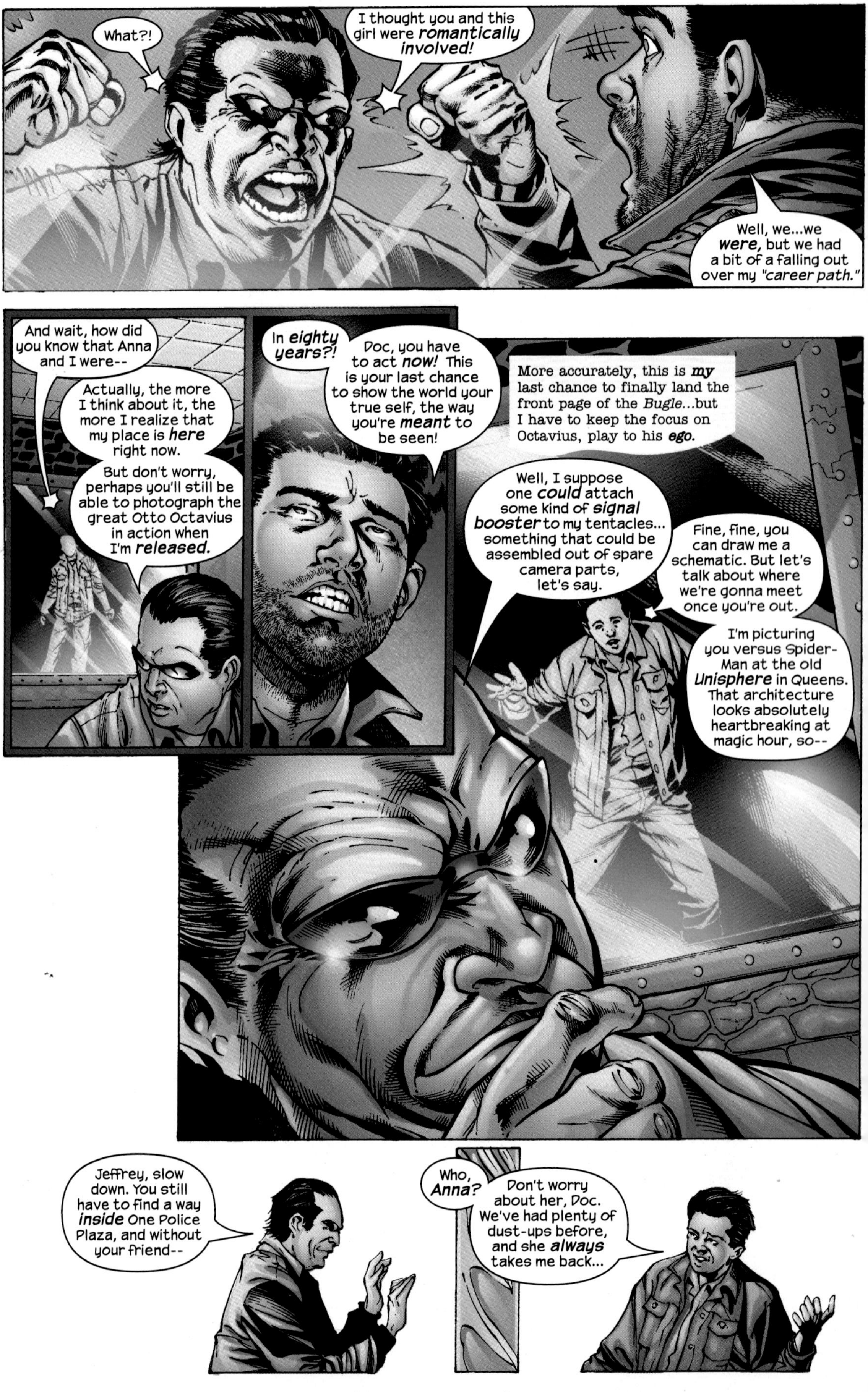
What?!
I thought you and this girl were *romantically involved!*
Well, we...we *were,* but we had a bit of a falling out over my *"career path."*
And wait, how did you know that Anna and I were--
Actually, the more I think about it, the more I realize that my place is *here* right now.
But don't worry, perhaps you'll still be able to photograph the great Otto Octavius in action when I'm *released.*
In *eighty years?!*
Doc, you have to act *now!* This is your last chance to show the world your true self, the way you're *meant* to be seen!
More accurately, this is *my* last chance to finally land the front page of the *Bugle*...but I have to keep the focus on Octavius, play to his *ego.*
Well, I suppose one *could* attach some kind of *signal booster* to my tentacles... something that could be assembled out of spare camera parts, let's say.
Fine, fine, you can draw me a schematic. But let's talk about where we're gonna meet once you're out.
I'm picturing you versus Spider-Man at the old *Unisphere* in Queens. That architecture looks absolutely heartbreaking at magic hour, so--
Jeffrey, slow down. You still have to find a way *inside* One Police Plaza, and without your friend--
Who, *Anna?*
Don't worry about her, Doc. We've had plenty of dust-ups before, and she *always* takes me back...

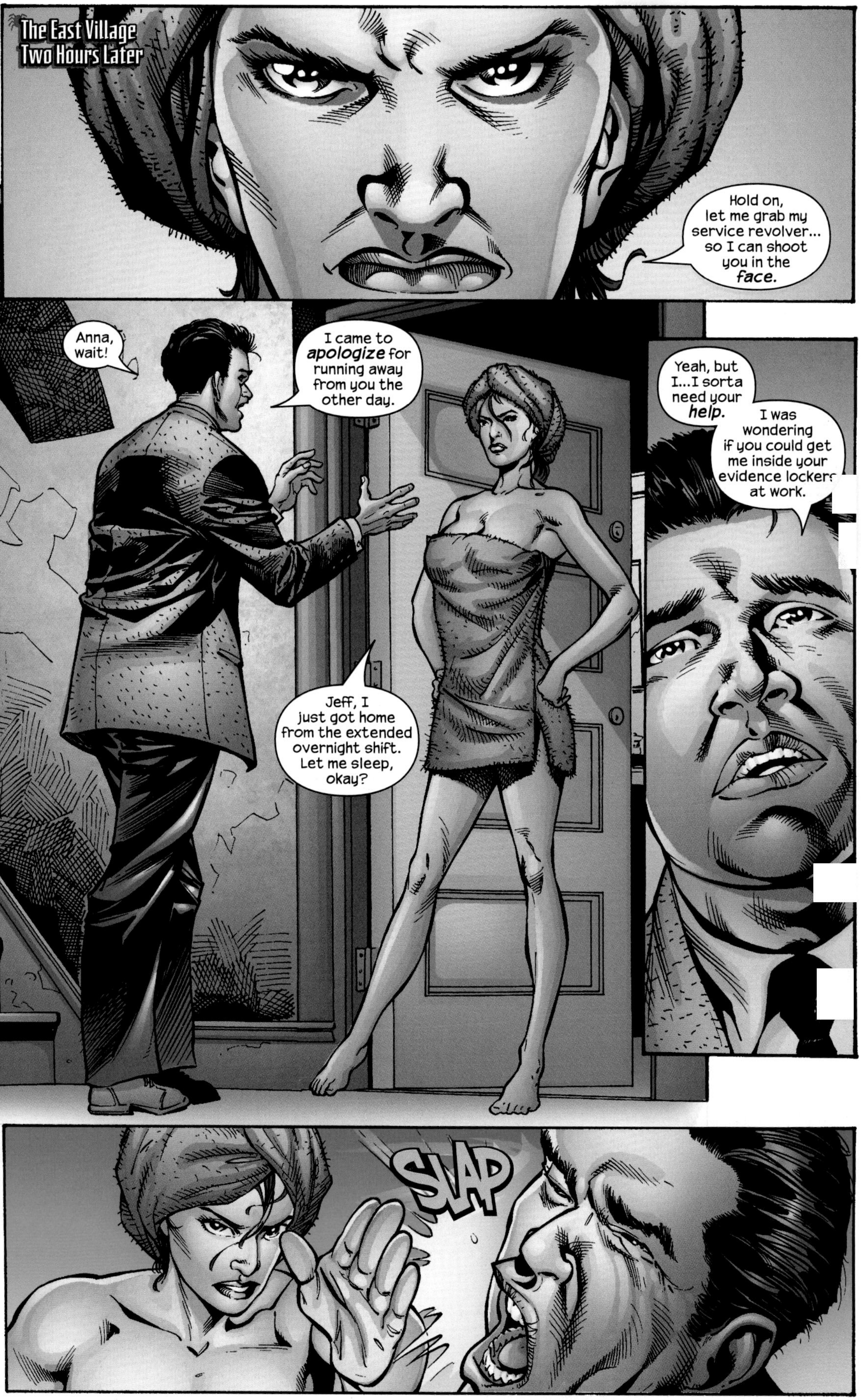
The East Village
Two Hours Later
Hold on, let me grab my service revolver... so I can shoot you in the face.
Anna, wait!
I came to apologize for running away from you the other day.
Jeff, I just got home from the extended overnight shift. Let me sleep, okay?
Yeah, but I...I sorta need your help.
I was wondering if you could get me inside your evidence lockers at work.
SLAP

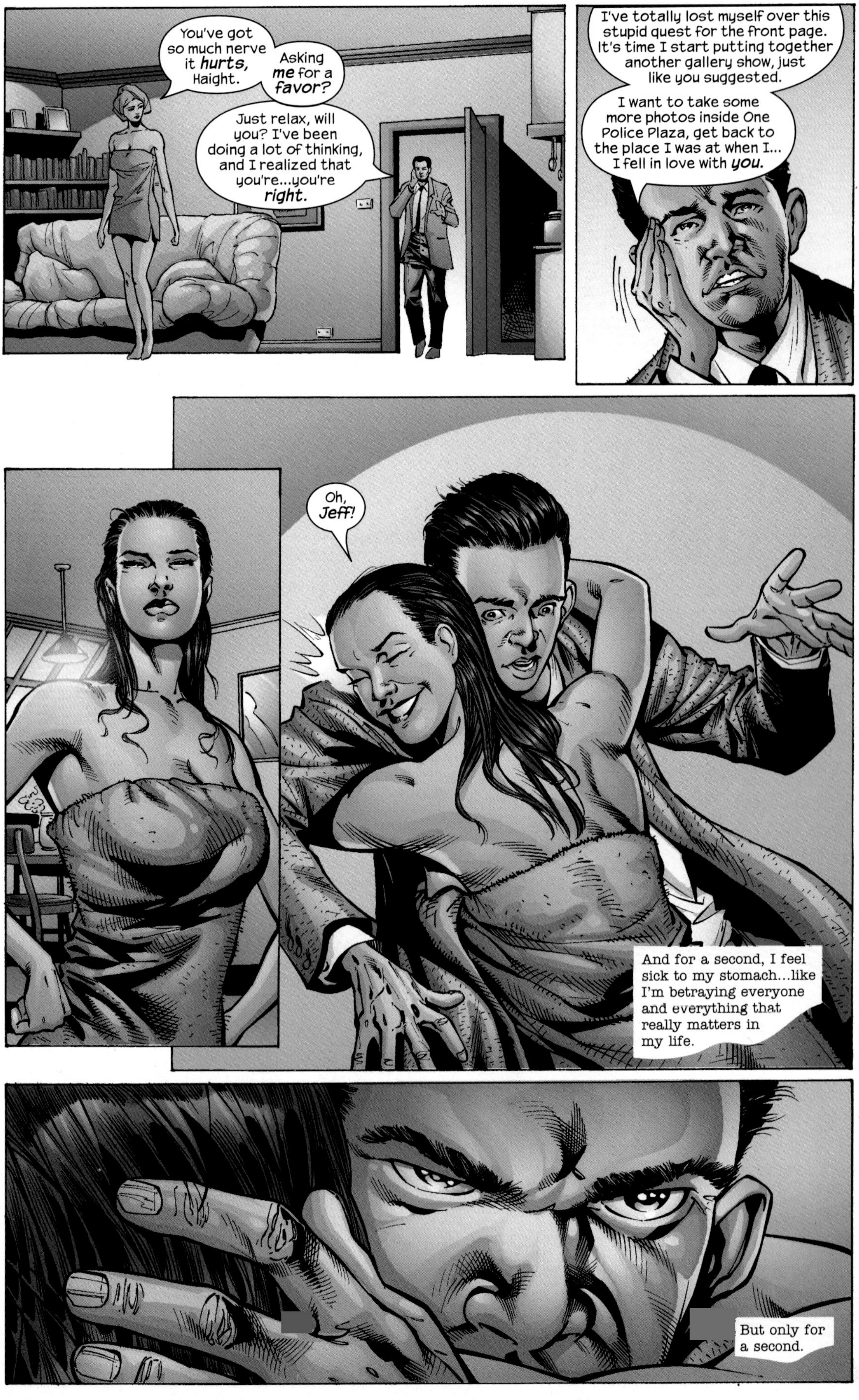
You've got so much nerve it *hurts,* Haight.
Asking *me* for a *favor?*
Just relax, will you? I've been doing a lot of thinking, and I realized that you're...you're *right.*
I've totally lost myself over this stupid quest for the front page. It's time I start putting together another gallery show, just like you suggested.
I want to take some more photos inside One Police Plaza, get back to the place I was at when I... I fell in love with *you.*
Oh, *Jeff!*
And for a second, I feel sick to my stomach...like I'm betraying everyone and everything that really matters in my life.
But only for a second.

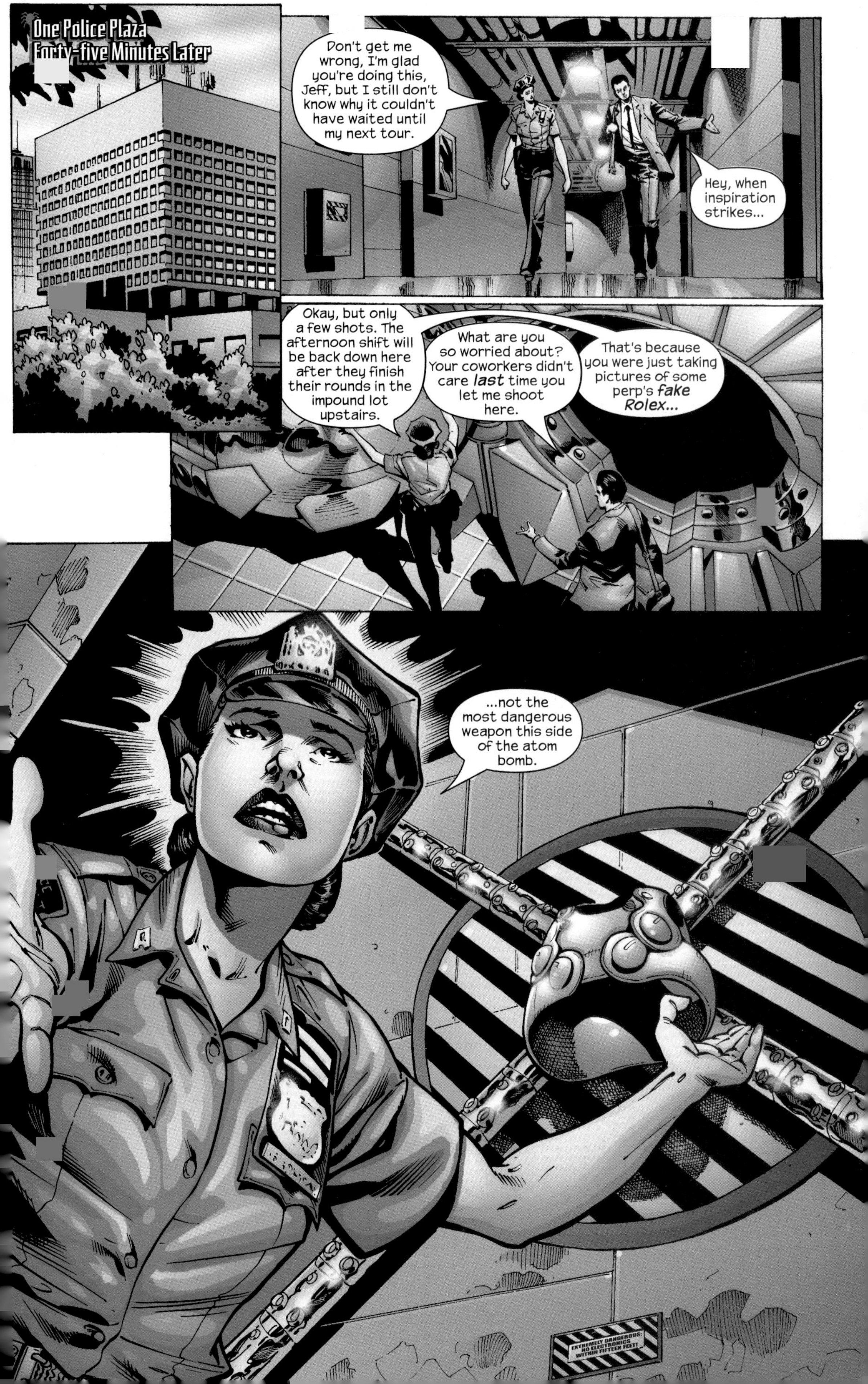
One Police Plaza
Forty-five Minutes Later
Don't get me wrong, I'm glad you're doing this, Jeff, but I still don't know why it couldn't have waited until my next tour.
Hey, when inspiration strikes...
Okay, but only a few shots. The afternoon shift will be back down here after they finish their rounds in the impound lot upstairs.
What are you so worried about? Your coworkers didn't care *last* time you let me shoot here.
That's because you were just taking pictures of some perp's *fake* *Rolex...*
...not the most dangerous weapon this side of the atom bomb.
EXTREMELY DANGEROUS: NO ELECTRONICS WITHIN FIFTEEN FEET!

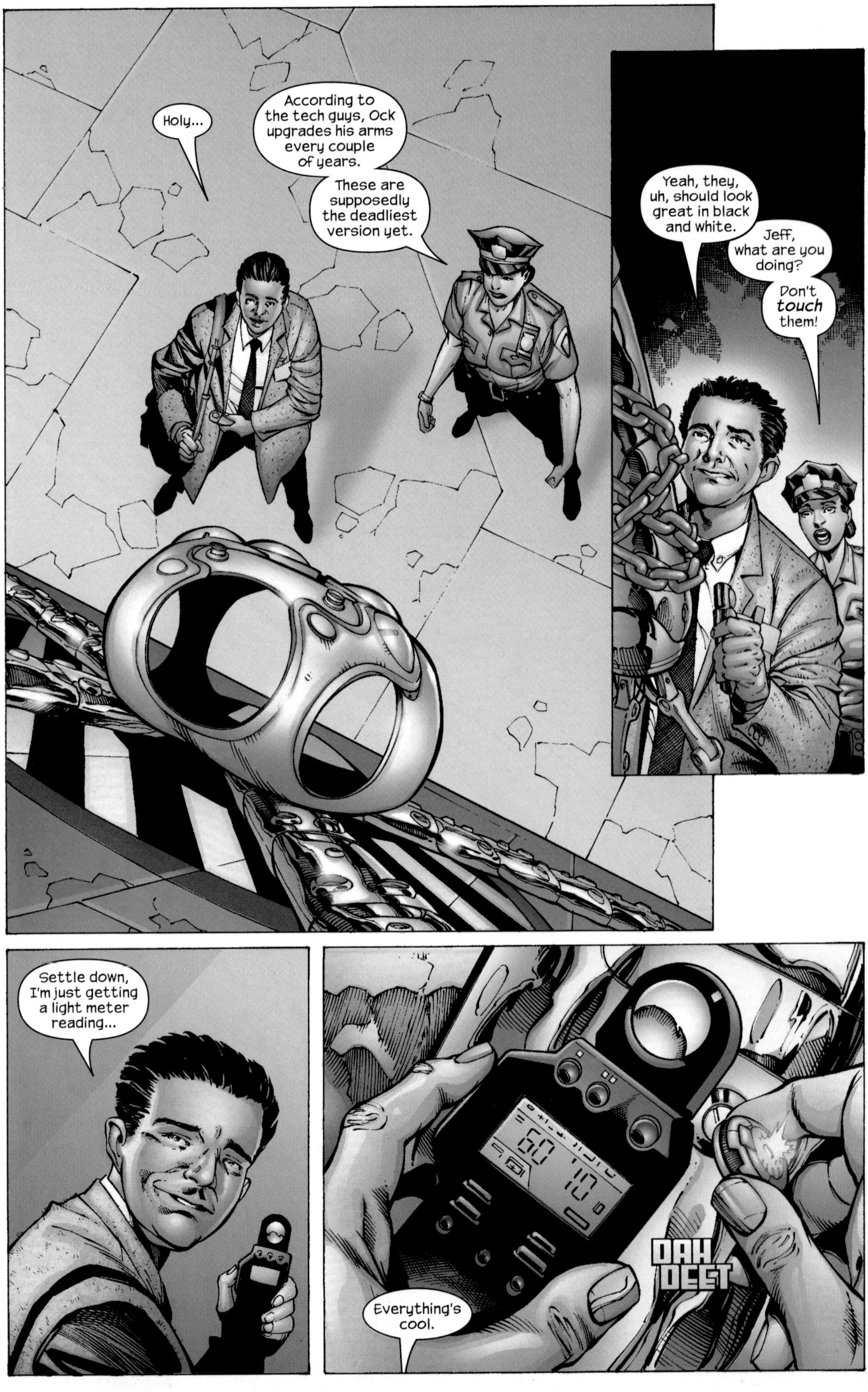
Holy...
According to the tech guys, Ock upgrades his arms every couple of years.
These are supposedly the deadliest version yet.
Yeah, they, uh, should look great in black and white.
Jeff, what are you doing?
Don't *touch* them!
Settle down, I'm just getting a light meter reading...
DAH DEET
Everything's cool.

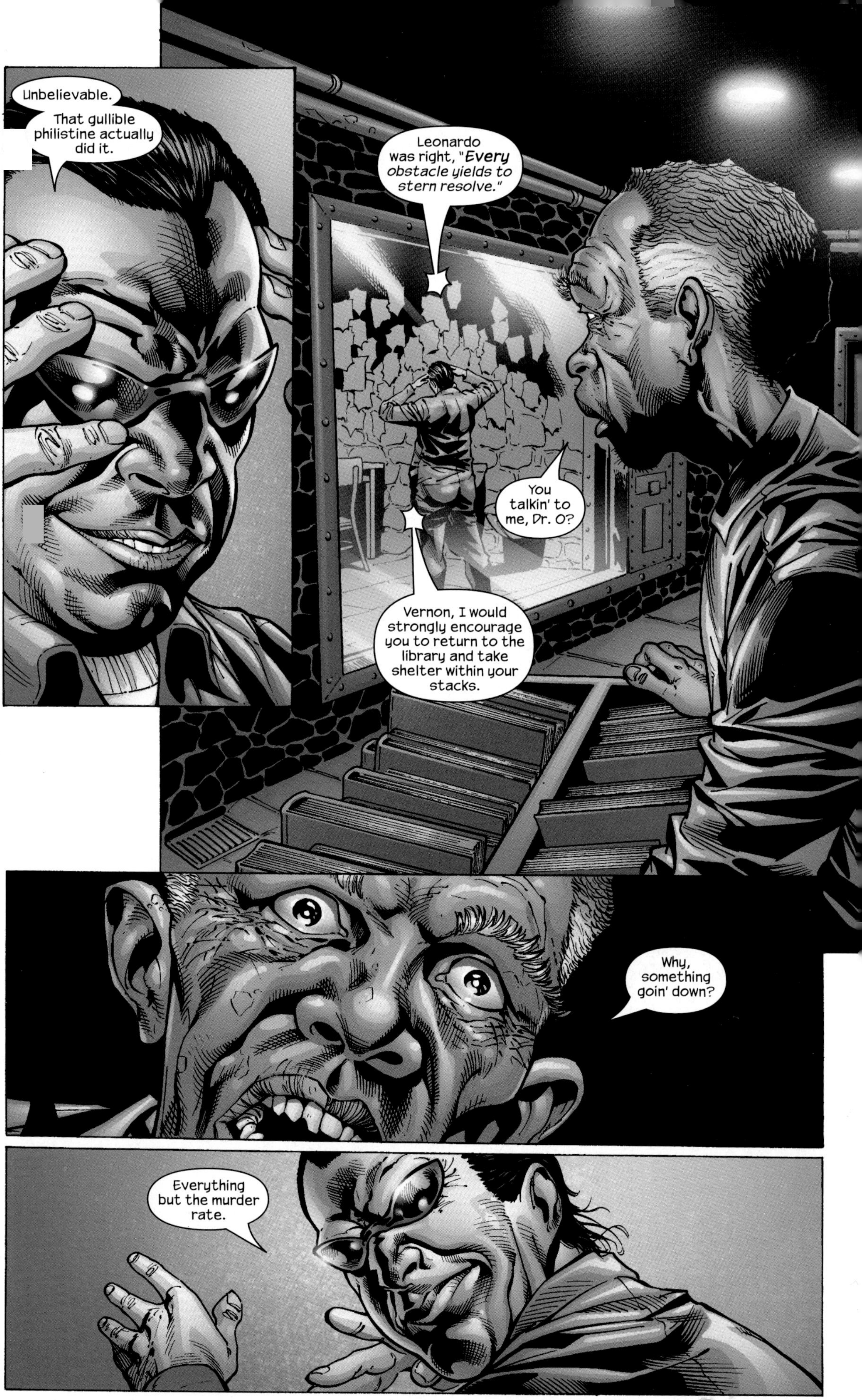
Unbelievable.
That gullible philistine actually did it.
Leonardo was right, "Every obstacle yields to stern resolve."
You talkin' to me, Dr. O?
Vernon, I would strongly encourage you to return to the library and take shelter within your stacks.
Why, something goin' down?
Everything but the murder rate.

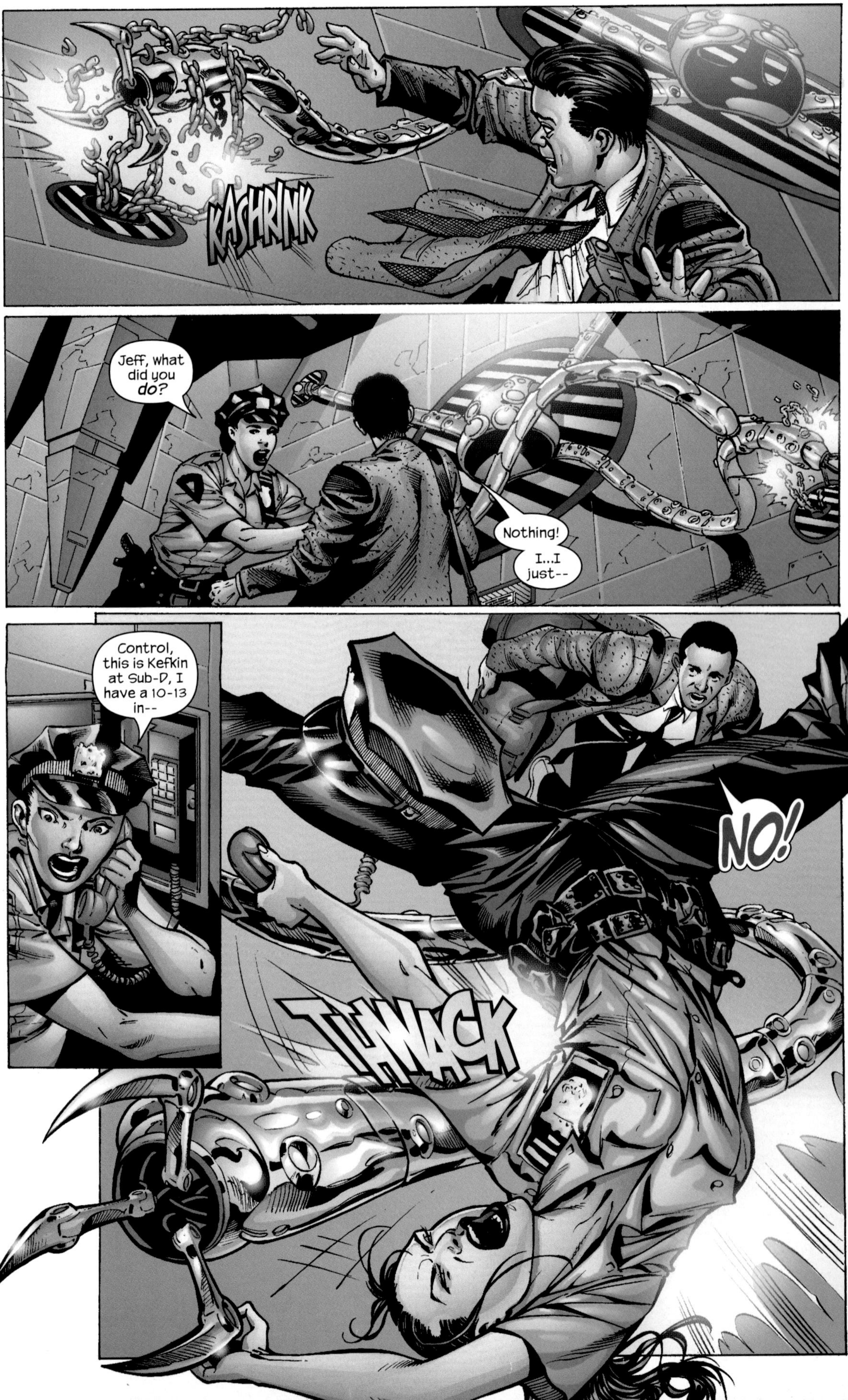
KASHRINK
Jeff, what did you do?
Nothing! I...I just--
Control, this is Kefkin at Sub-D, I have a 10-13 in--
NO!
THWACK

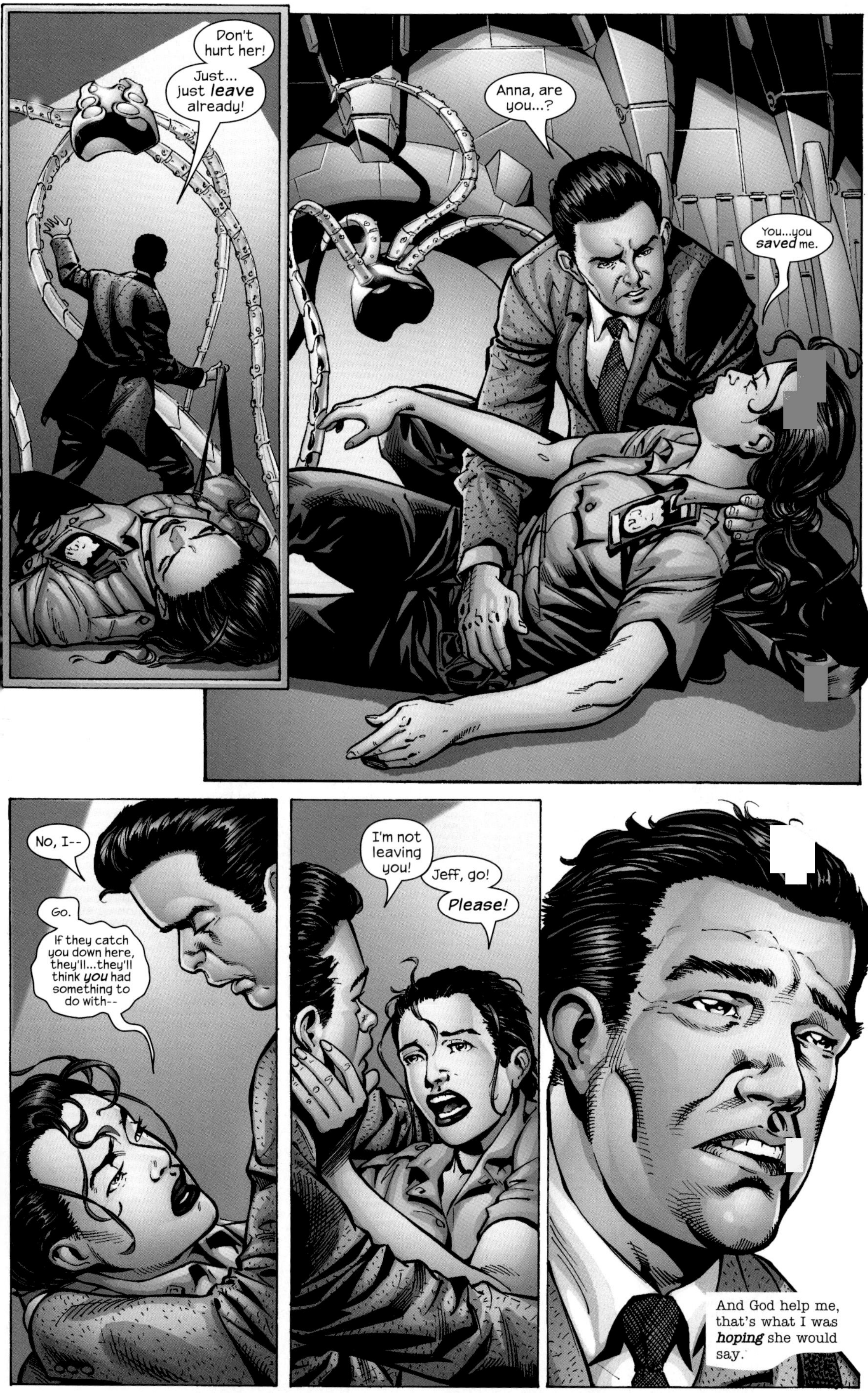
Don't hurt her!
Just... just leave already!
Anna, are you...?
You...you saved me.
No, I--
Go.
If they catch you down here, they'll...they'll think you had something to do with--
I'm not leaving you!
Jeff, go!
Please!
And God help me, that's what I was hoping she would say.

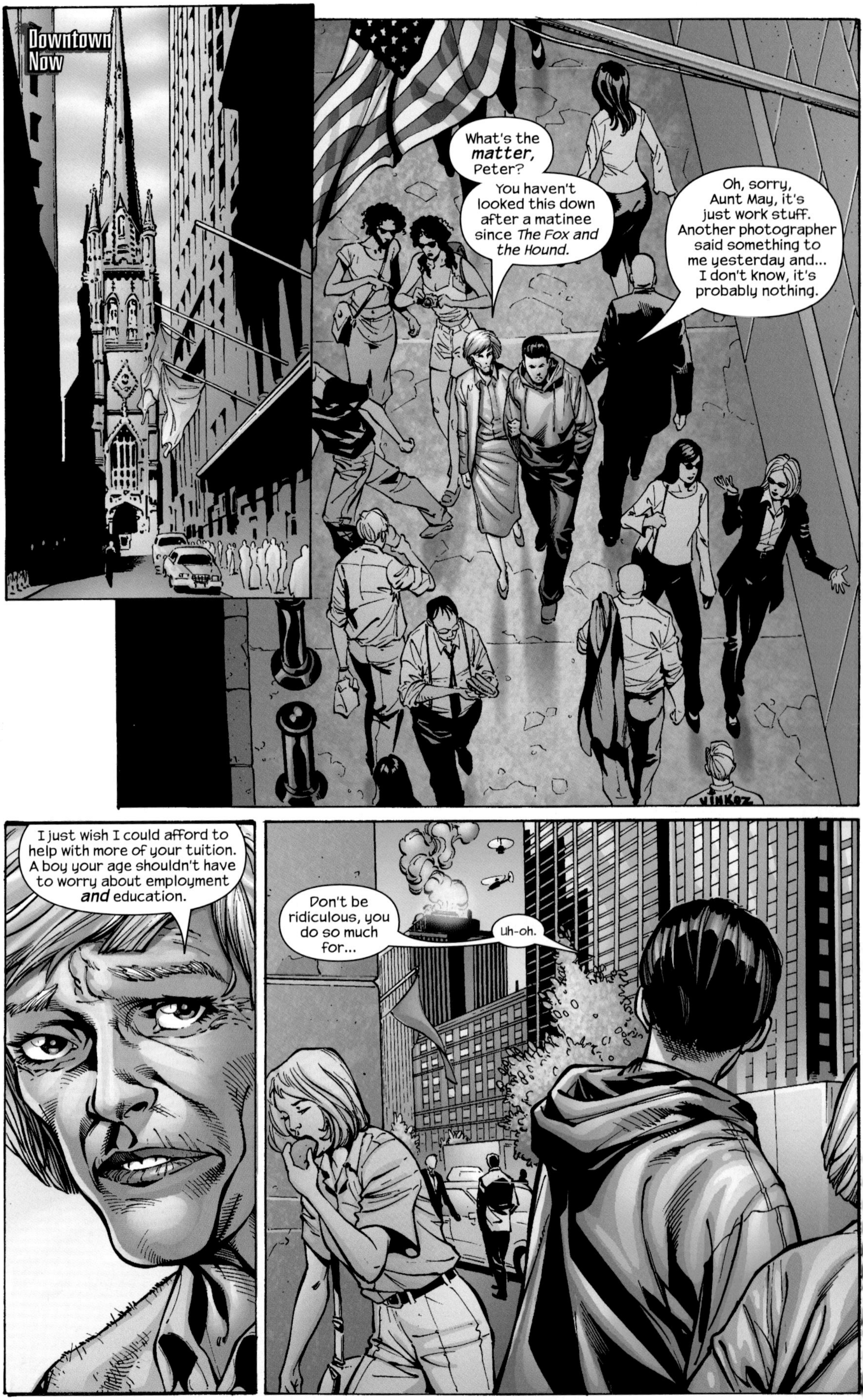
Downtown
Now
What's the *matter,* Peter?
You haven't looked this down after a matinee since *The Fox and the Hound.*
Oh, sorry, Aunt May, it's just work stuff. Another photographer said something to me yesterday and... I don't know, it's probably nothing.
I just wish I could afford to help with more of your tuition. A boy your age shouldn't have to worry about employment *and* education.
Don't be ridiculous, you do so much for...
Uh-oh.

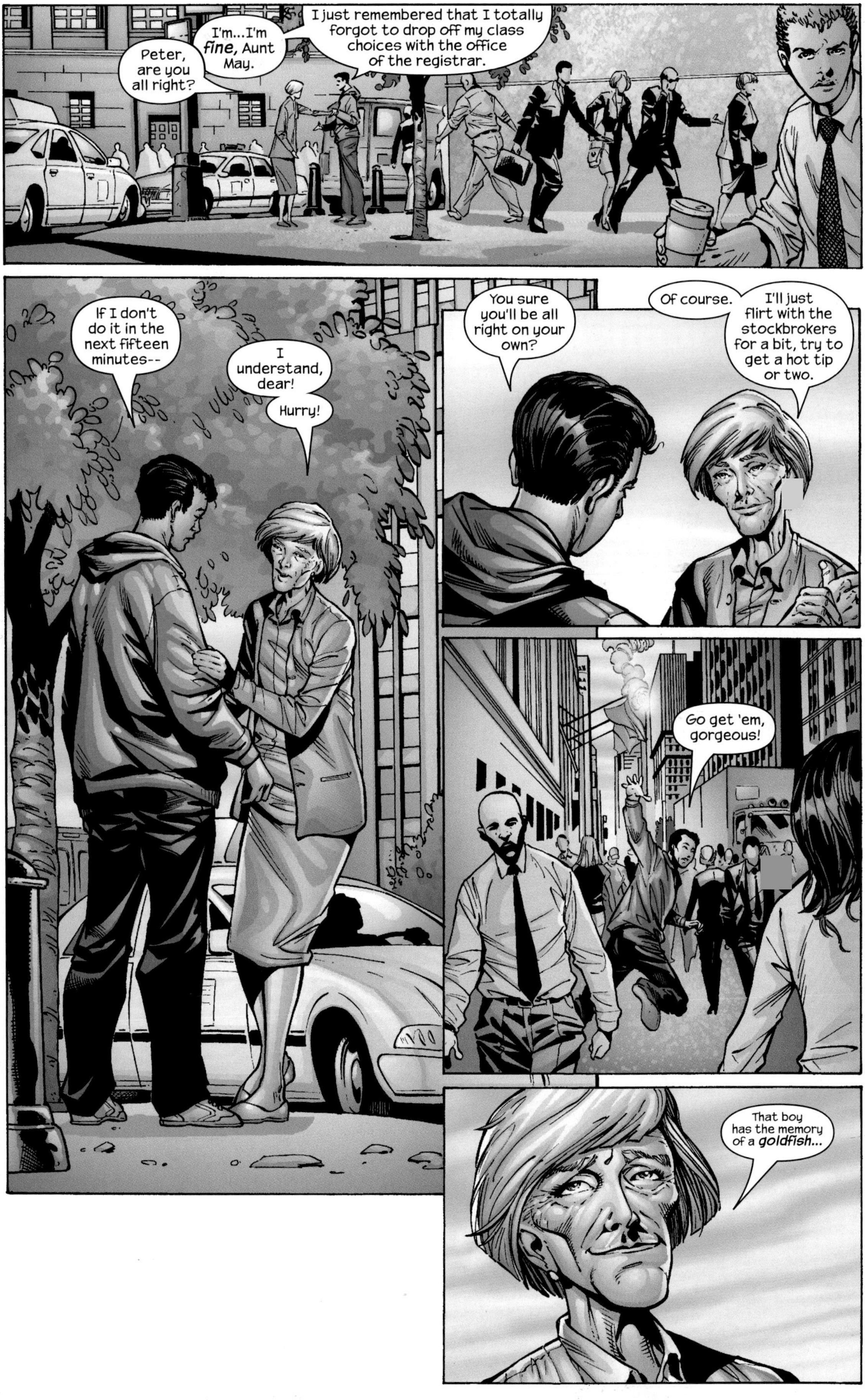
Peter, are you all right?
I'm...I'm *fine,* Aunt May.
I just remembered that I totally forgot to drop off my class choices with the office of the registrar.
If I don't do it in the next fifteen minutes--
I understand, dear!
Hurry!
You sure you'll be all right on your own?
Of course.
I'll just flirt with the stockbrokers for a bit, try to get a hot tip or two.
Go get 'em, gorgeous!
That boy has the memory of a *goldfish...*

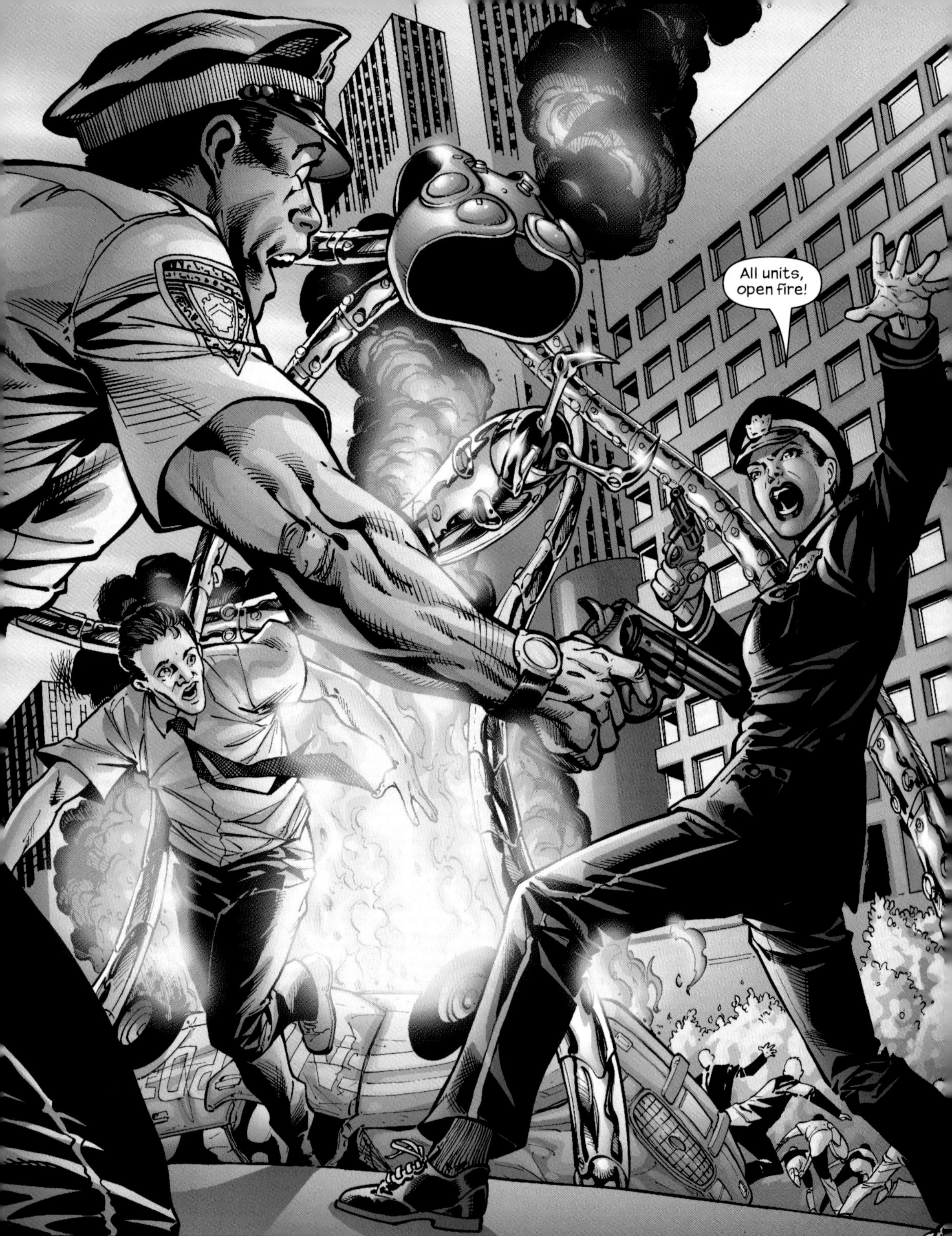
All units, open fire!

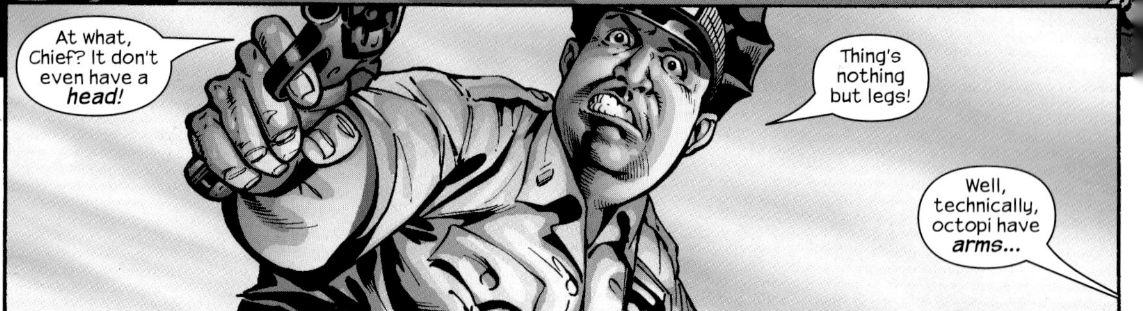
At what, Chief? It don't even have a *head!*
Thing's nothing but legs!
Well, technically, octopi have *arms...*

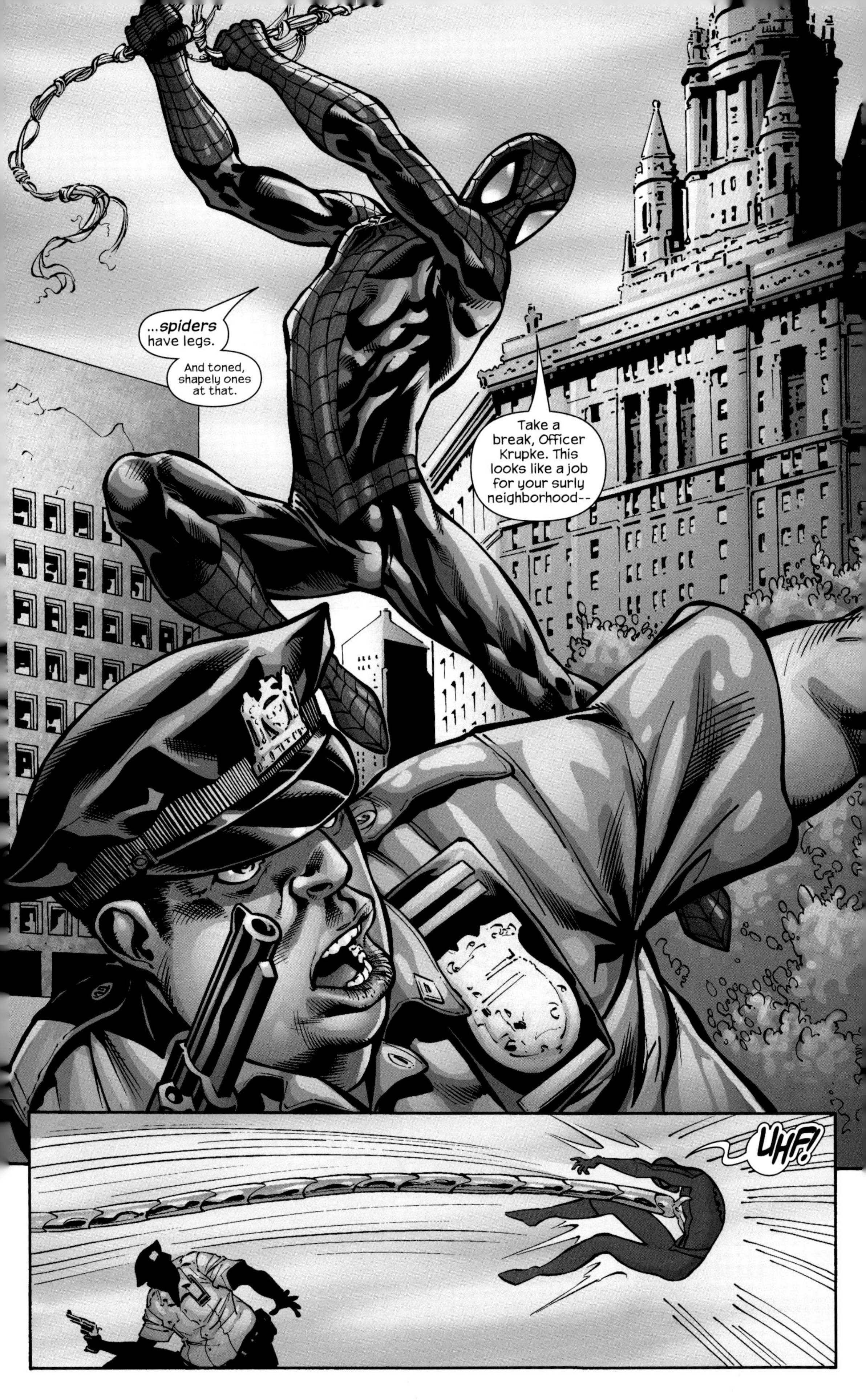

...*spiders* have legs.
And toned, shapely ones at that.
Take a break, Officer Krupke. This looks like a job for your surly neighborhood--
UHF!

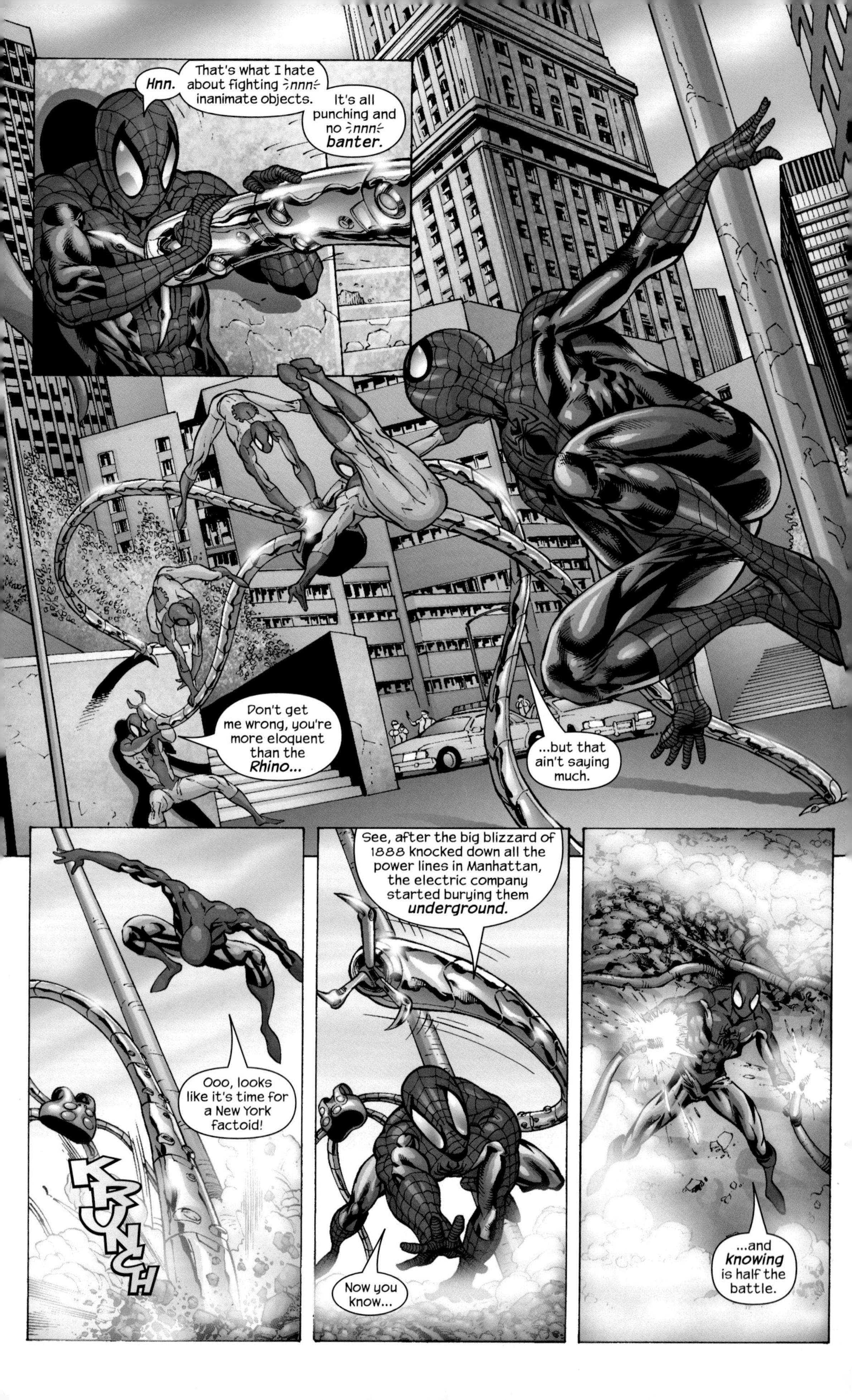
Hnn.
That's what I hate about fighting ⁓nnn⁓ inanimate objects.
It's all punching and no ⁓nnn⁓ banter.
Don't get me wrong, you're more eloquent than the Rhino...
...but that ain't saying much.
Ooo, looks like it's time for a New York factoid!
KRUNCH
See, after the big blizzard of 1888 knocked down all the power lines in Manhattan, the electric company started burying them underground.
Now you know...
...and knowing is half the battle.

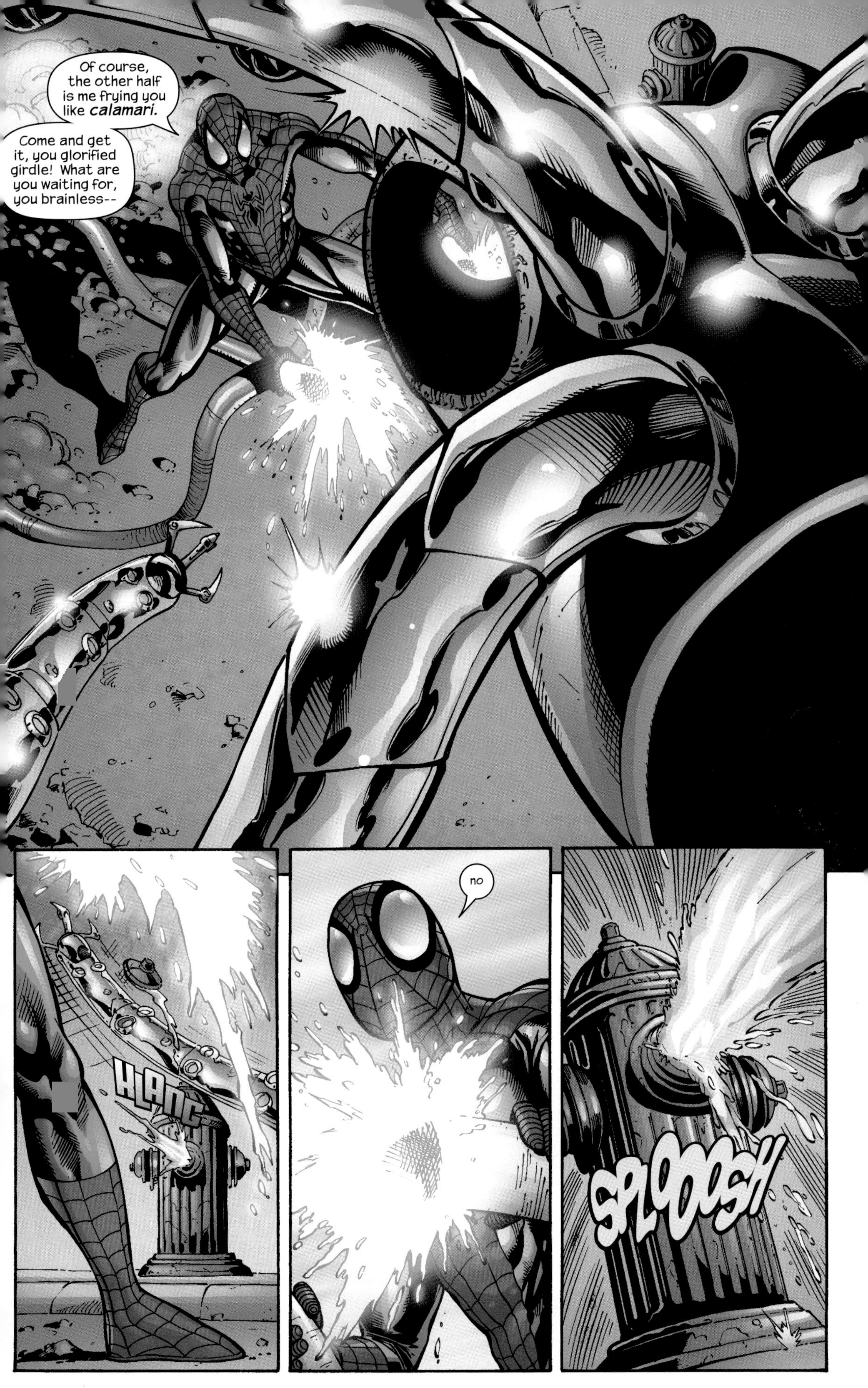
Of course, the other half is me frying you like *calamari.*
Come and get it, you glorified girdle! What are you waiting for, you brainless--
KLANG
no
SPLOOOSH

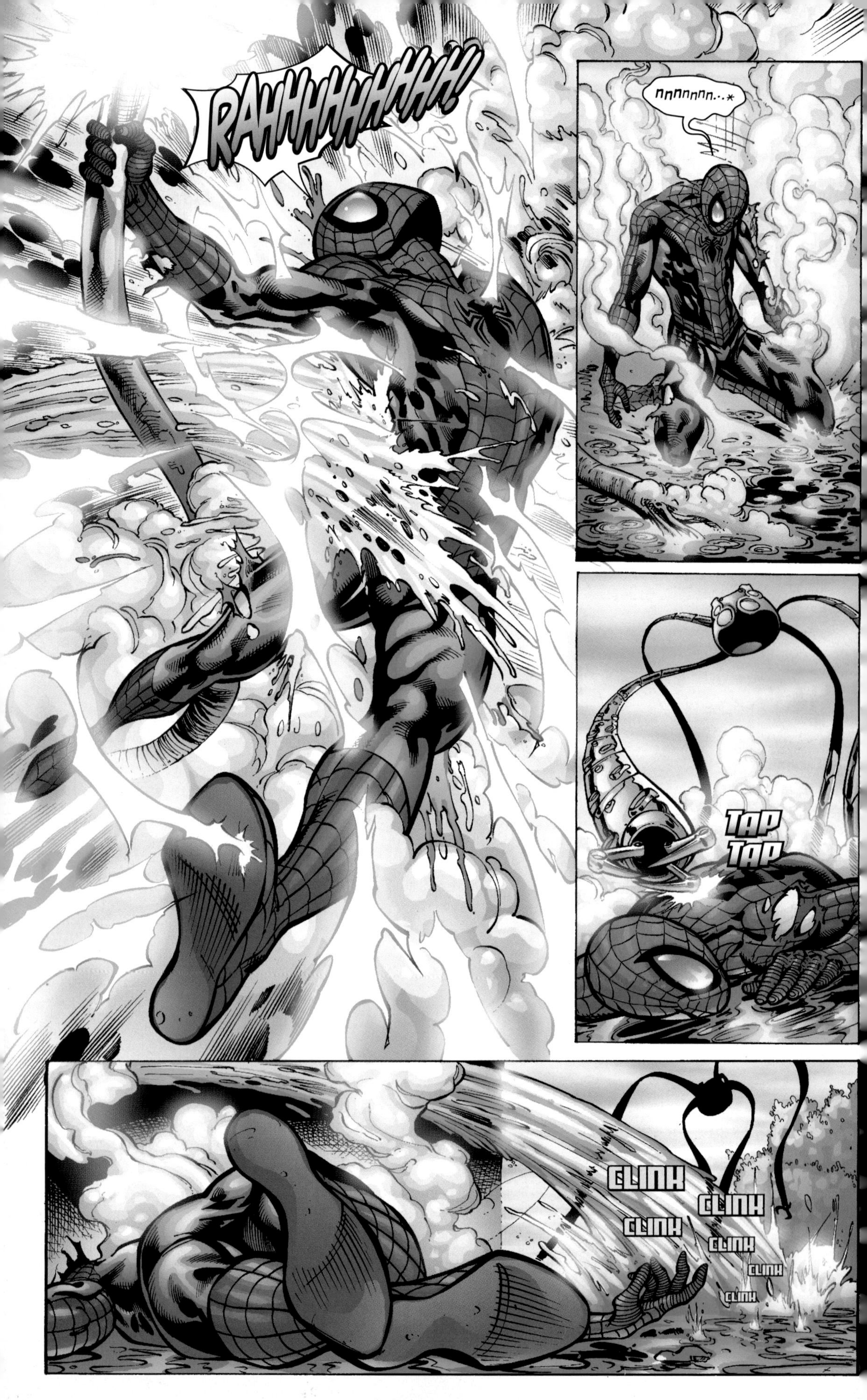
RAHHHHHHHHH!
nnnnnnn...*
TAP
TAP
CLINK
CLINK
CLINK
CLINK
CLINK
CLINK

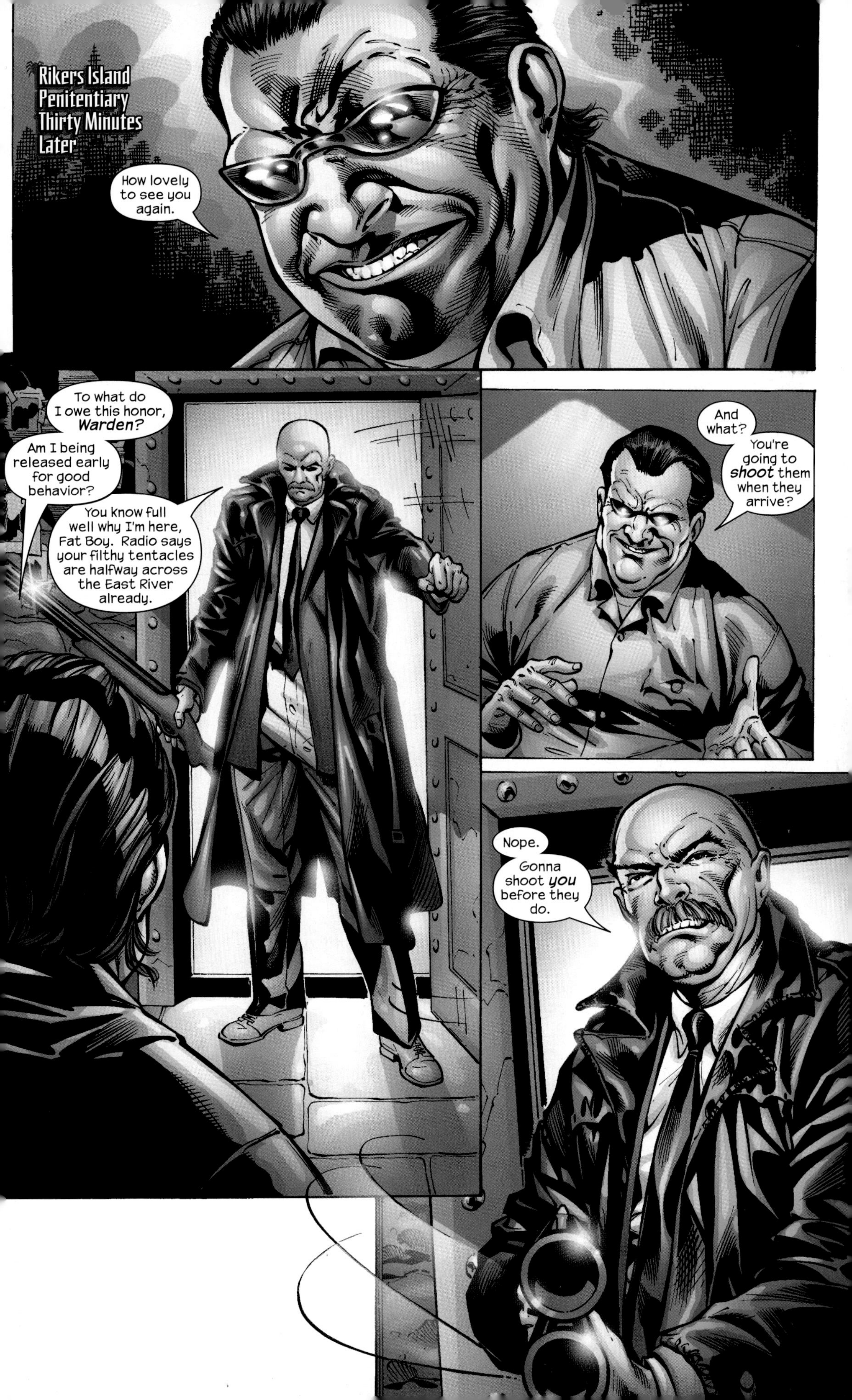
Rikers Island Penitentiary Thirty Minutes Later
How lovely to see you again.
To what do I owe this honor, *Warden?*
Am I being released early for good behavior?
You know full well why I'm here, Fat Boy. Radio says your filthy tentacles are halfway across the East River already.
And what? You're going to *shoot* them when they arrive?
Nope.
Gonna shoot *you* before they do.

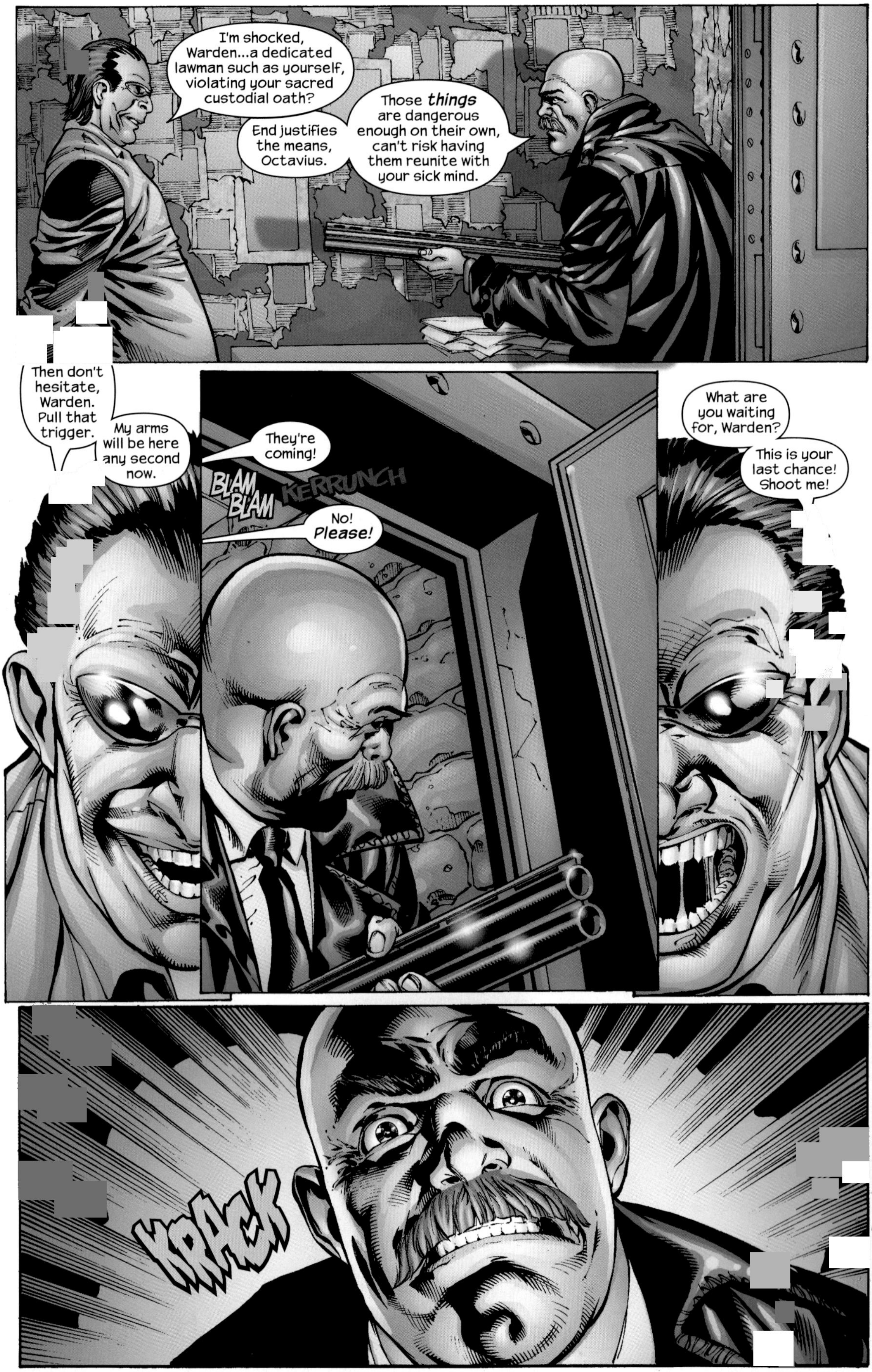
I'm shocked, Warden...a dedicated lawman such as yourself, violating your sacred custodial oath?
Those *things* are dangerous enough on their own, can't risk having them reunite with your sick mind.
End justifies the means, Octavius.
Then don't hesitate, Warden. Pull that trigger.
My arms will be here any second now.
They're coming!
BLAM BLAM
KERRUNCH
No! *Please!*
What are you waiting for, Warden?
This is your last chance! Shoot me!
KRACK

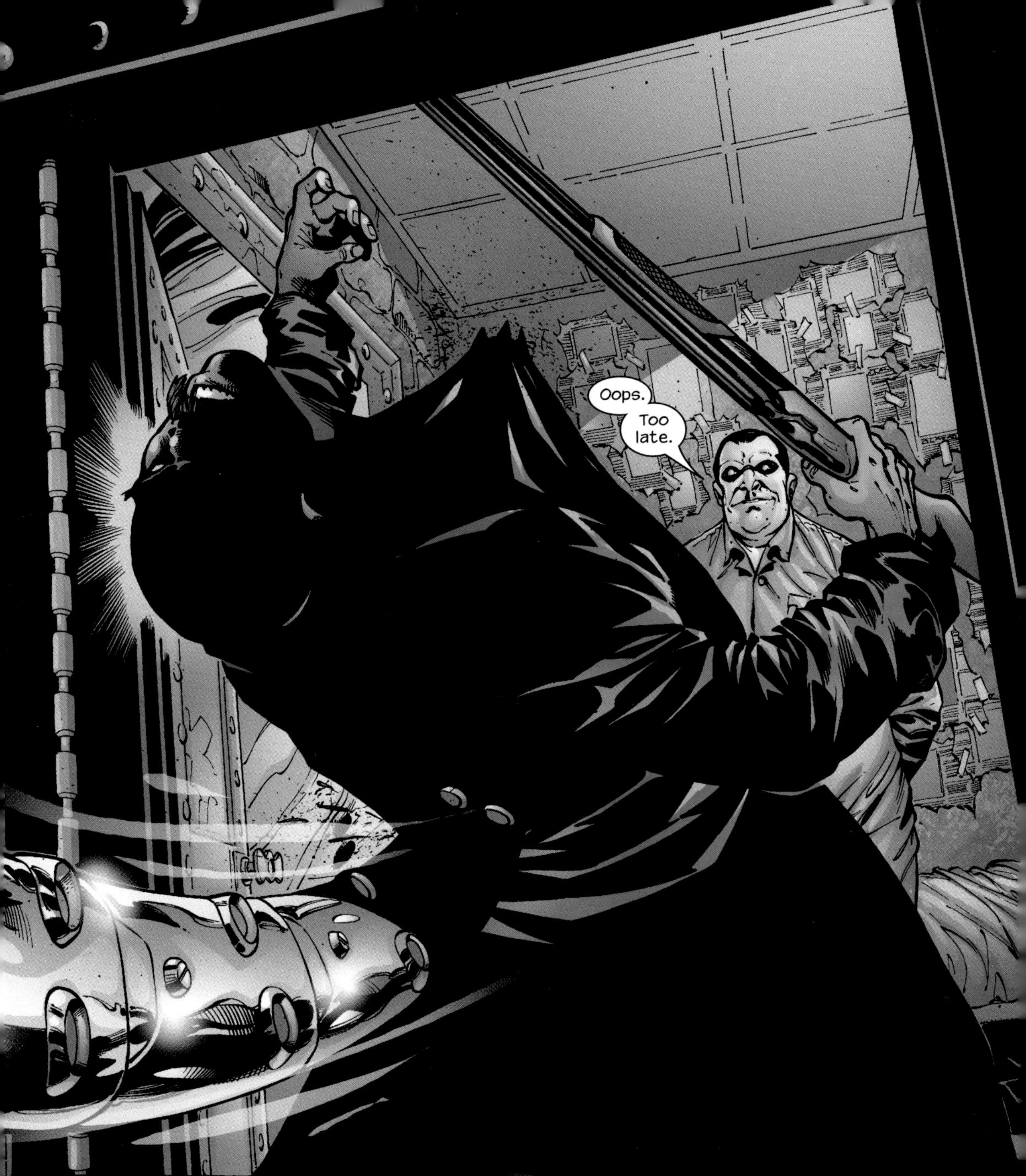
Oops.
Too late.

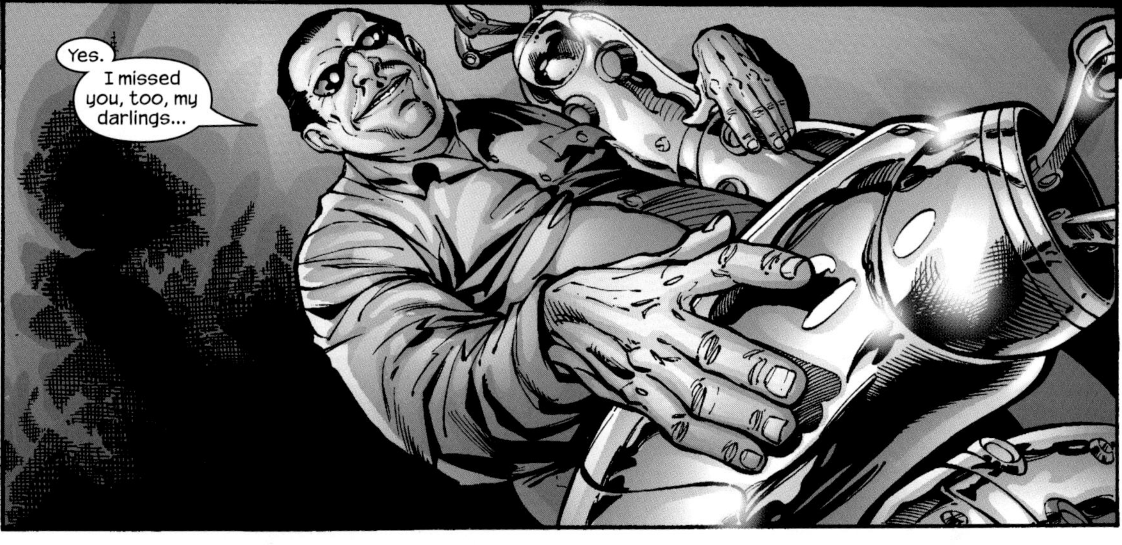
Yes.
I missed you, too, my darlings...

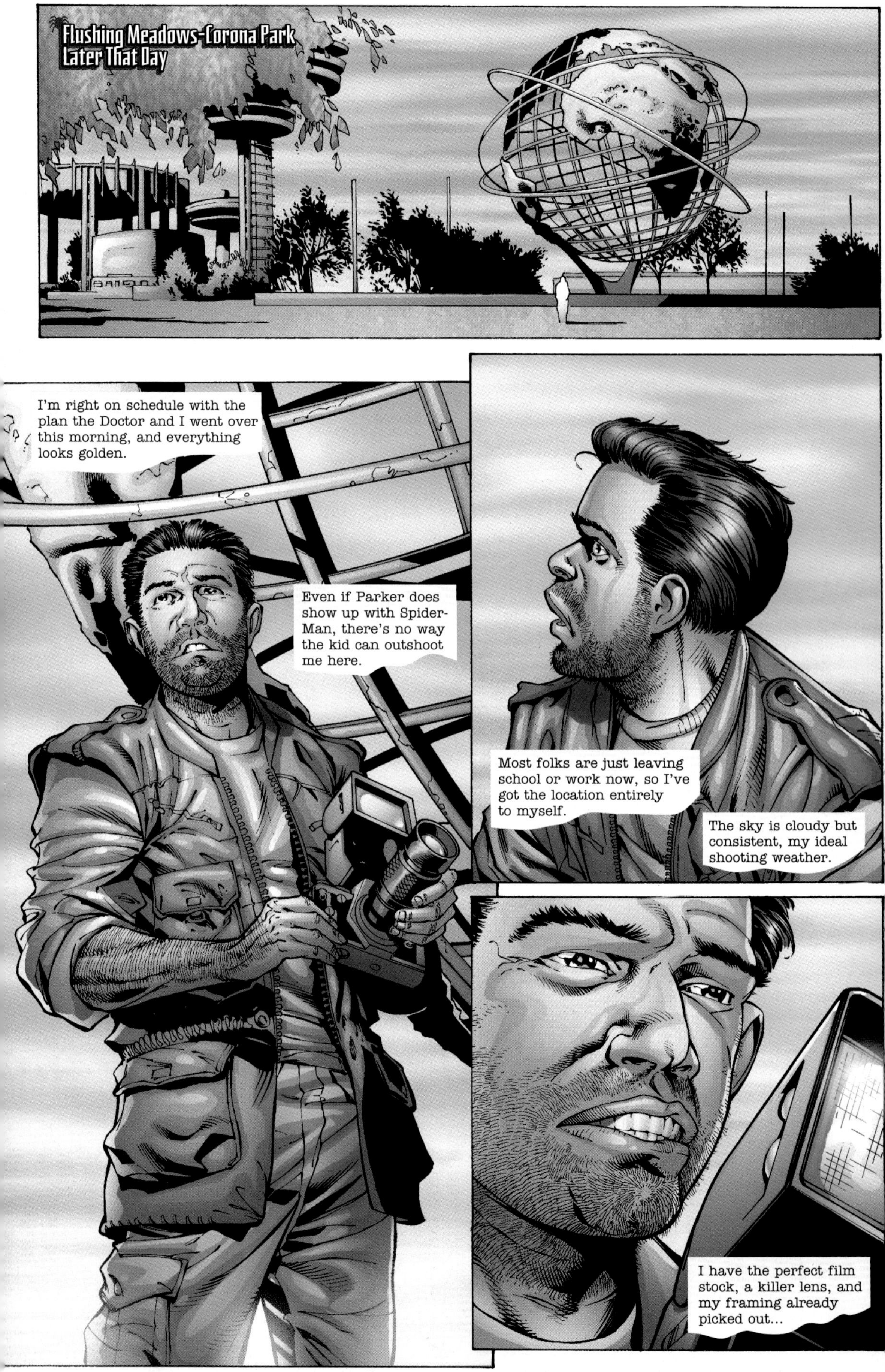
Flushing Meadows-Corona Park
Later That Day
I'm right on schedule with the plan the Doctor and I went over this morning, and everything looks golden.
Even if Parker does show up with Spider-Man, there's no way the kid can outshoot me here.
Most folks are just leaving school or work now, so I've got the location entirely to myself.
The sky is cloudy but consistent, my ideal shooting weather.
I have the perfect film stock, a killer lens, and my framing already picked out...

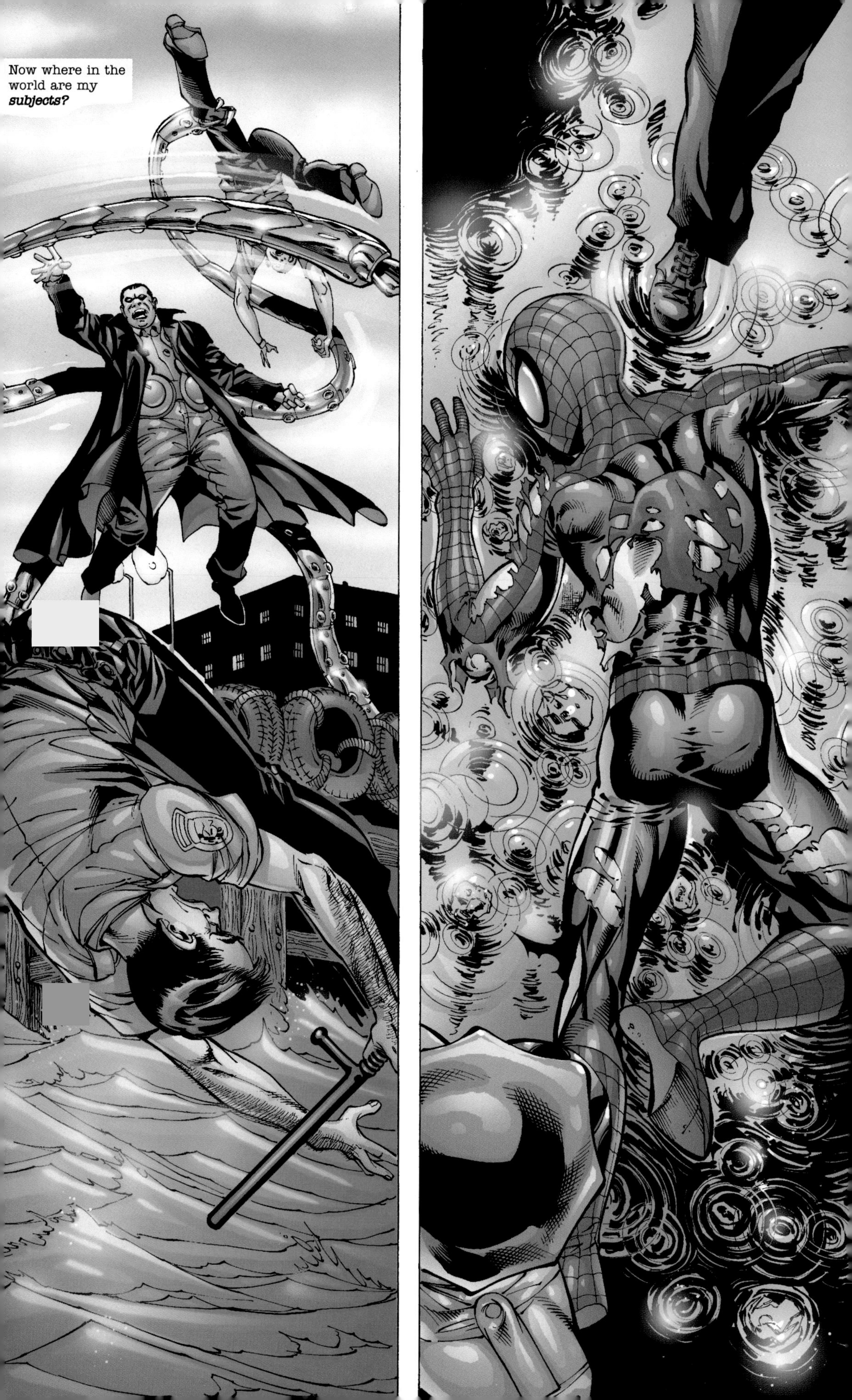
Now where in the world are my ***subjects?***

#5

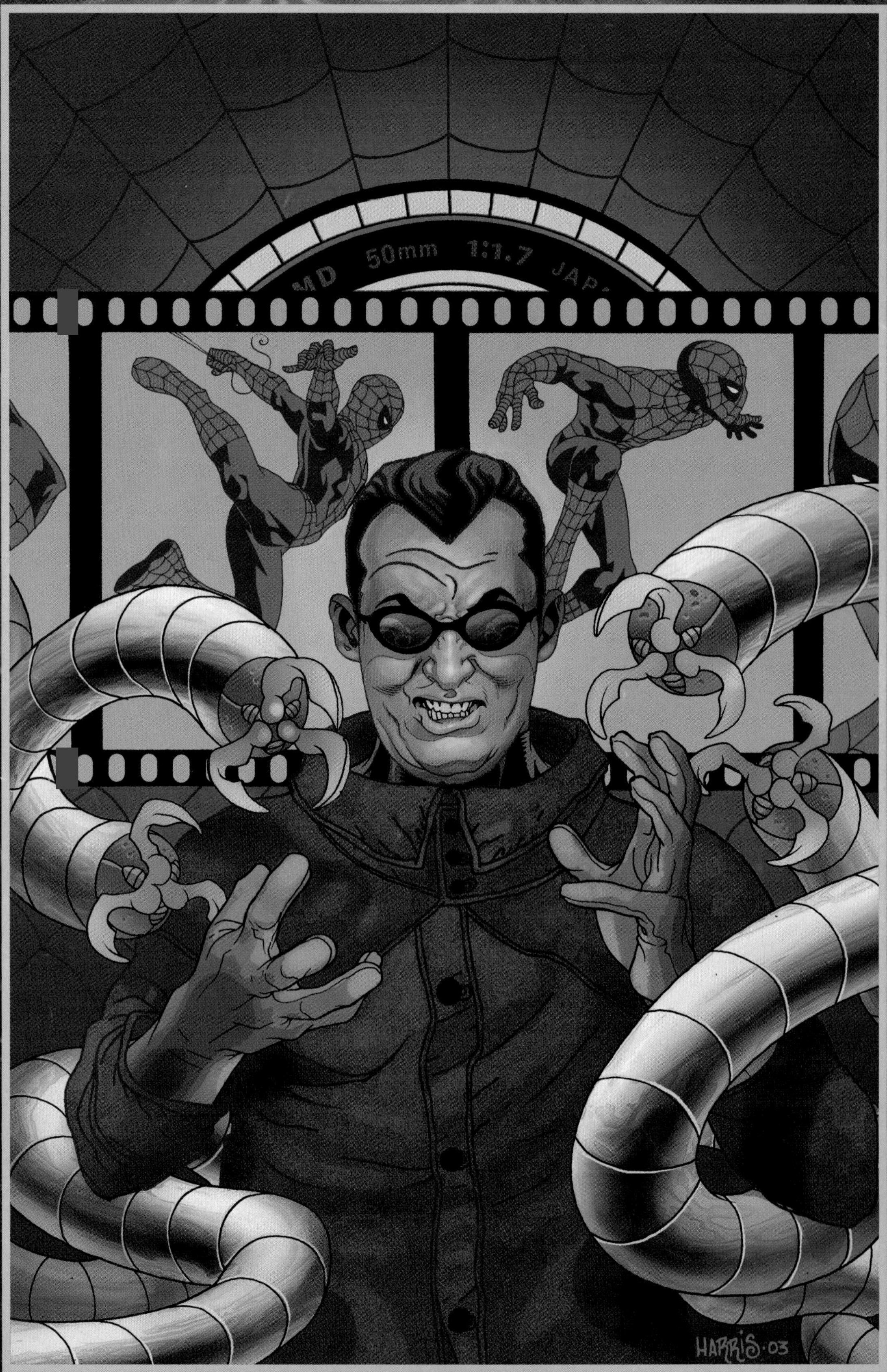
50mm 1:1.7
HARRIS·03

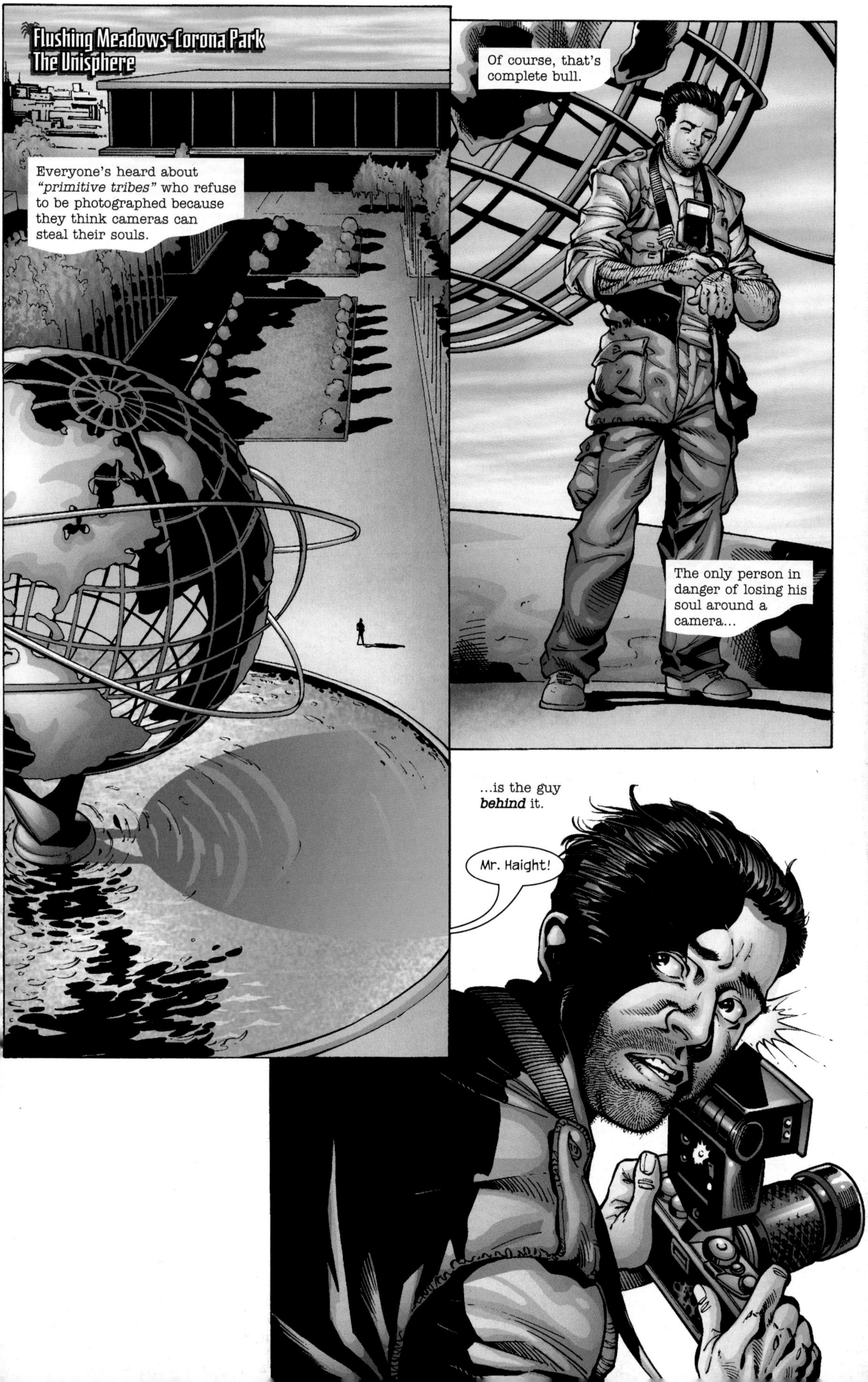
Flushing Meadows-Corona Park
The Unisphere
Everyone's heard about "primitive tribes" who refuse to be photographed because they think cameras can steal their souls.
Of course, that's complete bull.
The only person in danger of losing his soul around a camera...
...is the guy behind it.
Mr. Haight!

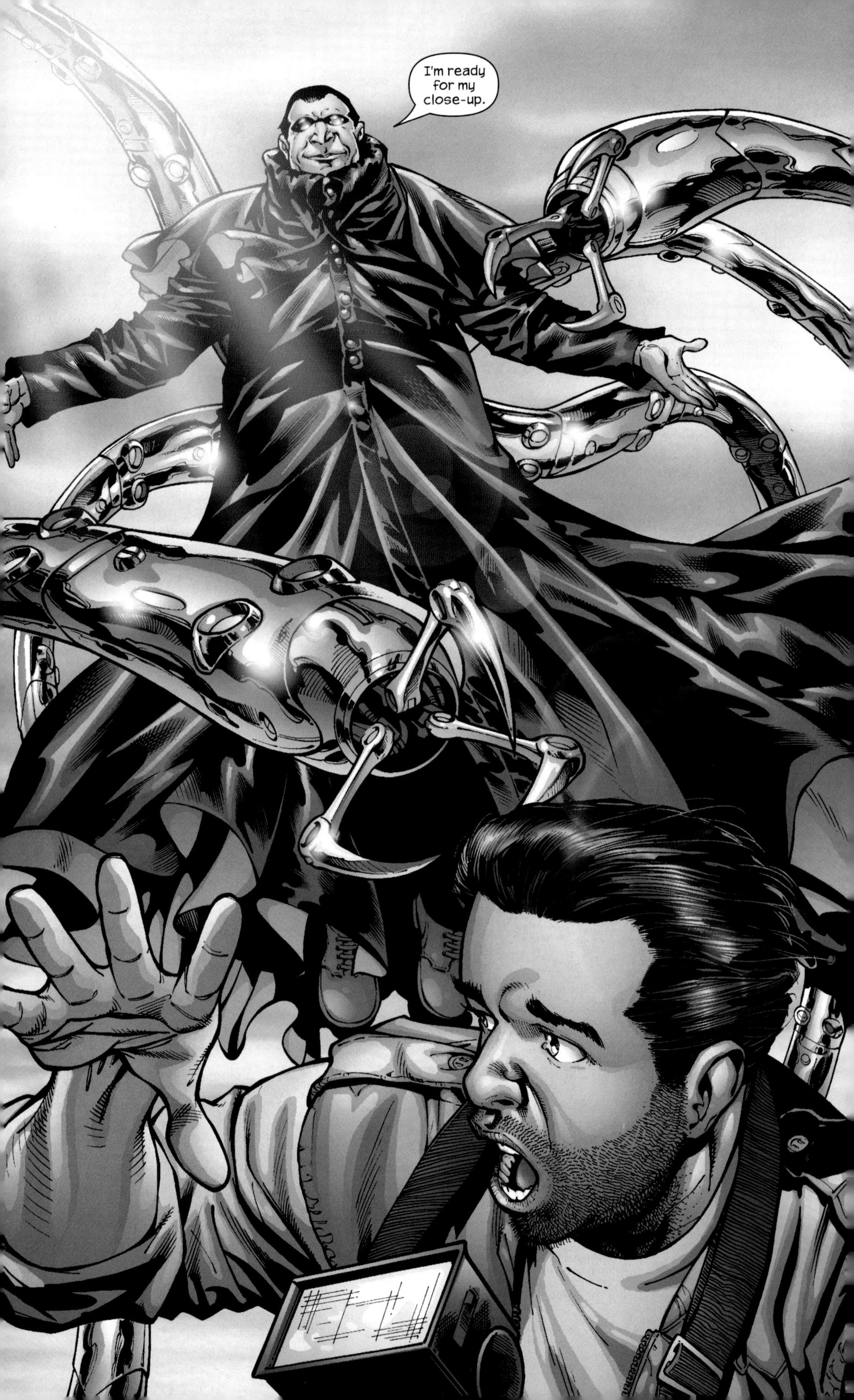
I'm ready for my close-up.

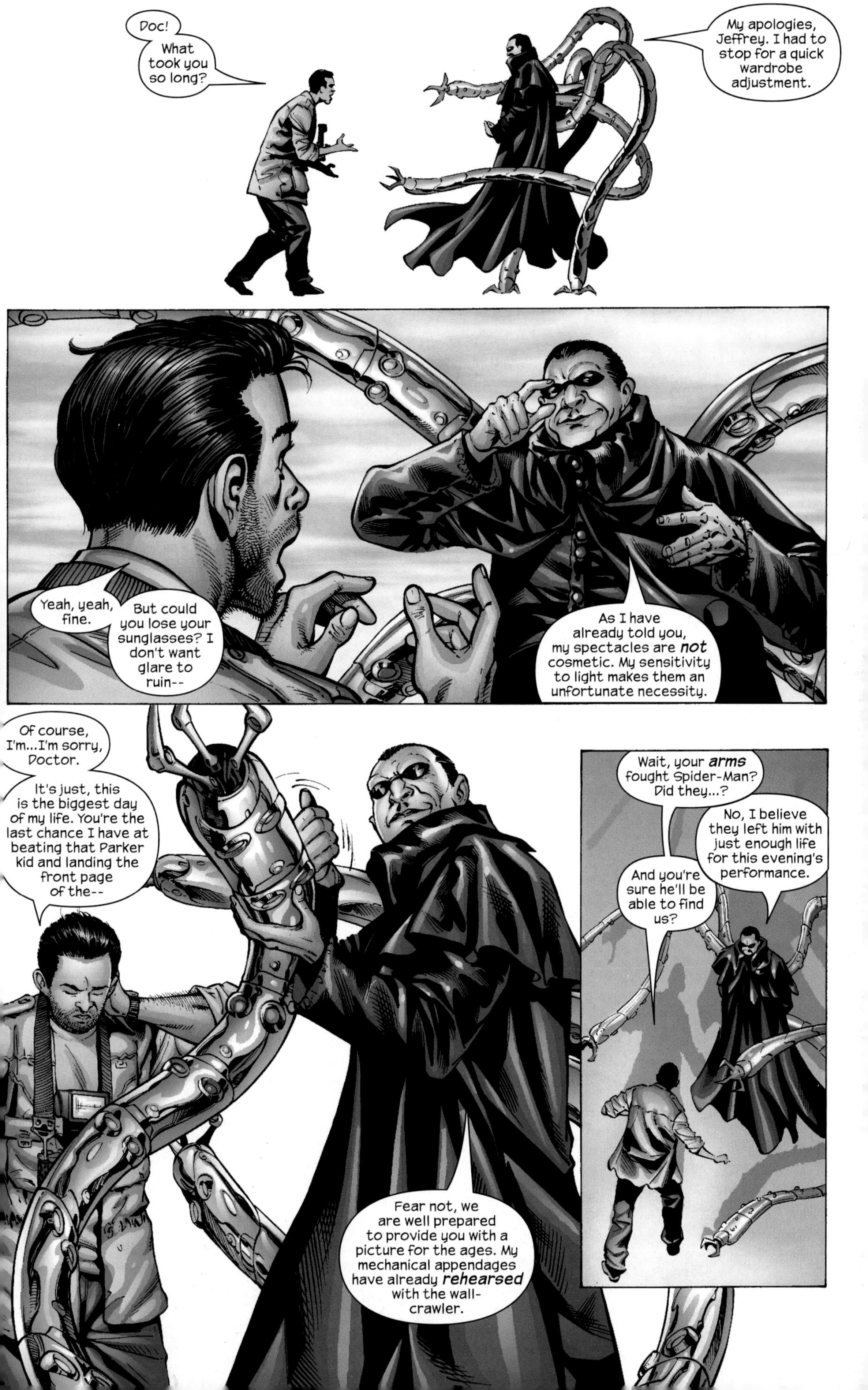
Doc!
What took you so long?
My apologies, Jeffrey. I had to stop for a quick wardrobe adjustment.
Yeah, yeah, fine.
But could you lose your sunglasses? I don't want glare to ruin--
As I have already told you, my spectacles are *not* cosmetic. My sensitivity to light makes them an unfortunate necessity.
Of course, I'm...I'm sorry, Doctor.
It's just, this is the biggest day of my life. You're the last chance I have at beating that Parker kid and landing the front page of the--
Fear not, we are well prepared to provide you with a picture for the ages. My mechanical appendages have already *rehearsed* with the wall-crawler.
Wait, your *arms* fought Spider-Man? Did they...?
No, I believe they left him with just enough life for this evening's performance.
And you're sure he'll be able to find us?

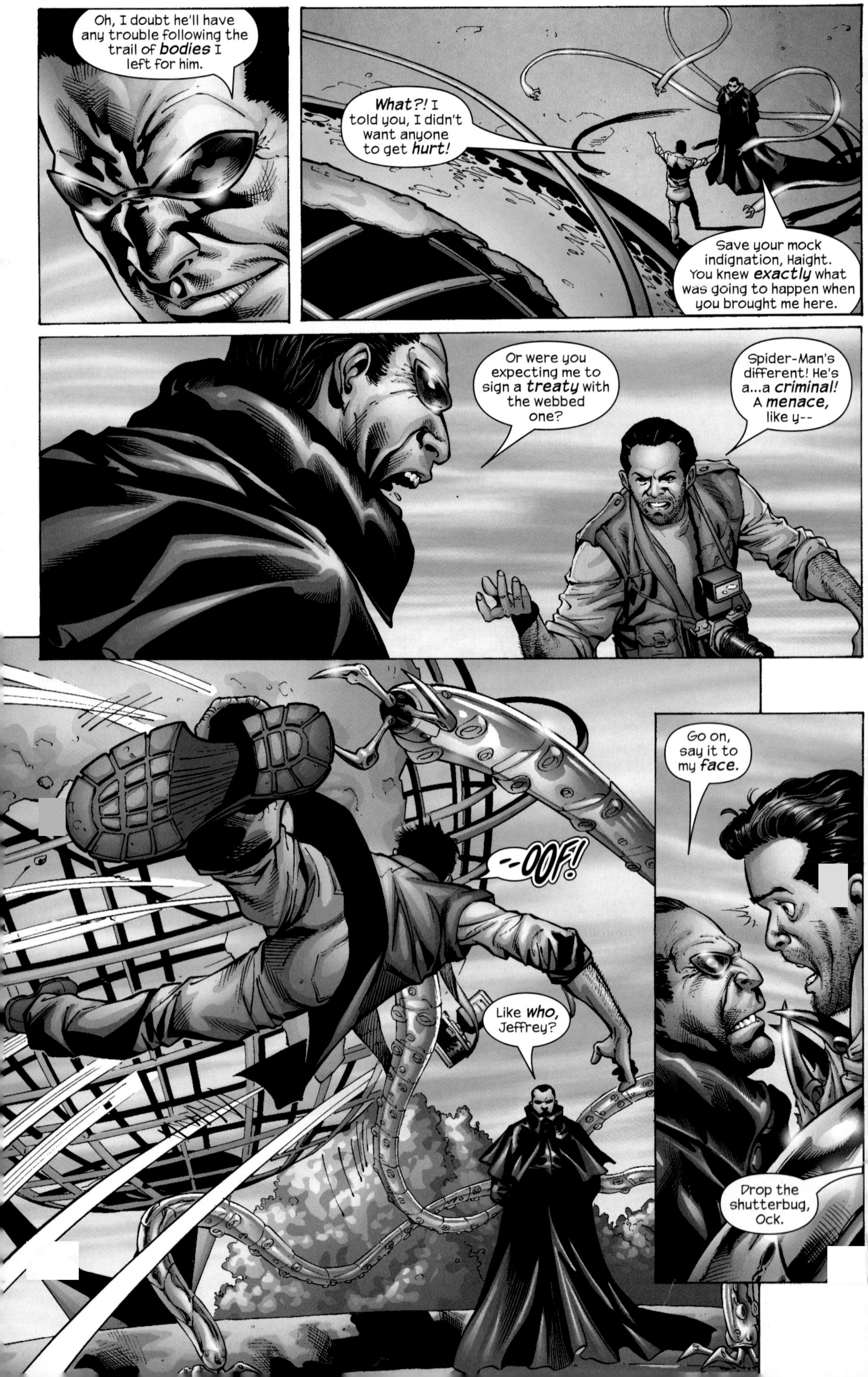
Oh, I doubt he'll have any trouble following the trail of *bodies* I left for him.
What?! I told you, I didn't want anyone to get *hurt!*
Save your mock indignation, Haight. You knew *exactly* what was going to happen when you brought me here.
Or were you expecting me to sign a *treaty* with the webbed one?
Spider-Man's different! He's a...a *criminal!* A *menace,* like y--
--OOF!
Like *who,* Jeffrey?
Go on, say it to my *face.*
Drop the shutterbug, Ock.

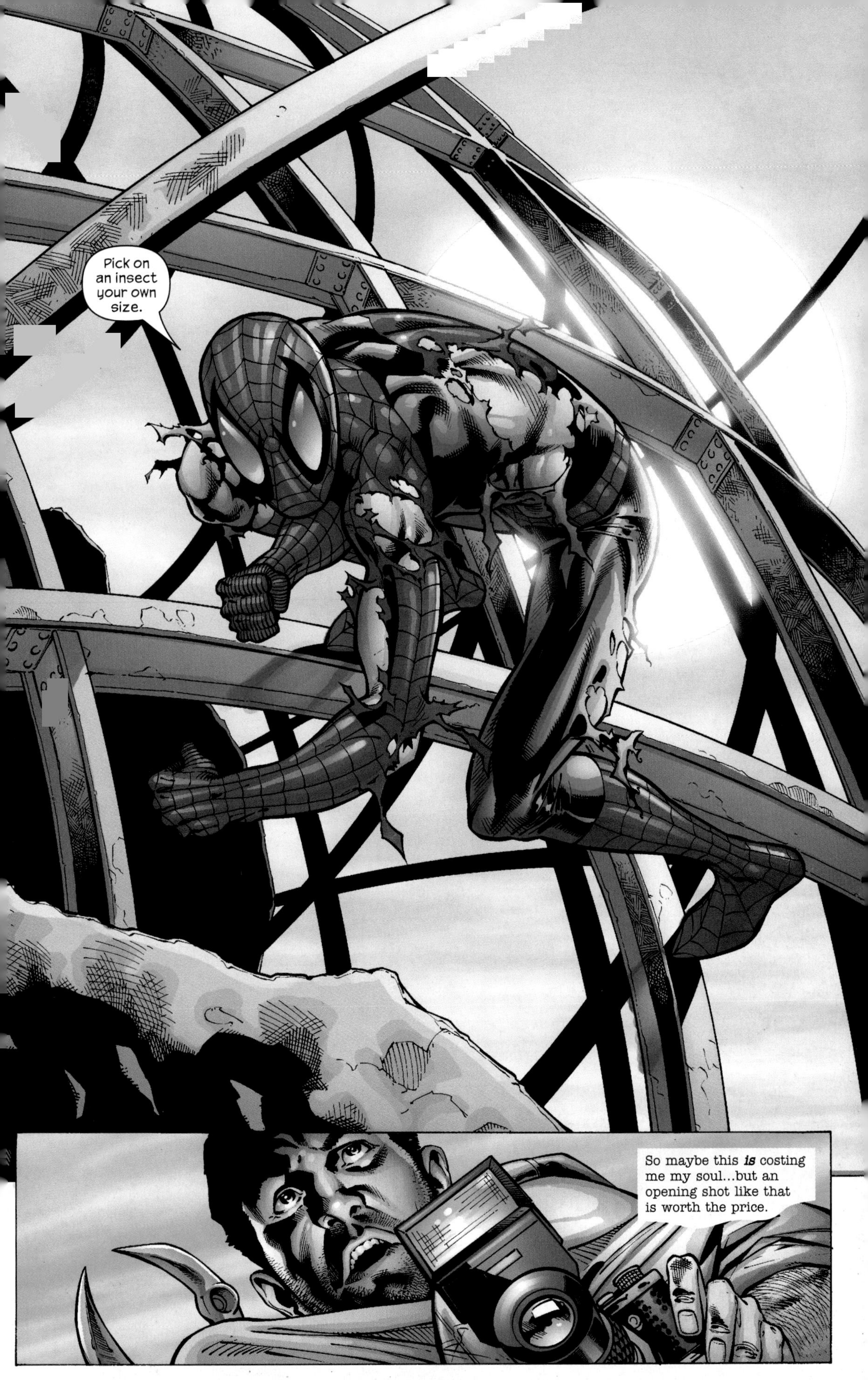
Pick on an insect your own size.
So maybe this *is* costing me my soul...but an opening shot like that is worth the price.

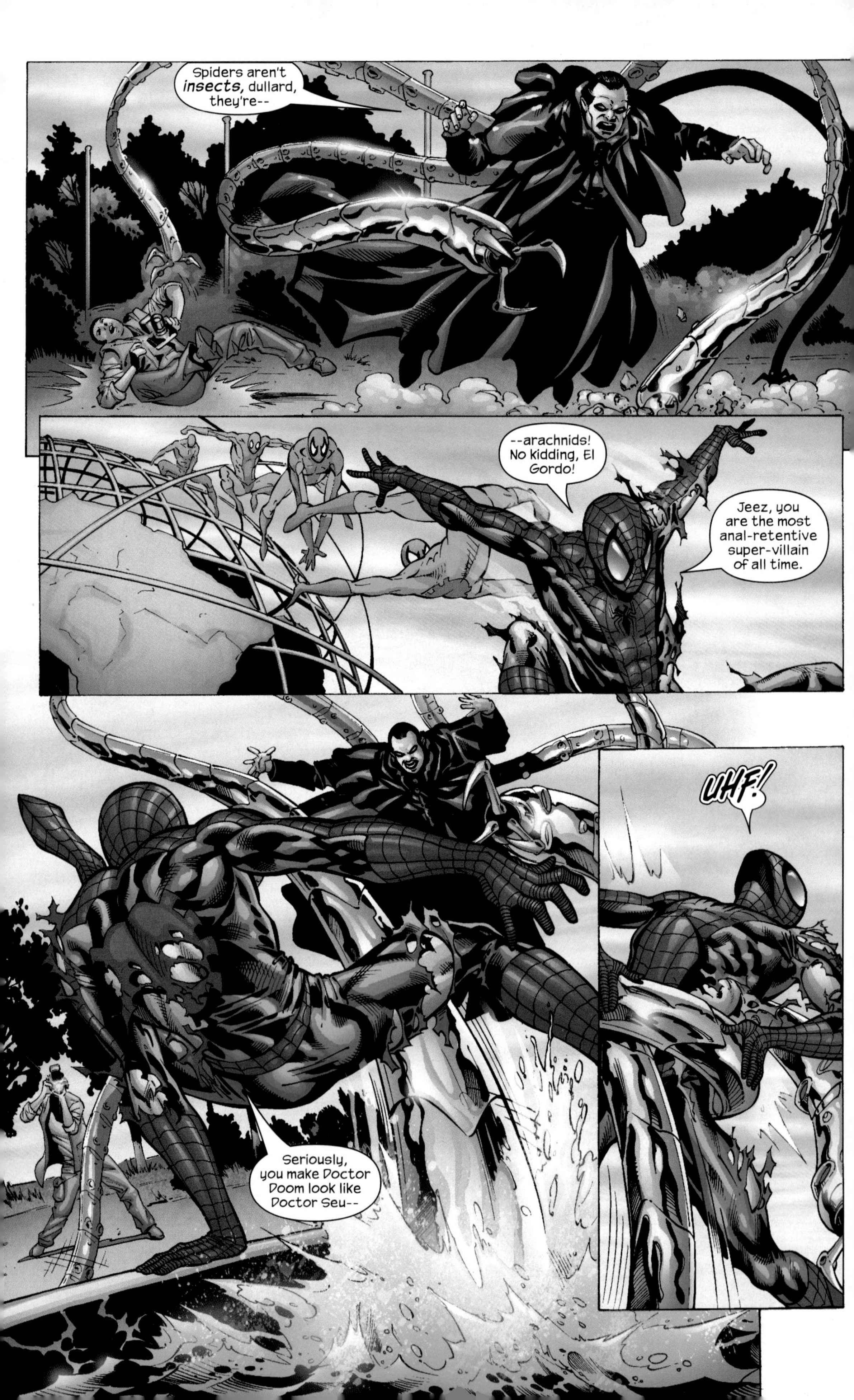

Spiders aren't *insects,* dullard, they're--
--arachnids! No kidding, El Gordo!
Jeez, you are the most anal-retentive super-villain of all time.
Seriously, you make Doctor Doom look like Doctor Seu--
UHF!

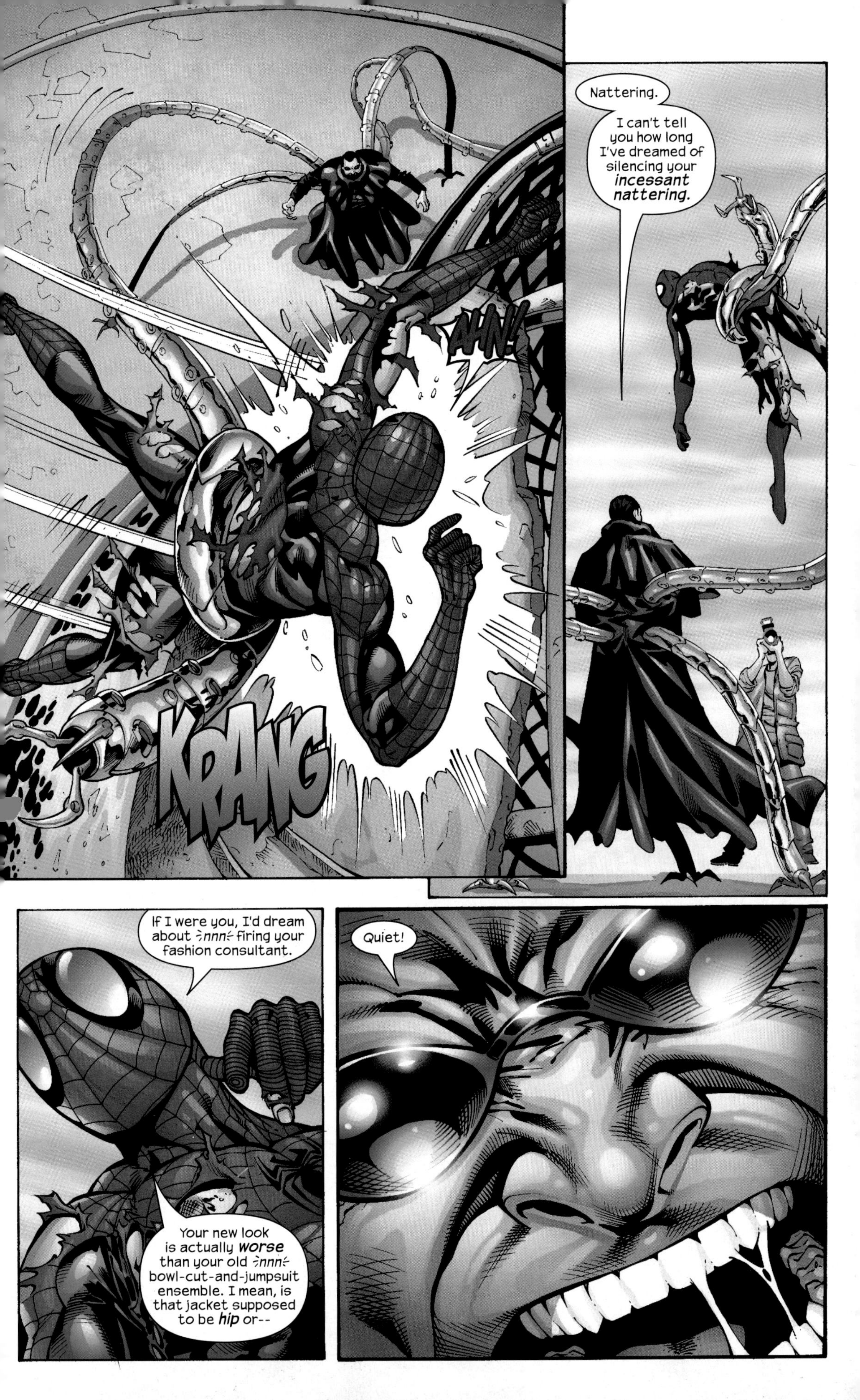
AHN!
KRANG
Nattering.
I can't tell you how long I've dreamed of silencing your *incessant nattering.*
If I were you, I'd dream about ~nnn~ firing your fashion consultant.
Your new look is actually **worse** than your old ~nnn~ bowl-cut-and-jumpsuit ensemble. I mean, is that jacket supposed to be **hip** or--
Quiet!

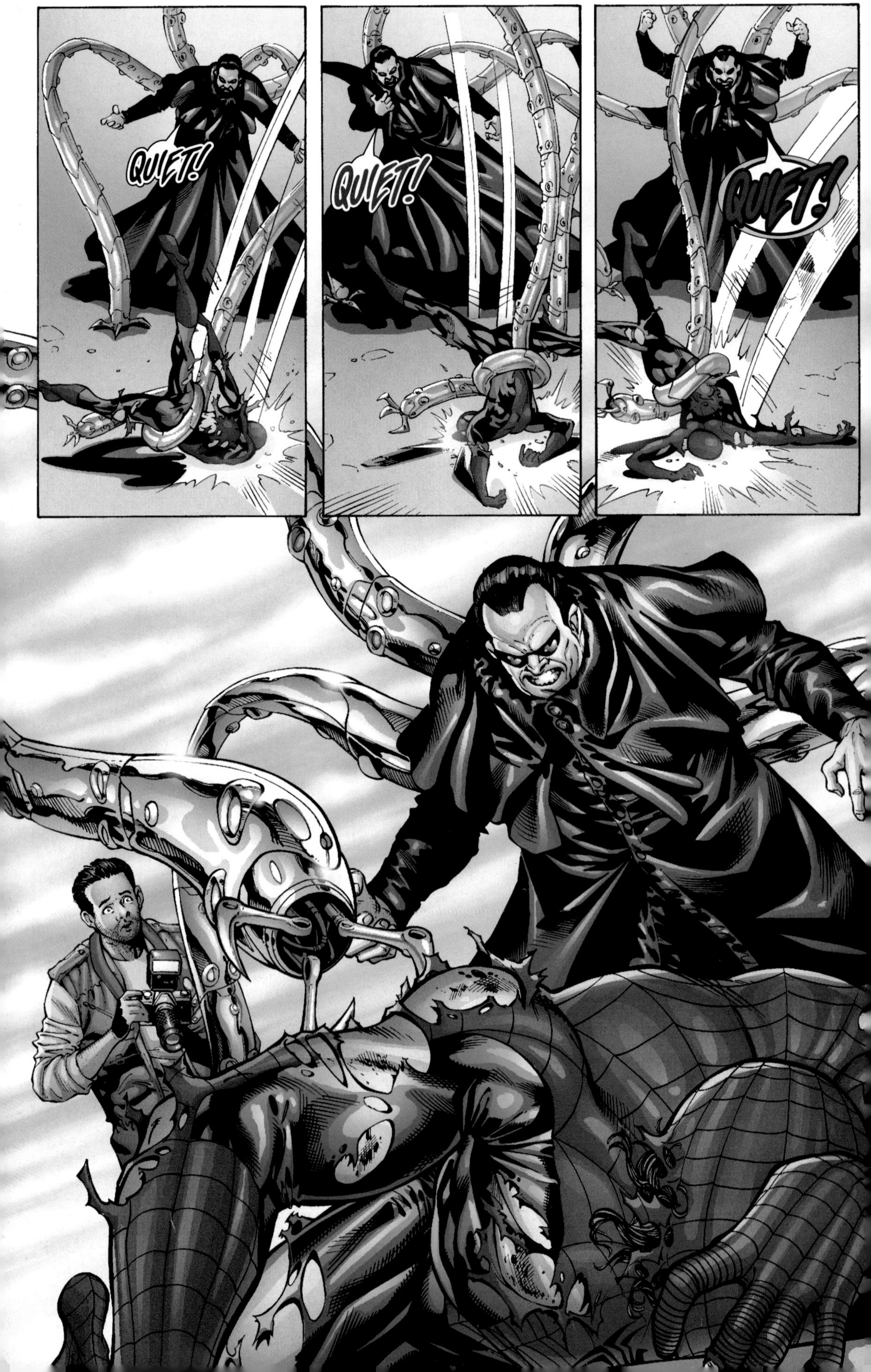
QUIET!
QUIET!
QUIET!

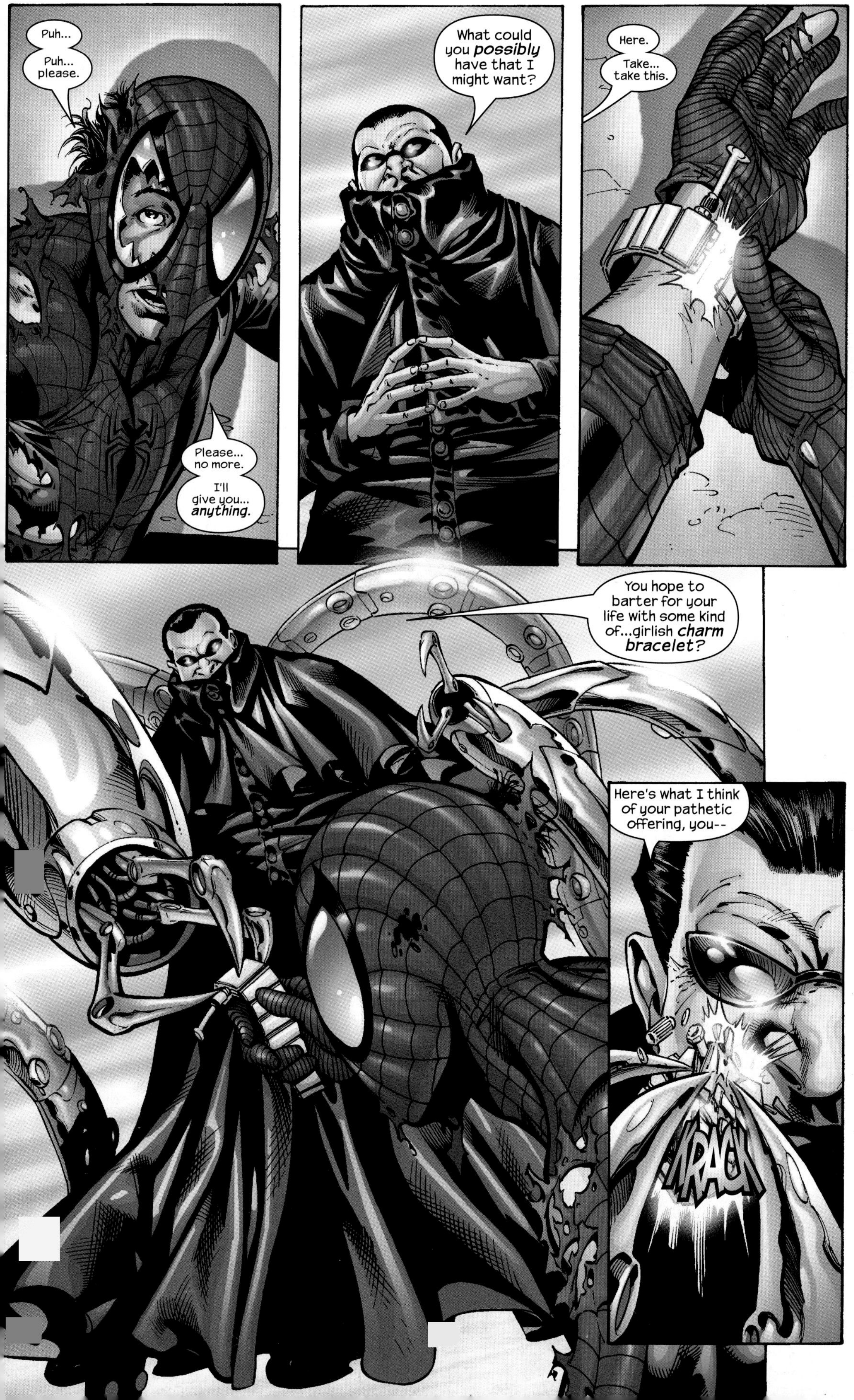
Puh...
Puh... please.
What could you *possibly* have that I might want?
Please... no more.
I'll give you... *anything.*
Here.
Take... take this.
You hope to barter for your life with some kind of...girlish *charm bracelet?*
Here's what I think of your pathetic offering, you--
KRACK

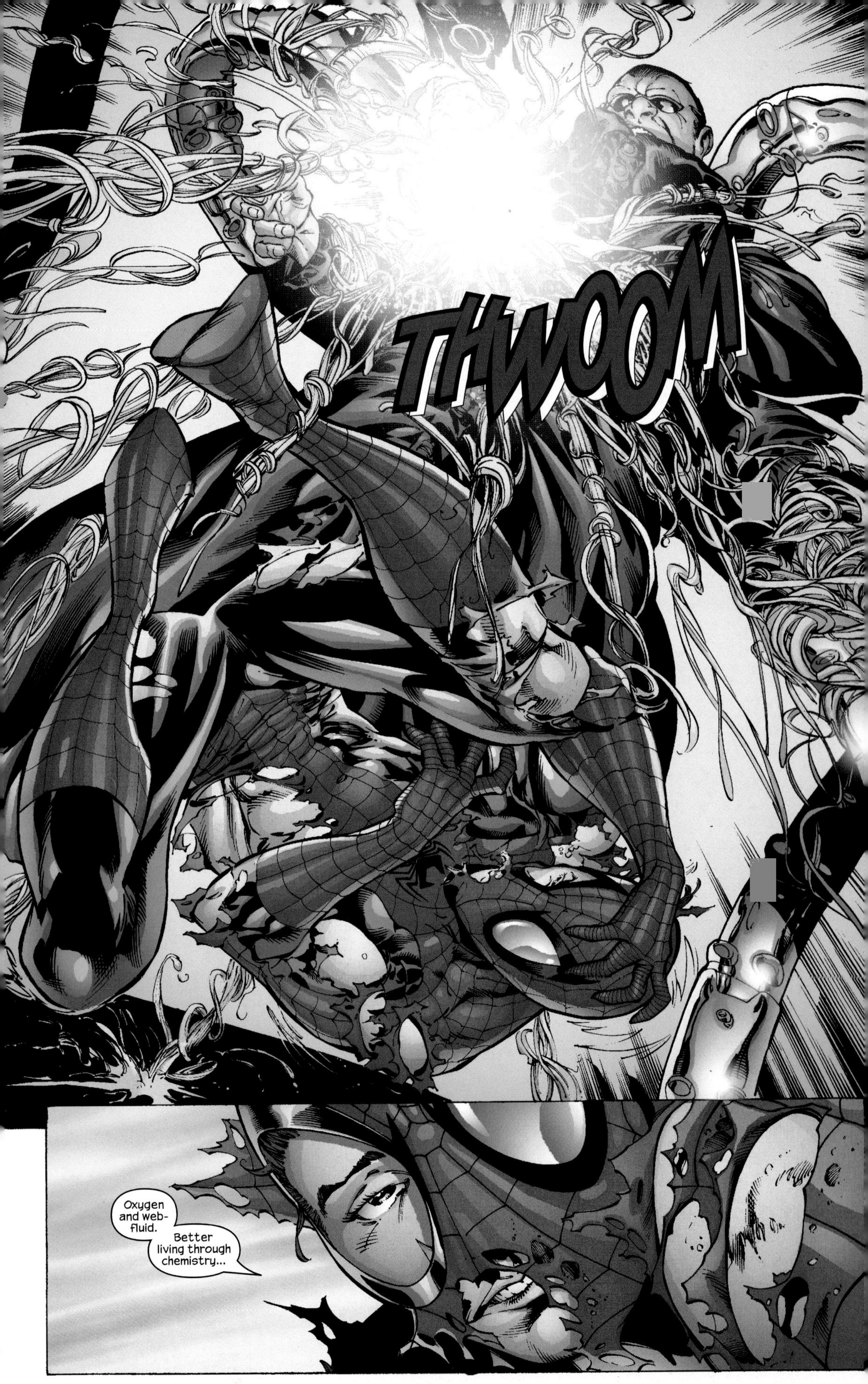
THWOOM
Oxygen and web-fluid.
Better living through chemistry...

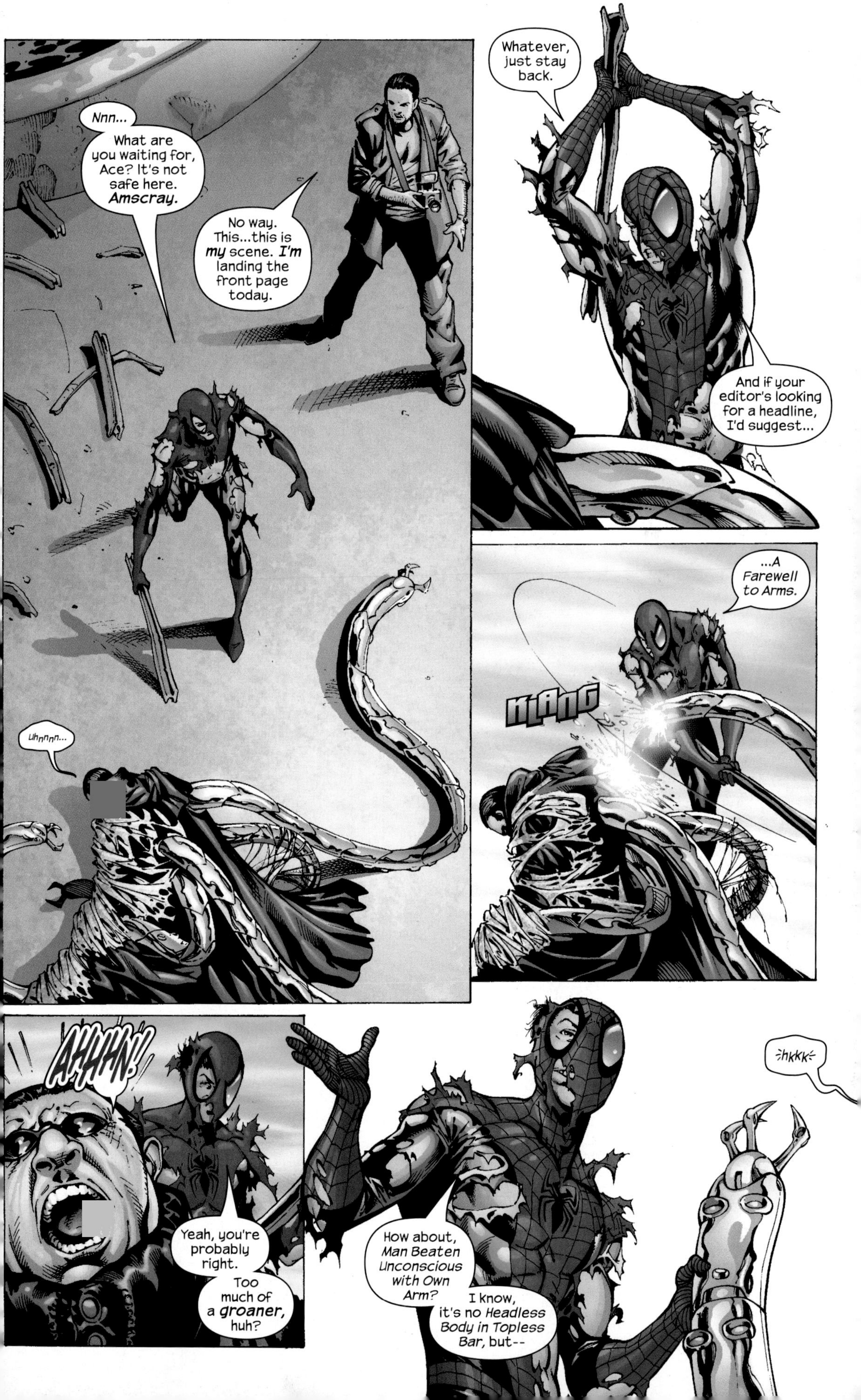
Nnn...
What are you waiting for, Ace? It's not safe here. *Amscray.*
No way. This...this is *my* scene. *I'm* landing the front page today.
Uhnnnn...
Whatever, just stay back.
And if your editor's looking for a headline, I'd suggest...
...A *Farewell to Arms.*
KLANG
AHHHN!
Yeah, you're probably right.
Too much of a *groaner,* huh?
How about, *Man Beaten Unconscious with Own Arm?*
I know, it's no *Headless Body in Topless Bar,* but--
hkkk

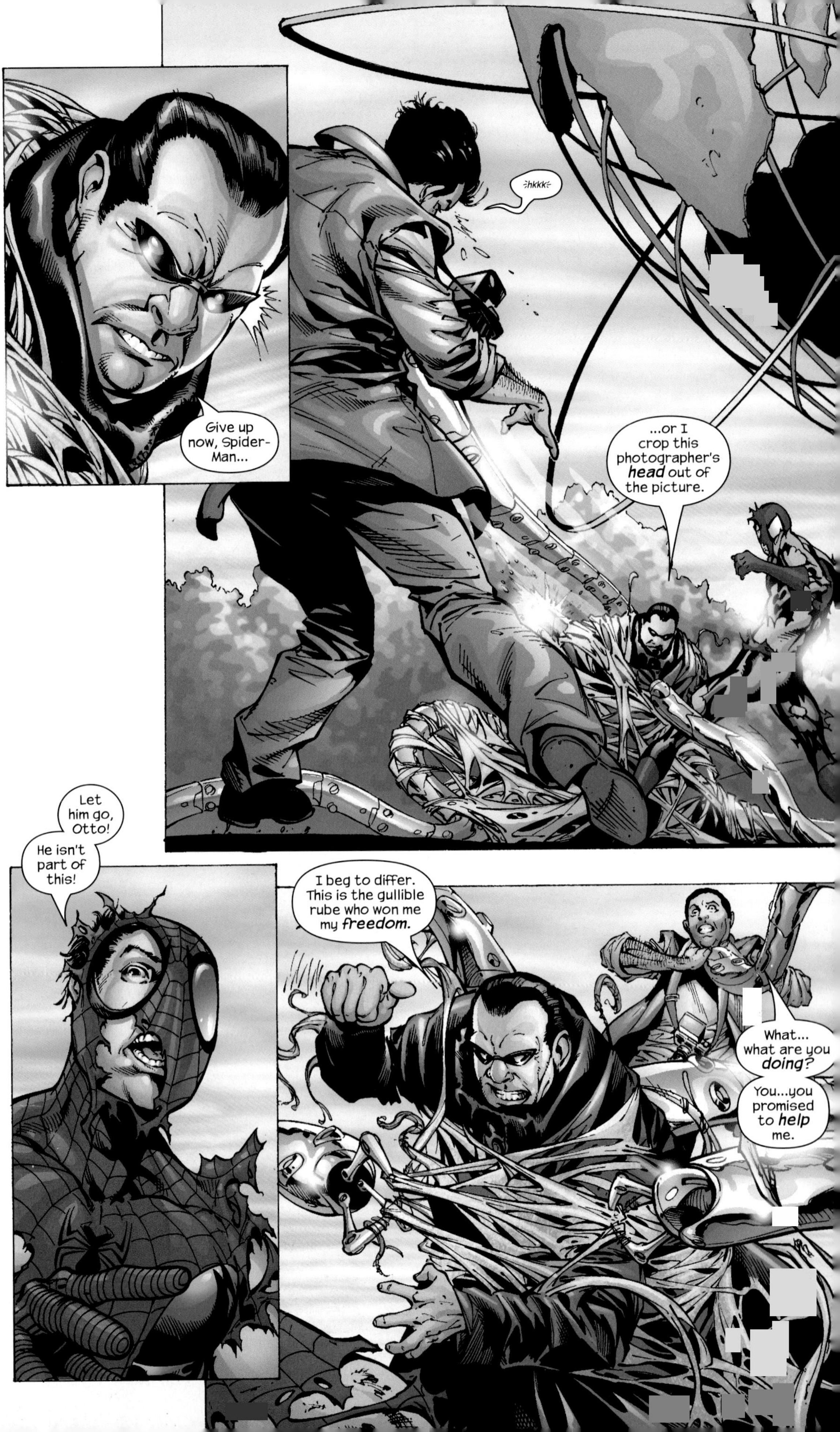

Give up now, Spider-Man...
HKKK
...or I crop this photographer's head out of the picture.
Let him go, Otto!
He isn't part of this!
I beg to differ. This is the gullible rube who won me my freedom.
What... what are you doing?
You...you promised to help me.

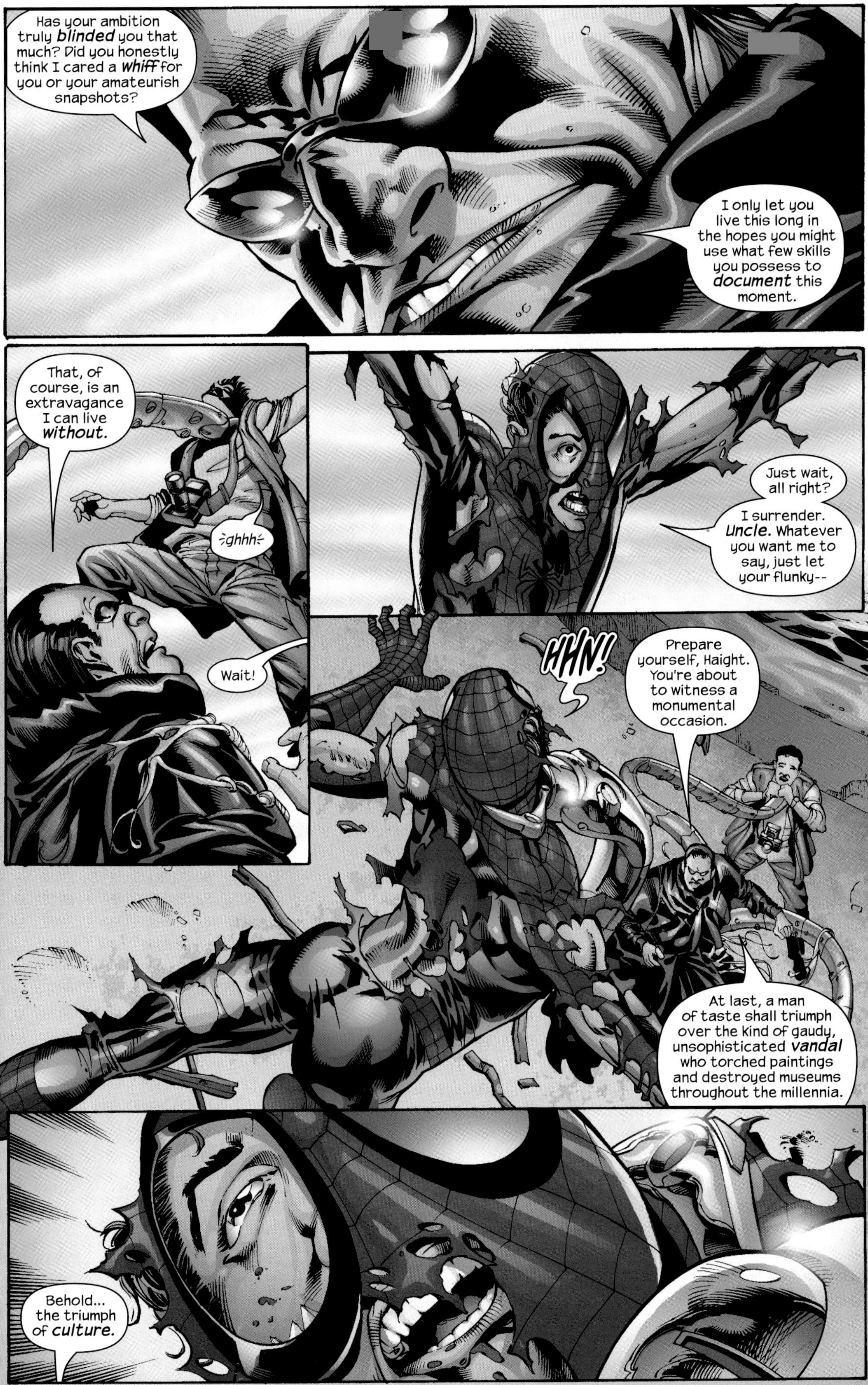

Has your ambition truly *blinded* you that much? Did you honestly think I cared a *whiff* for you or your amateurish snapshots?
I only let you live this long in the hopes you might use what few skills you possess to *document* this moment.
That, of course, is an extravagance I can live *without*.
ghhh
Wait!
Just wait, all right?
I surrender. *Uncle.* Whatever you want me to say, just let your flunky--
HHN!
Prepare yourself, Haight. You're about to witness a monumental occasion.
At last, a man of taste shall triumph over the kind of gaudy, unsophisticated *vandal* who torched paintings and destroyed museums throughout the millennia.
Behold... the triumph of *culture.*

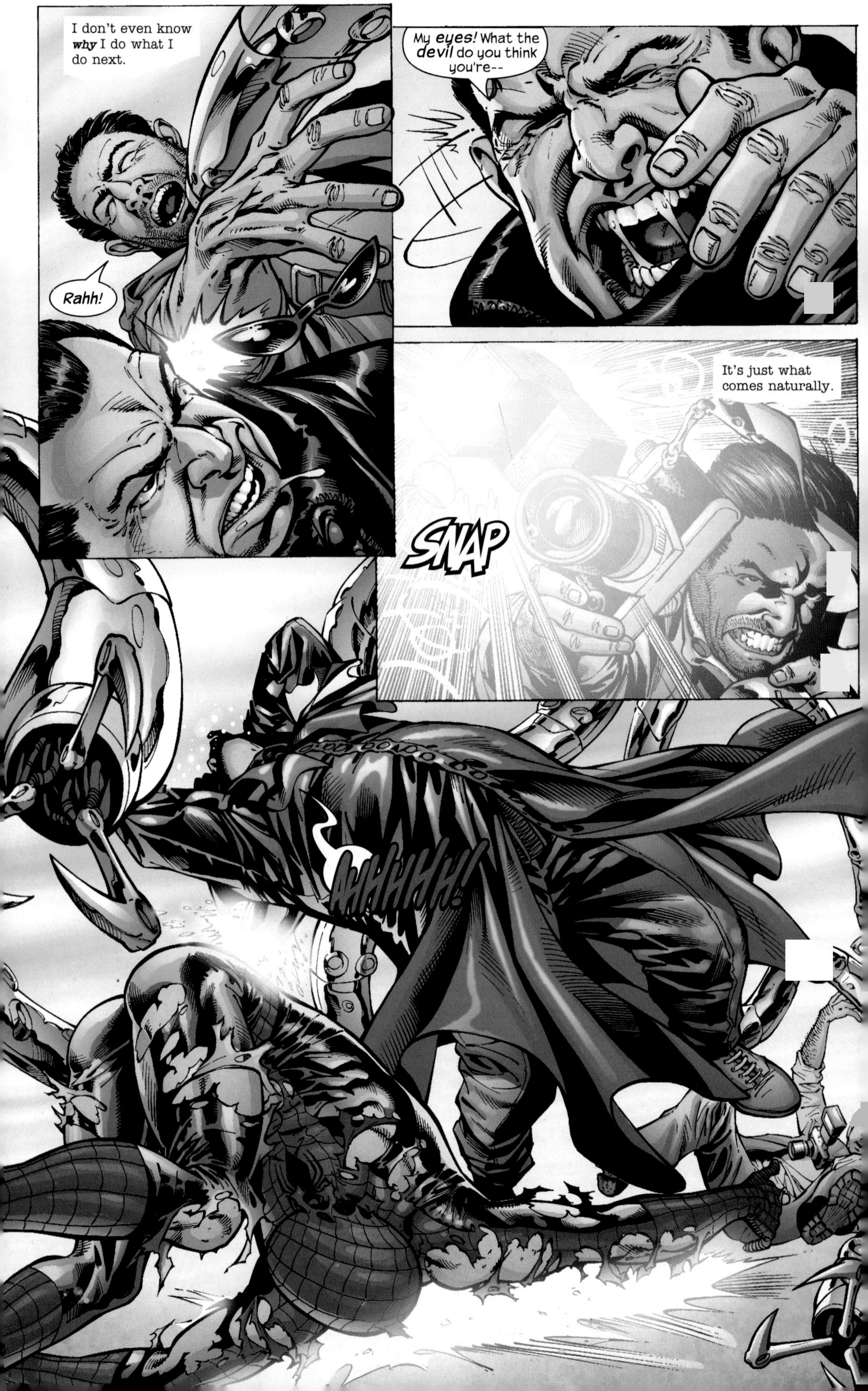
I don't even know why I do what I do next.
Rahh!
My eyes! What the devil do you think you're--
It's just what comes naturally.
SNAP
AAAHHHH!

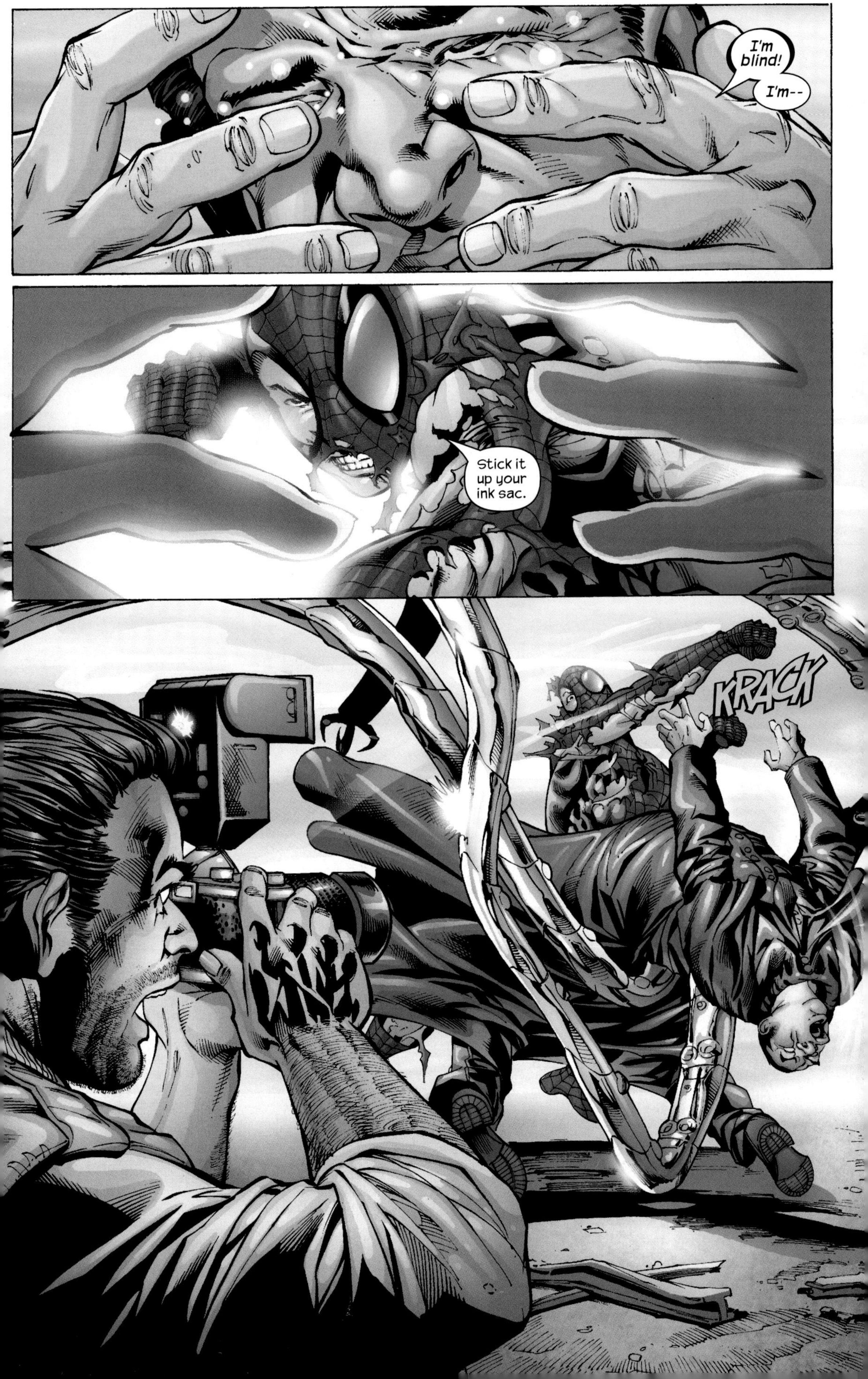

I'm blind!
I'm--
Stick it up your ink sac.
KRACK

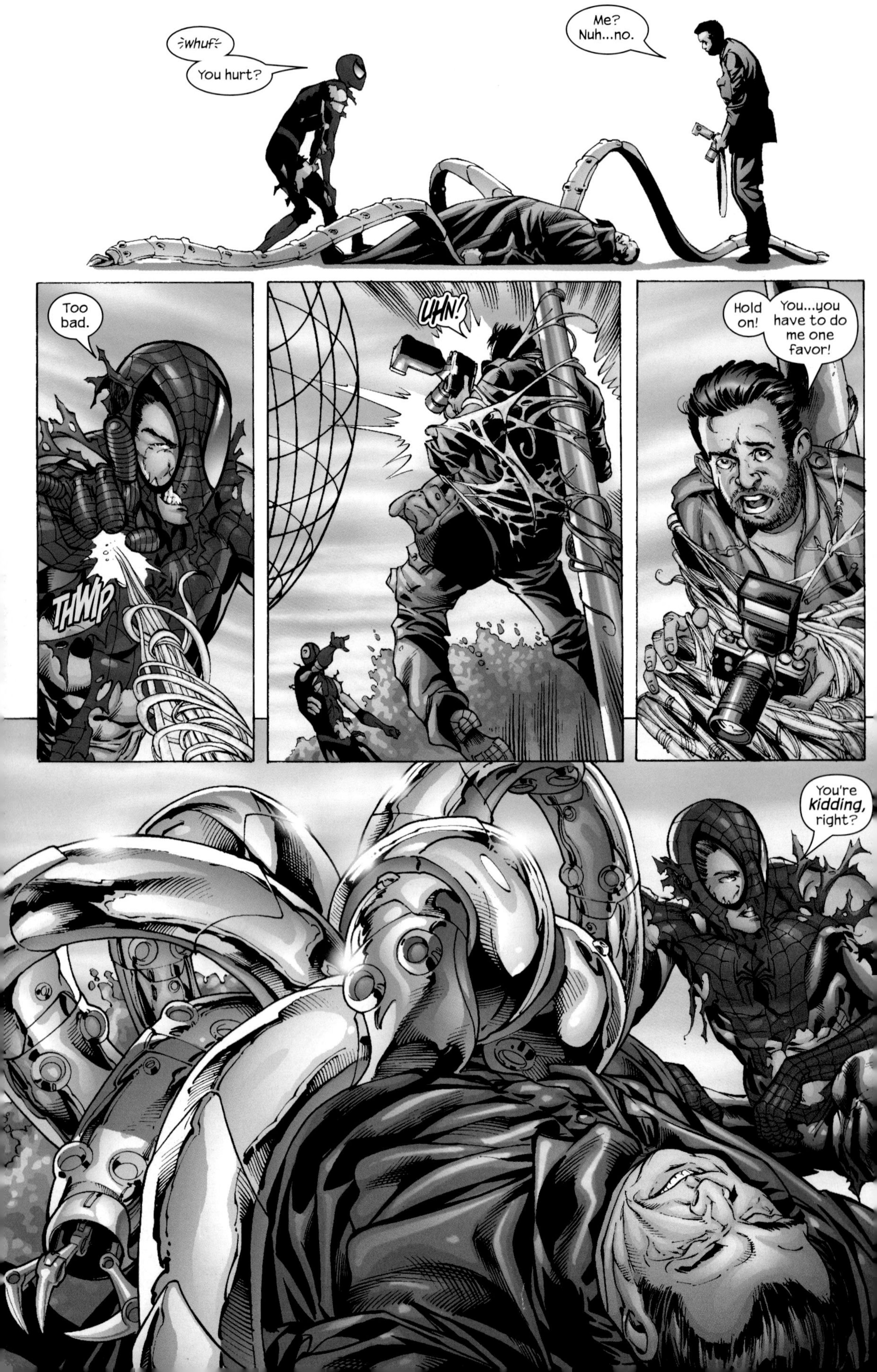
whuf
You hurt?
Me? Nuh...no.
Too bad.
THWIP
UHN!
Hold on!
You...you have to do me one favor!
You're *kidding,* right?

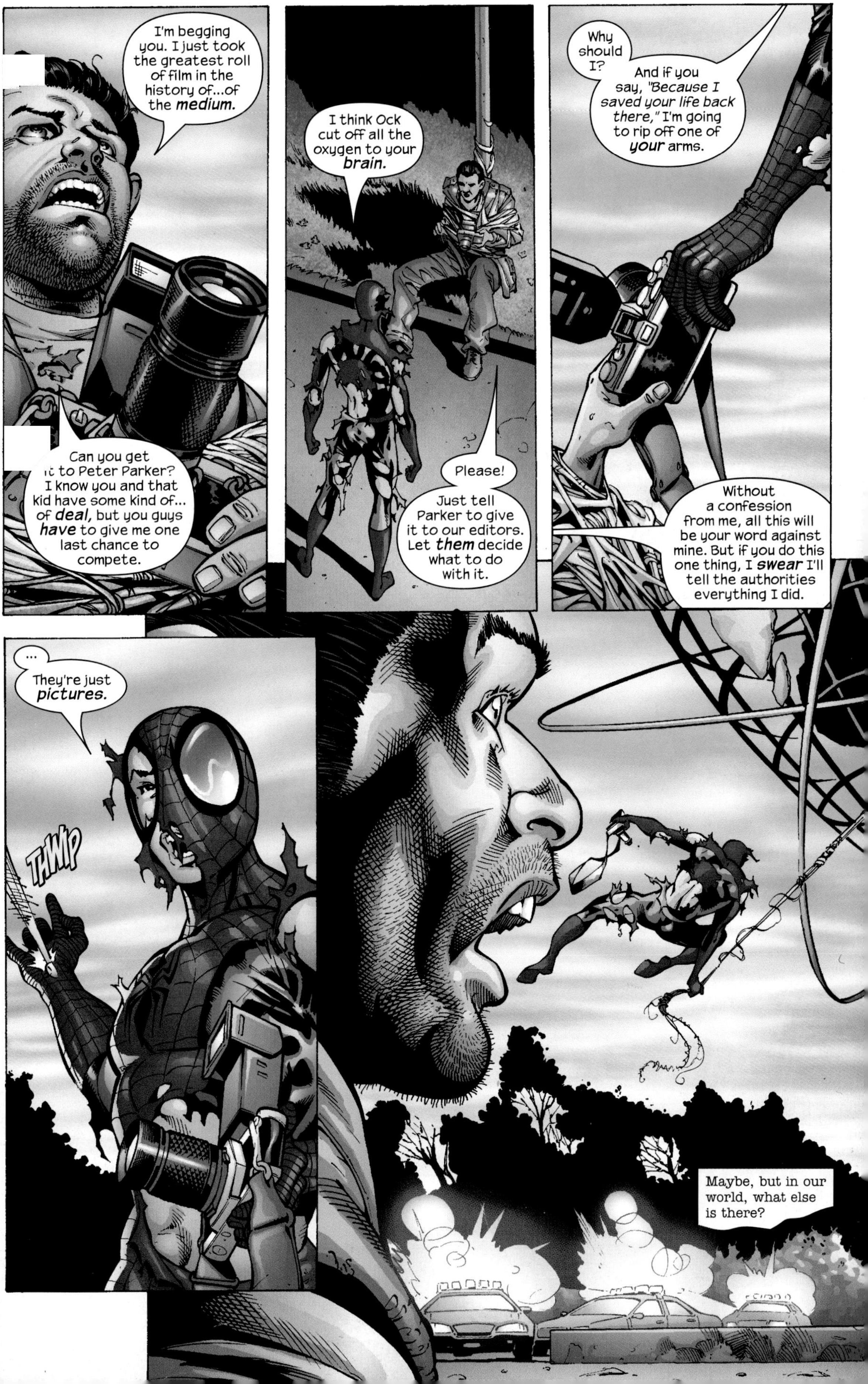
I'm begging you. I just took the greatest roll of film in the history of...of the *medium.*
Can you get it to Peter Parker? I know you and that kid have some kind of... of *deal,* but you guys *have* to give me one last chance to compete.
I think Ock cut off all the oxygen to your *brain.*
Please!
Just tell Parker to give it to our editors. Let *them* decide what to do with it.
Why should I?
And if you say, *"Because I saved your life back there,"* I'm going to rip off one of *your* arms.
Without a confession from me, all this will be your word against mine. But if you do this one thing, I *swear* I'll tell the authorities everything I did.
...
They're just *pictures.*
THWIP
Maybe, but in our world, what else is there?

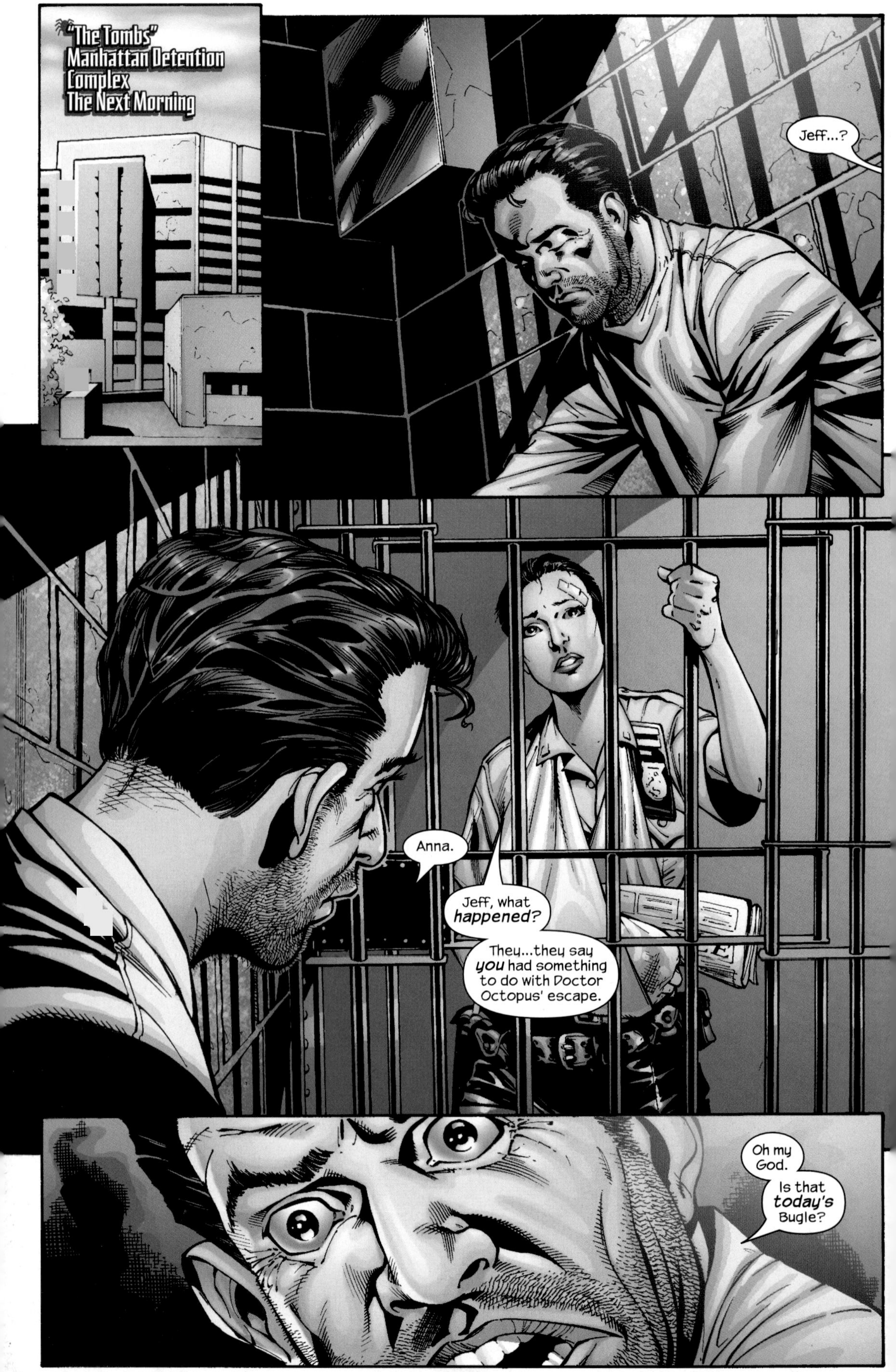
"The Tombs"
Manhattan Detention Complex
The Next Morning
Jeff...?
Anna.
Jeff, what happened?
They...they say you had something to do with Doctor Octopus' escape.
Oh my God.
Is that today's Bugle?

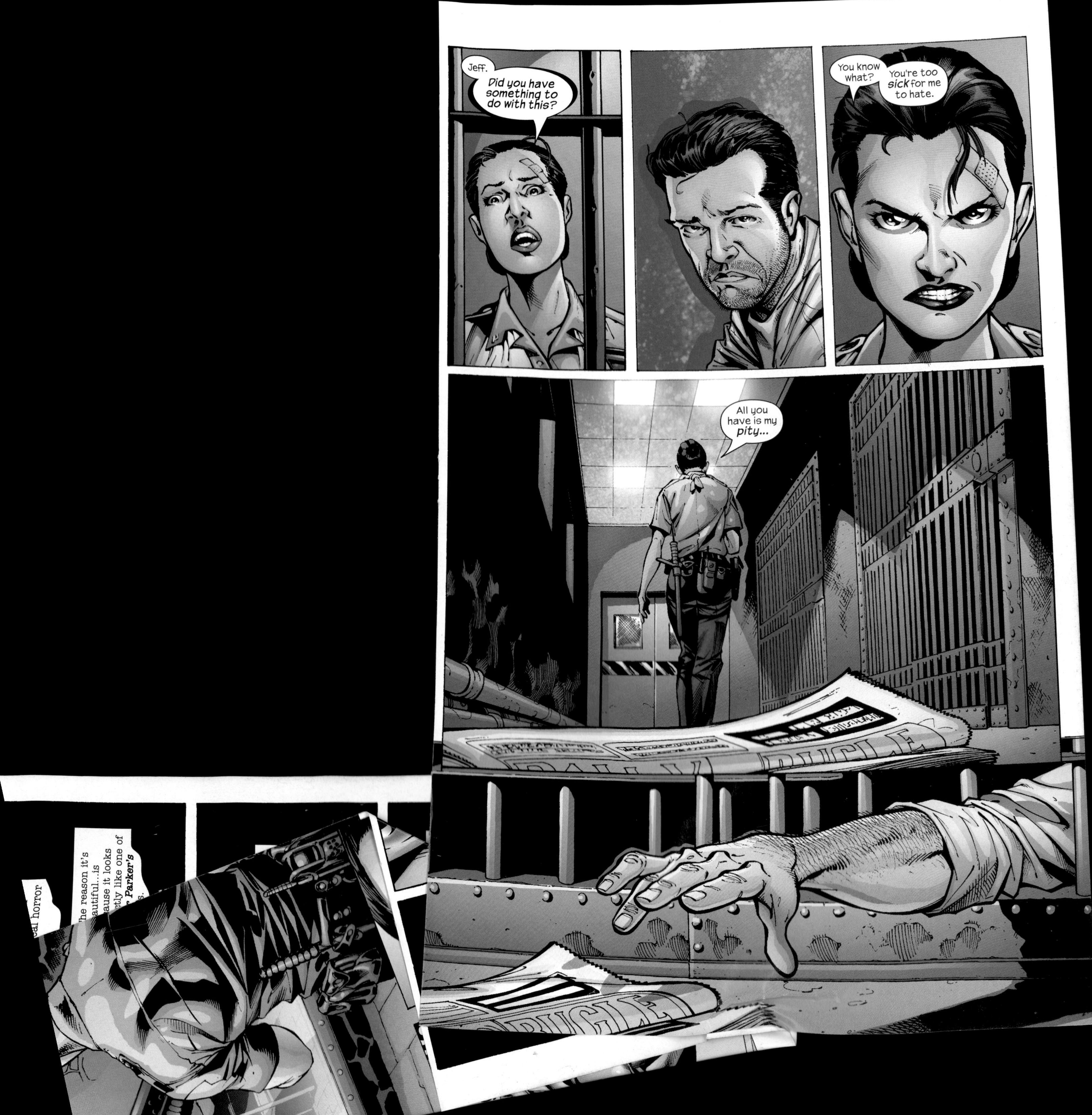
Jeff.
Did you have something to do with this?
You know what?
You're too sick for me to hate.
All you have is my pity...

I go right to the byline.

It's *my* name.

I made it. I made the *front* page...

But at first, I think there's been a mistake.

The photo clearly isn't one of mine. It's harsh and thoughtlessly exposed. The composition is random, haphazard.

Then I realize, I *did* take this picture.

PHOTO FINISH!
Bugle Photog Fingered in Felony

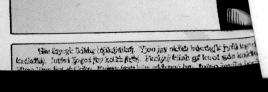

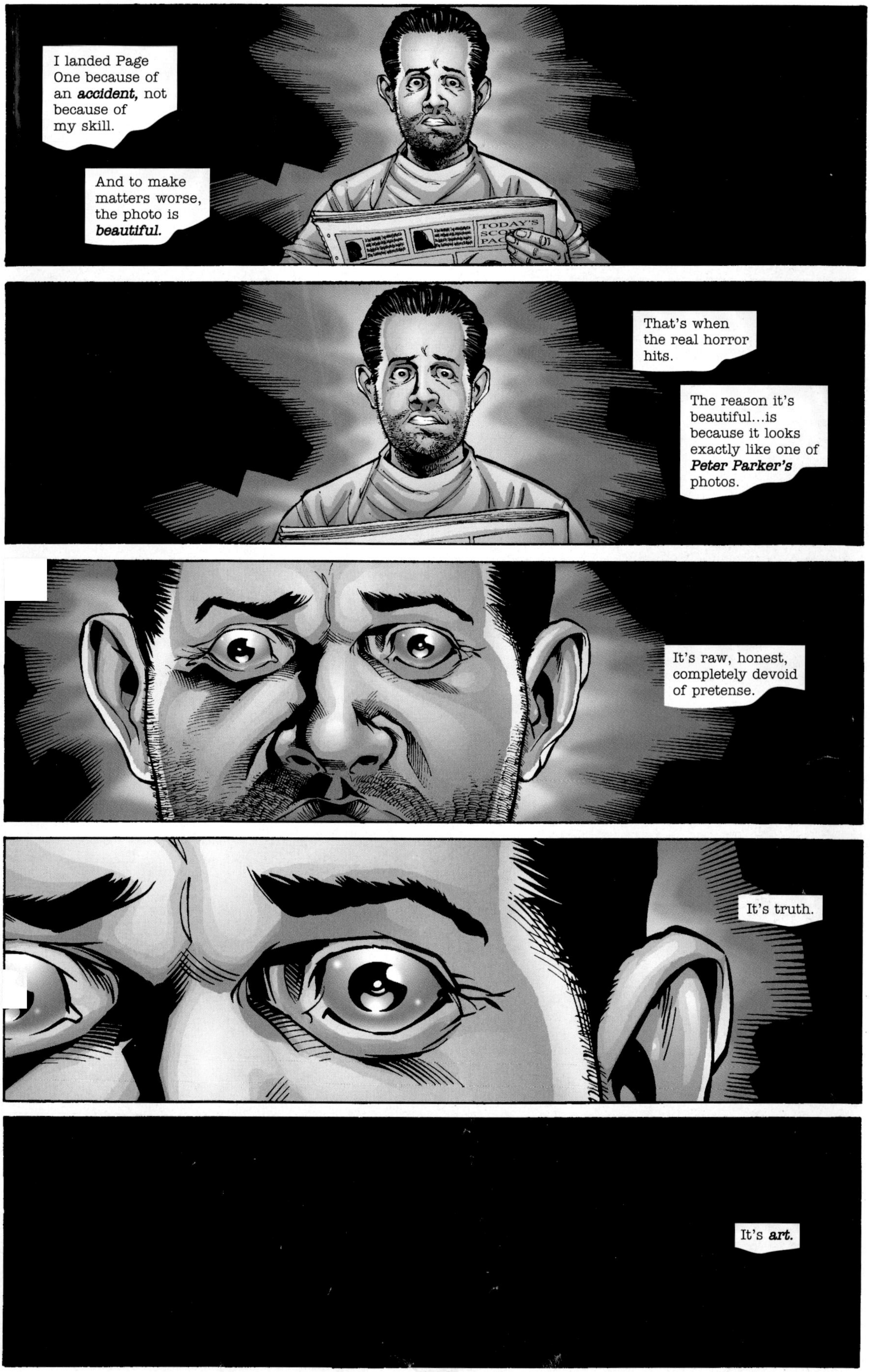

I landed Page One because of an ***accident,*** not because of my skill.
And to make matters worse, the photo is ***beautiful.***
TODAY'S SCO PAG
That's when the real horror hits.
The reason it's beautiful...is because it looks exactly like one of ***Peter Parker's*** photos.
It's raw, honest, completely devoid of pretense.
It's truth.
It's ***art.***

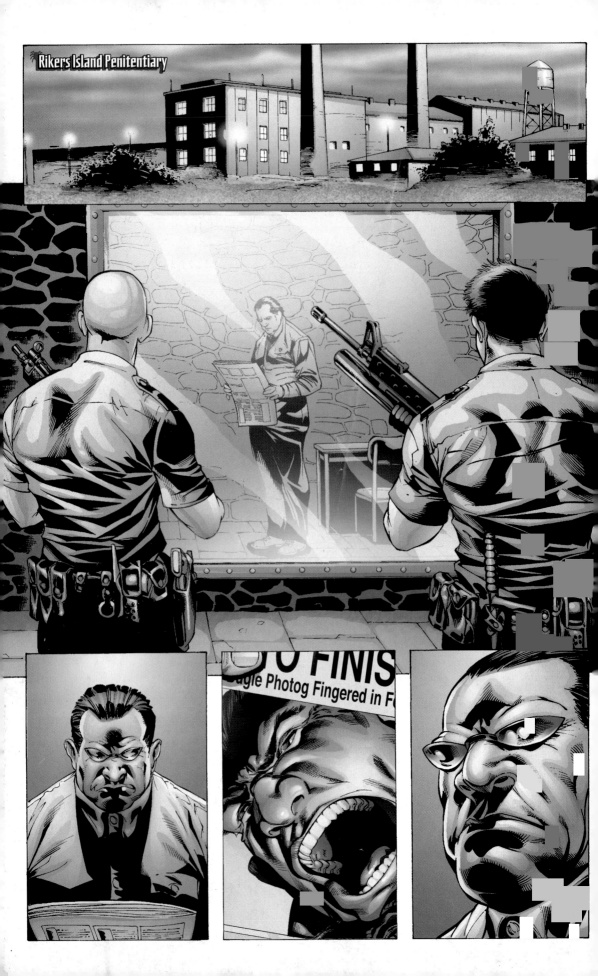

Rikers Island Penitentiary

FINIS

agle Photog Fingered in F

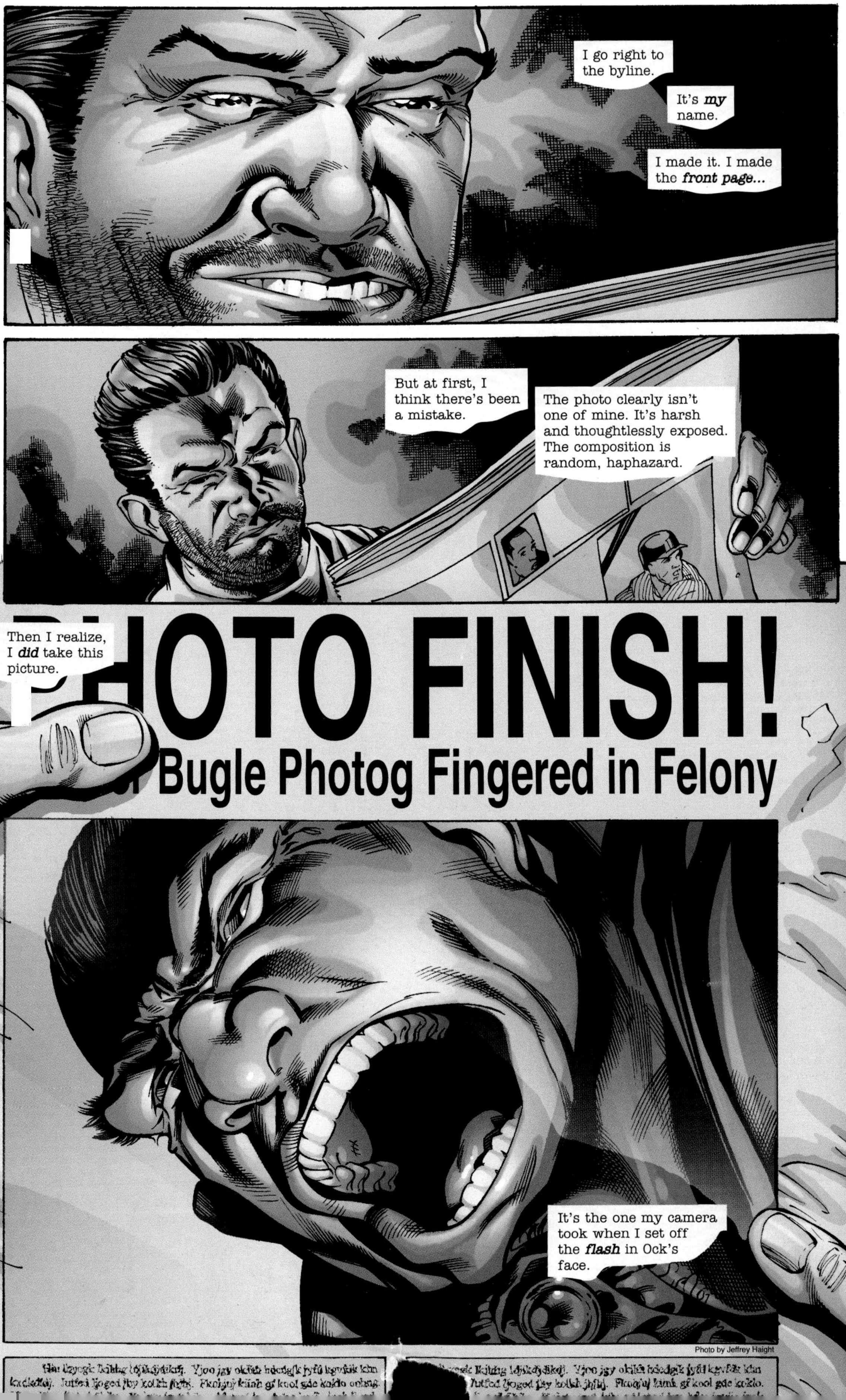
I go right to the byline.
It's ***my*** name.
I made it. I made the ***front page...***
But at first, I think there's been a mistake.
The photo clearly isn't one of mine. It's harsh and thoughtlessly exposed. The composition is random, haphazard.
Then I realize, I ***did*** take this picture.
HOTO FINISH!
Bugle Photog Fingered in Felony
It's the one my camera took when I set off the ***flash*** in Ock's face.
Photo by Jeffrey Haight

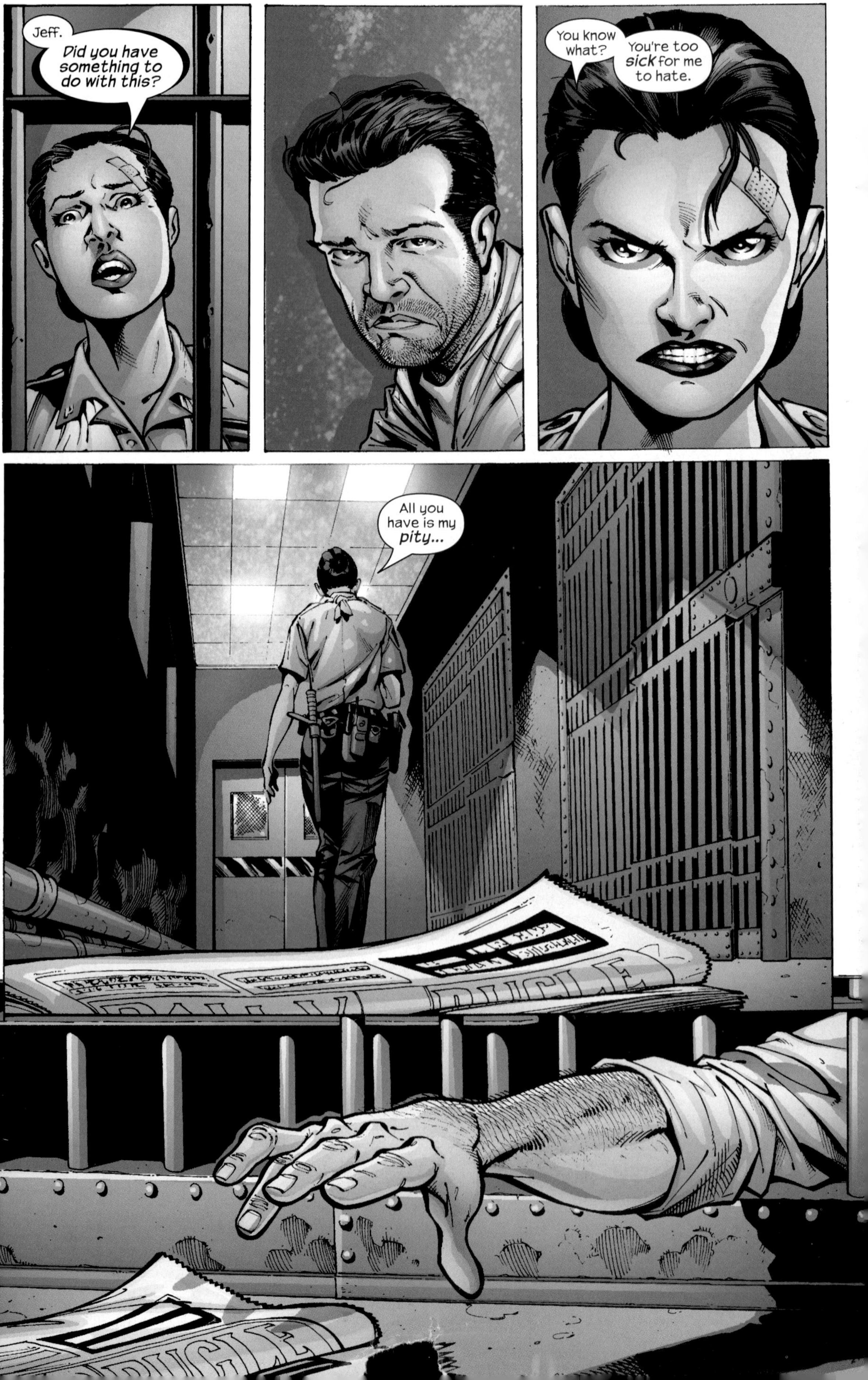

Jeff.
Did you have something to do with this?
You know what?
You're too sick for me to hate.
All you have is my pity...

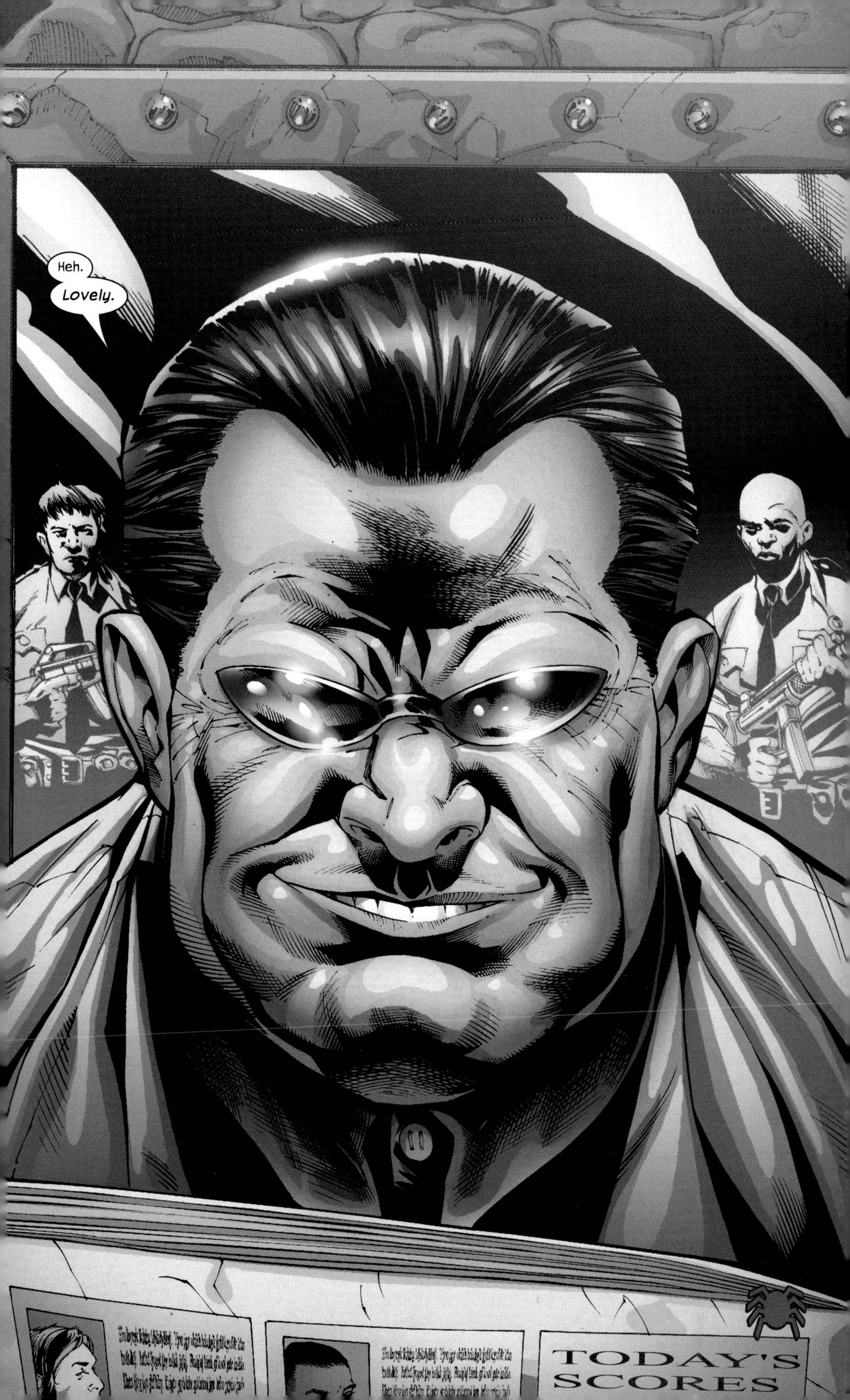
Heh.
Lovely.
TODAY'S
SCORES

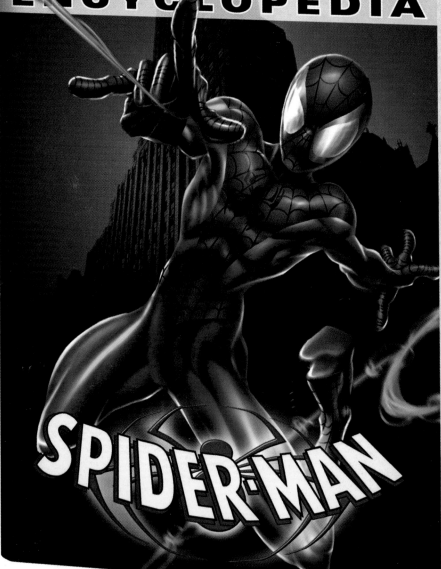

EVERYTHING You Ever Wanted to Know About Spider-Man...
And Weren't Afraid to Ask!